Jean-Jacques Rousseau

MODERNITY AND POLITICAL THOUGHT

Series Editor: Morton Schoolman
State University of New York at Albany

This unique collection of original studies of the great figures in the history of political and social thought critically examines their contributions to our understanding of modernity, its constitution, and the promise and problems latent within it. These works are written by some of the finest theorists of our time for scholars and students of the social sciences and humanities.

The following titles are available as New Editions from
Rowman & Littlefield Publishers, Inc.

The Augustinian Imperative: A Reflection on the Politics of Morality
by *William E. Connolly*

Emerson and Self-Reliance
by *George Kateb*

Edmund Burke: Modernity, Politics, and Aesthetics
by *Stephen K. White*

Jean-Jacques Rousseau: The Politics of the Ordinary
by *Tracy B. Strong*

Michel Foucault and the Politics of Freedom
by *Thomas L. Dumm*

Reading "Adam Smith": Desire, History, and Value
by *Michael J. Shapiro*

Thomas Hobbes: Skepticism, Individuality, and Chastened Politics
by *Richard E. Flathman*

Thoreau's Nature: Ethics, Politics, and the Wild
by *Jane Bennett*

Jean-Jacques Rousseau

The Politics of the Ordinary

New Edition

TRACY B. STRONG

Modernity and Political Thought Series

ROWMAN & LITTLEFIELD PUBLISHERS, INC.
Lanham • Boulder • New York • Oxford

ROWMAN & LITTLEFIELD PUBLISHERS, INC.

Published in the United States of America
by Rowman & Littlefield Publishers, Inc.
A Member of the Rowman & Littlefield Publishing Group
4720 Boston Way, Lanham, Maryland 20706
www.rowmanlittlefield.com

12 Hid's Copse Road
Cumnor Hill, Oxford OX2 9JJ, England

Originally published in 1994 by Sage Publications, Inc.
Reprinted in 2000 by AltaMira Press
New Preface and Introduction Copyright © 2002 by
Rowman & Littlefield Publishers, Inc.

British Library Cataloguing in Publication Information Available

The Library of Congress has cataloged the previous edition as follows:

Strong, Tracy B.
  Jean-Jacques Rousseau: the politics of the ordinary / Tracy B. Strong.
    p. cm.—(Modernity and political thought: 6)
  Includes bibliographical references and index.
  1. Rousseau, Jean-Jacques, 1712–1778—Contributions in political science.
2. Political science—France—History—18th century. I. Title. II. Series:
Modernity and political thought: vol. 6.
  JC179.R9S77   1994
  320'.092—dc20   94-4599

ISBN 0-7425-2142-7 (cloth : alk. paper)
ISBN 0-7425-2143-5 (paper : alk. paper)

Printed in the United States of America

♾™ The paper used in this publication meets the minimum requirements of
American National Standard for Information Sciences—Permanence of Paper
for Printed Library Materials, ANSI/NISO Z39.48-1992.

In memoriam
Judith Nisse Shklar

"It is modest of the nightingale not
to require any one to listen to it;
but it is also proud of the nightingale
not to care whether any one listens to it or not."

S. Kierkegaard
On the Difference Between a Genius and an Apostle

Contents

Series Editor's Introduction

racy B. Strong's *Jean-Jacques Rousseau: The Politics of the Ordinary* is the fourth volume in the Rowman & Littlefield series **Modernity and Political Thought** to be published in a second edition, and follows publication of the new editions of William E. Connolly's *The Augustinian Imperative: A Reflection on the Politics of Morality*, Richard E. Flathman's *Thomas Hobbes: Skepticism, Individuality, and Chastened Politics*, and Michael Shapiro's *Reading "Adam Smith": Desire, History, and Value*.[1] Each of the remaining six original volumes belonging to **Modernity and Political Thought,** studies of G. W. F. Hegel, by Fred Dallmayr, Edmund Burke, by Stephen White, Henry David Thoreau, by Jane Bennett, Ralph Waldo Emerson, by George Kateb, Michel Foucault, by Thomas Dumm, and Hannah Arendt, by Seyla Benhabib, also are scheduled to appear in a second edition in the fall of 2001.[2] In addition, new works for **Modernity and Political Thought** are underway, and among others will focus on such diverse thinkers as Plato, Aristotle, Thomas Aquinas, Thomas More, Niccolo Machiavelli, John Locke, Karl Marx, Friedrich

Nietzsche, and John Stuart Mill, as well as a selection of contemporary political thinkers. As those who are familiar with the previous works of series authors will expect, taken together their studies adopt a variety of approaches and pose importantly different questions. As contributors to **Modernity and Political Thought,** however, their efforts also are commonly devoted to effecting critical examinations of major political theorists who have shaped our understanding of modernity—its constitution, problems, promises, and dangers that are latent within it.

The rich and fertile qualities of Strong's earlier writings make it a simple matter to discover theoretical interests that run through them to anchor the study of Jean-Jacques Rousseau. His first major work, *Friedrich Nietzsche and the Politics of Transfiguration,* was one of the first English language examinations to recognize the importance of Nietzsche for political theory.[3] Noted especially for the complexity and range of its analysis, Strong's text focused on Nietzsche's philosophy of "eternal return" as a procedure for transfiguration. Perhaps reflecting the spirit of the 1960s, Strong embraced the notion of transfiguration enthusiastically, arguing that eternal return ought to be construed as a form of praxis rather than as a passive attitude toward the world. In the course of developing this argument, Strong also illuminated dimensions of Nietzsche's work that now play an equally provocative but far more prominent role in *Jean-Jacques Rousseau.* Among these dimensions, of particular interest for the present study is Strong's exploration, in Nietzsche's thought, of the relationship between modernity and what it means to be human.

Taking Nietzsche's work as a whole, Strong argues that an aim of his enterprise was to show that whatever culturally had bound together men and women in Western society has broken down. Moreover, all that has been dominant in the politics, religion, and morality of Western culture is of a piece, and no one part of it will pass away without the rest eventually following. Signaled by the death of God, as this crisis marking the veritable end of Western culture and the precipitous slide into nihilism unfolds, men and women gradually will discover, as Strong poignantly expresses it, that they "no longer know their way about with themselves, or with others."

As Strong describes it, the crisis of Western culture emerges because the presuppositions that constitute its foundations and on which individuals base their thought and action are no longer available. Yet, the source of the problems and of the discontents characterizing modernity's decline is seen by Nietzsche as running far deeper, so deep, in Strong's words, that it is "incarnate in humans themselves, or, at least, in humans as they are now." Departing from usual philosophical practices, Nietzsche does not offer us new answers to profound problems, but rather a mode of human archeology, an analysis of the particular "soil"—that is, of the sorts of *beings* men were—from which these problems have sprung.

This analytical turn, Strong presumes, is the point of departure for Nietzsche's strictures against the "human-all-too-human," and provides the foundations for two seminal theoretical conceptions. It is the ground for Nietzsche's call for something or someone who is not similarly human, but rather "overman." And it is the basis for his projection of a form of life that renders obsolete the need for answers to chronic historical problems by depriving them of their "necessity." This would be a form of life that would possess as little as possible of what afflicts men and women at present. Indeed, because Nietzsche's genealogical critiques established the extent to which the past so aggressively informs and thus contributes to the decline of the present and future, it would have to be a form of life that would constitute nothing less than a qualitative break with the past. Even an emphatic denial of the past by the human so powerfully tied to it would be insufficient to break its hold over everything that follows or to measure the change entailed by his conception of a new form of life. To alter so dramatically a form of life that has held us prisoner, in other words, is to bring about a metamorphosis—a transformation—in those to whom this life belongs. Strong explains all of this by saying that

> it is a mistake to think that Nietzsche criticizes morality, or politics or any other traits of Western man, as "simply" illusions, which can be wiped away with bold words. His critique is of us, the men and women for whom that morality is *not* "childish" nonsense, but actual. Morality is real because of the sort of people we are. A critique of morality, or of politics, or religion, cannot stop with the institution or practice; for Nietzsche, it must continue on to the beings of whose life it is a necessary part.[4]

With this, it is easy to see why Strong underscores how deficient are philosophies and psychologies that stress the acquisition of self-knowledge as either an end to which humans ought to aspire or as a means to an end when there is posted a demonstrable need for radical change. From Nietzsche's standpoint, the self that can be known might well prove to be flawed profoundly. If so, then its beliefs and truths, or that of which the self is, quite literally, constructed, might also be flawed. Knowing such a self, therefore, holds no promise for reform and cannot stand in place of a self fully transfigured. But a self who must press far beyond self-knowledge will be left without borders and horizons to which it is accustomed. It will not, Strong contends eloquently, "know [its] way about, and what will count as a question, or an answer, or indeed as truth itself, is not clear." Strong's Nietzsche thus "seeks to show us that a world we have thought familiar has, in fact, become strange, even though we have yet to acknowledge this. Then, having shown us that we have and will become strangers to ourselves, he would show us a world where we might, once again, and for the first time, come to be ourselves."[5]

In "Nietzsche's Political Aesthetics," an essay composed several years after the appearance of *Friedrich Nietzsche and the Politics of Transfiguration*, Strong sets for himself the task of trying to understand, in relation to Nietzsche's life's work, the political position he appeared to adopt at the end of his life when he may have been overcome by his madness.[6] Along the way of this difficult investigation, Strong takes the opportunity to revisit some of the arguments he made in his own first study as well as to look anew at other facets of Nietzsche's thought. Both of these objectives succeed in bringing into even sharper relief his earlier concern with modernity and the nature of the human.

The singular problem for modernity, as Nietzsche understood it, Strong contends, is that we have lost the human capacity for accepting justification, that is, the ability to recognize in oneself the validity of another's judgment. Thus Strong roots the heart of this problem, the status and standing of authority in the modern world, in the *human*. For it is precisely this human capacity for engaging in human relationships that establishes authority that modernity first erodes, and finally destroys. The immediate consequence of modernity's achievement is that no longer can anything stand authoritatively for us. Of far greater consequence, however, is that absent the establishment of authority through relations between and among selves and others, no form of life can be grounded legitimately, that is, authoritatively. Such an authoritative grounding roots a form of life so deeply in human being as to place it beyond question. Indeed, Strong weights this depth dimension of the grounding of a form of life by saying that "were we able to question it we would literally be another being," that is, other than human being. Essentially and most importantly, then, by destroying the capacity for judgment and justification modernity spoils the possibility to craft a common authority in common, and to live a common form of life.

Aesthetics, Strong argues, could in Nietzsche's view lead the way to a recovery of common authority by restoring the capacity for judgment, but only if we could first imagine an aesthetic that ceased to equate art with its representational orientation toward the world. Art must be conceived as an activity that constructs, rather than imitates or represents, the very world to which it refers. Tragedy, in particular, can be so conceived, Nietzsche proposes in *The Birth of Tragedy*, because it "establishes the authority of a human sense before the audience in a manner that this sense can be experienced both as something external and found in oneself."[7] Through tragedy, in other words, one is taught to interpret the experience that one has with another as authoritative and thus learns to recognize and to acknowledge judgment and justification. The aesthetics of tragedy accomplishes what Strong refers to as the "Emersonian moment of transfiguration." Emerson had considered the only legitimate authority to be that which can be found inside the self. Tragedy allows us to take that necessary preliminary step, in effect to undergo a transfiguration, which makes it possible to discover authority inside the self and thus to form relations of authority with others. By renewing the capacity for judgment and justification in this way, tragedy lays the groundwork for a reconstitution of individual and social identity and for a new form of life. The aesthetic mode thus provides Nietzsche with a world that is human. Moreover, it is a world that is securely grounded in that it does not point nor seek to point beyond itself for authority, that is, beyond the forms of life that a restored human capacity for judgment has made possible.

Strong suggests that at the end of his life the promise of renewal that Nietzsche held for art is relinquished. Just as modernity destroys our capacity for justification, Nietzsche feared, it likewise disfigures our capacity for aesthetic experience. Nietzsche then turns instead to politics to recreate the possibility for aesthetic reflection—unfortunately, to a politics of domination. Strong's work clearly shows us that, the faults that attend the diseases of the mind aside, Nietzsche's entire enterprise of transfiguration, whether conceived as the engendering of an "overman" or of beings who could again bear witness to the presence of authority in their lives, was directed toward the revivication of what is truly human.

Without intending to diminish in the least the significance of this examination of Nietzsche, it is apparent that one of its finest accomplishments was to lay the foundations for a subsequent and uniquely creative interpretive project. Although there are prolific and theoretically interesting differences between Strong's Rousseau and his Nietzsche, *Jean-Jacques Rousseau: The Politics of the Ordinary* is a beautifully constructed argument that sustains Strong's interest in the relationship between modernity and humanity.

Strong uses the term *ordinary* in no ordinary sense to describe Rousseau's undertaking. Rousseau, he explains, attached the greatest possible significance to what he believed to be the most profound experience we, as human beings, can have—the experience of the "ordinary," of the "common," or, to be precise, the *experience of the human.* Modernity is characterized by the loss of our human capacity to have this experience of the human in another, to acknowledge our commonalty, to acknowledge, in other words, the way in which another is exactly the same as I.

From the start Rousseau's similarity to Nietzsche is distinctive. He speaks to the eclipse of capacities to discover in all of its forms the other in myself and myself in the other, to recognize humanness and to make it available for experience in all of its potentiality and multiplicity. At the same time as it spoils the capacity to experience commonalty, modernity opposes its discovery by concealing the multiplicity of human being beneath the proliferation of personal identities. Identity is opposed to the human by making that which is many into the one. Identity imposes unity, coherence, and consistency on being that in its own protean self-sameness is essentially in excess of and inimical to the limitation that identification and representation entails. Modernity, in light of Strong's reading of Rousseau, never has afforded us the Shakespearean choice "to be, or not to be." Rather, in the modern world, to be is *always also* not to be. For to be something or someone is not to be something or someone *else,* not to be available in our multiplicity and in excess of any identity.

Although the experience of the ordinary is not our everyday experience, Rousseau, Strong argues, seeks to make it so. The human must become the stuff of politics, for the social contract will return the human to us. The political realm is thus legitimized on the basis of the human. The language of politics will be the language of the human and this, in turn, again striking a chord that resonates in Nietzsche, will have an aesthetic configuration. In addition, because politics thrives on the availability of the human and it is possible for everyone to be human (again), Strong makes an excellent case for the thoroughly democratic and egalitarian qualities of Rousseau's politics. The importance of Strong's contribution here cannot be overestimated. When at one point he says, in a particularly poignant expression of Rousseau's own humanity, that there is "meaning shining in every facet of Rousseau's existence," Strong appears to be speaking not just descriptively, but analytically, as well. Because if Rousseau is human and it is his humanness that is meaningful, then by virtue of their humanness every facet of every other human's existence is equally meaningful. As the basis of politics, then, the human would in no sense be diminished through political activity and find it anathema. The human would find politics to be the most accommodating vehicle for self-expression.

As Strong construes them, neither Rousseau's conception of humanity or of politics should be confused with utopian proposals that bear some superficial resemblance. On the contrary, it is one of Strong's most compelling insights that Rousseau confronts and even accepts the conditions that constitute modernity. Rousseau refuses to draw from the past, from nature or some other extrasocietal or transcendental source for philosophical grounding. Rather, the human is to be recovered from within modernity, a position that appears to leave the framework of the modern world standing.

The Rousseau Strong has presented us with, then, is a thinker for "we moderns," as Nietzsche would put it, and perhaps more than he has been understood to be. We can see clearly from Strong's analysis, for example, that Rousseau's critique of identity anticipates some of the most radical indictments of modernity by our contemporary postmodern and poststructuralist theorists. In addition, it confirms some of their worst fears about the human implications of modernity's structural imperatives. Rousseau directs our attention, for example, to structural factors that breed identity through processes of rationalization. Such processes individuate the self according to the limitless production of roles required to meet the imperatives of unbounded economic growth. And he leads us further to examine the function of knowledge-based disciplinary practices. These impel individuals to pursue ideals of selfhood that foreshorten the self while devaluing an other who serves instrumentally to maintain the identity in which the self becomes normatively encased.

And whereas Strong's exposition reveals Rousseau's affinity for post-modern and poststructuralist critique, he certainly figures, as well, as one of the earliest critics of Enlightenment rationalism. Rousseau draws our attention to positivist and metaphysical strains of rationalism that fix human identity either by construing it as "given" or by privileging certain moral and ethical categories. Rousseau also joins those few Enlightenment thinkers who are hostile to forms of thought that conceive of our relation-ship to the world as one of mastery. Here Rousseau's notion of the human would function very much like certain concepts in Burke's writings. As Stephen White has importantly shown in *Edmund Burke: Modernity, Poli-tics, and Aesthetics,* the aesthetic dimension of Burke's work opposes those modern forms of thought that represent or impose an identity on the world as some "thing" that can be infinitely mastered by a will not guided by a sense of "finitude."[8]

Finally, Strong's interpretation of Rousseau transcends the overused and stale framework of the individualism-communitarian debate, which by his reading of Rousseau is now shown to have only obscured the more complex and subtle dimensions of his thought. Rousseau's conception of the human illuminates a potential for each individual that exceeds the ambitions of contemporary theories of individuality. Yet, it is a potential that at the same time appears disposed to constituting a form of life that can tie rather than bind individuals together. And this potential is alien to such fetters, because the human is resistant to the denaturation of which Rousseau is accused by those who take his politics to be nothing more than another vehicle for the tyranny of the majority of the community.

This position that Rousseau enjoys above the individualism-communitar-ian debate enables us to renew our critical perspective on modern liberal democracy, as in different ways has each of the earlier contributions to **Modernity and Political Thought.** For liberal democratic society is the form of life that is frequently promoted as realizing the ends of both indi-viduality and community without becoming vulnerable to either communi-tarian or individualist critiques. It would be difficult, at best, to sustain unquestionably this favorable view of liberalism in light of the new require-ments for individuality and community outlined by Rousseau's conception of what is human. In the Rousseauian mirror that Strong has provided us, what sort of human reflection would liberal democracy cast today?

Part of the answer to that query lies in this. Rousseau and Nietzsche were both solitaries. As Strong explains, they stood as "other" in relation to the rest of us. Their "difference" presents special problems for the interpreter, who must find a way to represent it in terms sufficiently familiar for the reader to grasp, without at the same time giving that difference a new identity and betraying the intentions of the theorist. Strong accomplishes this admirably, perhaps because he never tries to abolish—but only to explain and to problematize—that irreducible distance between the reader and the text. Thus the reader is doubly fortunate in being able to be clear about what Strong makes perfectly intelligible, but paradoxically even clearer about what he leaves mysterious by locating it on the interpretive horizons of our own form of life. Liberalism, if only implicitly, is here chastened for its failure to accord difference the space warranted by that which stands apart and challenges us with an unfamiliar image of ourselves.

* * *

I am especially grateful to Steven Wrinn of Rowman & Littlefield for shepherding **Modernity and Political Thought** through the transitional stages to our new publisher and home, and for his thoughtfulness and professionalism that make it possible for editor and authors alike to produce their best work. And while each of the authors of series volumes will earn rewards and punishments commensurate with his or her contribution, as the hidden architects of the series each must also share credit with me for launching **Modernity and Political Thought.**

—Morton Schoolman
State University of New York at Albany

Notes

1. William E. Connolly, *The Augustinian Imperative: A Reflection on the Politics of Morality*; Richard E. Flathman, *Thomas Hobbes: Skepticism, Individuality, and Chastened Politics*; Michael Shapiro, *Reading "Adam Smith": Desire, History, and Value* (Lanham, Boulder, New York, Oxford: Rowman & Littlefield, 2001).

2. **Modernity and Political Thought** was first published by Sage Publications, Newbury Park, California. Volume 1, William E. Connolly, *The Augustinian Imperative: A Reflection on the Politics of Morality* (1993); Volume 2, Richard E. Flathman, *Thomas Hobbes: Skepticism, Individuality, and Chastened Politics* (1993); Volume 3, Fred Dallmayr, *G.W.F. Hegel: Modernity and Politics* (1993); Volume 4, Michael Shapiro, *Reading "Adam Smith": The Politics of Desire* (1993); Volume 5, Stephen K. White, *Edmund Burke: Modernity, Politics, and Aesthetics* (1994); Volume 6, Tracy Strong, *Jean-Jacques Rousseau: The Politics of the Ordinary* (1994); Volume 7, Jane Bennett, *Thoreau's Nature: Ethics, Politics, and the Wild* (1994); Volume 8, George Kateb, *Emerson and Self-Reliance* (1994); Volume 9, Thomas Dumm, *Michel Foucault and the Politics of Freedom* (1996); Volume 10, Seyla Benhabib, *Hannah Arendt's Reluctant Modernism* (1996).

3. Tracy B. Strong, *Friedrich Nietzsche and the Politics of Transfiguration* (Berkeley: University of California Press, 1975, Revised and expanded edition, 1988).

4. Ibid., xi.

5. Ibid., 19.

6. Tracy B. Strong, "Nietzsche's Political Aesthetics," in Michael A. Gillespie and Tracy B. Strong, eds. *Nietzsche's New Seas* (Chicago: University of Chicago Press, 1988).

7. Ibid., 164.

8. Stephen K. White, *Edmund Burke: Modernity, Politics, and Aesthetics.* **Modernity and Political Thought**, ed. Morton Schoolman (Lanham, Boulder, New York, Oxford: Rowman & Littlefield, 2001).

Preface to the New Edition

ON READING ROUSSEAU IN OUR TIMES

S ince writing this book, I have elsewhere pursued some of the questions left untreated here.[1] I should like in this new introduction to take up three related matters, each of which finds instantiation, albeit a brief one, in this book. I am grateful for the opportunity to extend my thoughts here.

Let me start with two texts not ordinarily associated with Rousseau. I do so because it is with texts such as these that I wish to read Rousseau; indeed, it is in resonance with texts such as these that I claim Rousseau should be read.

> You can find in a text whatever you bring, if you stand between it and the mirror of your imagination. You may not see your ears but they will be there.[2]
> —Mark Twain, 1909

> Ultimately, nobody can get more out of things, including books, than he already knows. For what one lacks access to from experience one will have

no ear. Now let us imagine an extreme case: that a book speaks of nothing but events that lie altogether beyond the possibility of any frequent or even rare experience—that it is the first language for a new series of experiences. In that case, simply nothing will be heard, but there will be the acoustic illusion that where nothing is heard, nothing is there.

This is, in the end, my average experience and, if you will the originality of my experience. Whoever thought he had understood me had made up something out of me after his own image.[3]

—Friedrich Nietzsche, 1888

Twain and Nietzsche tell us that if I stand between myself and the text—we might call this *inter*-pretation—I will hear only what my ears can already hear, although I will almost certainly be unaware that I am hearing myself. If we see books as containers of meaning from which we extract content, we will find only what we already have.[4] Rousseau gives us a similar warning. In his *Dialogues* a character makes reference to the fact that Jean-Jacques (who is the subject of the dialogue) has placed the following quatrain under one of the portraits that an admirer had commissioned of him. It reads:

> Those knowing in the art of pretense
> Who give me such gentle features,
> No matter how you wish to portray me
> You will have only displayed yourselves.[5]

My juxtaposition of these passages is intended to call preliminary attention to two claims of this book. The first claim has to do with what it means to read Rousseau, or any important text. All of these passages are about the relation of a text to those who read that text. Both of them suggest that if one approaches a text in such a matter as to interfere with it, either by standing between it and one's imagination or by bringing only experience of one's own to that text, one will find only what one already has. The text will do nothing to you, it will lack what Samuel Beckett called its "power to claw."

The point—one of the points—of these passages is to dissuade us from the idea that what we should do, or what we are doing, in reading a text that we find important, is to *interpret* it. When in the seventeenth-century Tyndale, Lilburne, and the others preached in favor of a literal reading of the Scriptures they had in mind something that they knew to be difficult.

Most people wanted to *interpret* the scriptures and as the verb itself indicates this meant that they wanted to put something between the text and the capacity of the text to work on them. Interpretation was a way of holding God's word at a distance, of not allowing an incarnate presence to it.[6]

Rousseau, I suggest below, does not want us to "interpret" him; more importantly, he writes so as to prevent that. In the *Essay on the Origin of Languages*, Rousseau writes of a fantasy first or natural language. Among its qualities would be a plethora of nouns so as to "express the same being in its different relations" and "instead of arguments it would have maxims (*sentences*), it would persuade without convincing and depict (*peindrait*) without reasoning. . . . "[7] Rousseau hopes that his own writing will achieve this effect. It is noteworthy that in the *Social Contract*, during his discussion of the legislator figure, some of the same distinctions recur. As the legislator can use "neither force nor reason, it is from necessity that he has recourse to another kind of authority, that can bring others along without violence and persuade without convincing."[8]

What is wrong with interpretation as a way of approaching a text? Instead of a text, think of a human being. You are my good and trusted friend; you approach me accompanied by another person, whom I do not know. You say: "Tracy, I would like you to meet Jean-Jacques—you two should get to know each other." I do not—I hope—for the least moment entertain the idea of *interpreting* this other person: to the degree that I do I will never come to know nor will I be moved by that person. Can one, however, respond to a text as one can to a person? Can I be called out, provoked by a text in the way that I can be by a teacher or lover or a friend? I note in chapter 1 below that already in Rousseau's time his writing made available to some an immediacy of response that passed all rational understanding.

Why though is this important? Or: why should one speak approvingly of it at all? Is not rationality and argument the best foundation for a civilized society? I argue in this book that while Rousseau does not reject rationality or argument, he is convinced that the crisis of society is such that a kind of new beginning, a recommencement, is necessary and that for this something other than rational argumentation will be required. This conviction means that the terms of argumentation that are acceptable in society will be inadequate, precisely because they are the terms of that society. Rousseau's concern with language is a concern to find a way to make his thought available without it being strained through the constraints of the corrupt world in which he lived and of which most of those he knew were. The refusal of interpretation is thus a radical move, a proposal for a kind of revolution or the world in its foundations and depth. As Wittgenstein remarks in a notebook: "Grasping the difficulty in its depth is what is hard. For if you interpret it in a shallow way the difficulty just remains. It has to be pulled out by the root; and that means, you have to start thinking about these things in a new way."[9] Rousseau calls for a change that surpasses past assessment and thus becomes part of assessment itself. "Unless the idea that strikes the brain . . . penetrate[s] to the heart, it is nothing."[10]

The above gives some sense of the range and daring of Rousseau's project. As should now be becoming clear, the second intention of my choice of epigraphs is to signal the resonance that I find in Rousseau to those who come after him, and more precisely to those who come considerably after him. Part of my intent in writing this book has been to try and show that Rousseau can be read as a *modern*.

What does it mean to read someone as a modern? It means at least to find that that person or that text is in important conversation with oneself, but oneself as a historical being of the period of human history that starts loosely with World War I and continues at least until 1989. It does not mean simply to read as a person who lives *in* that period, but to read as a person *of* that period. This does not mean that some of those who lived before might not have had a sensibility that was fundamentally out of their season, "untimely" as Nietzsche called them. A reason for calling upon Hölderlin's "Rousseau" poem as epigraph for my final chapter is the line "And some see over their own time." Rousseau is untimely much in the manner that Nietzsche thought himself to be. Only the untimely can have the unkind fate to set straight that which is out of joint.

To be modern—that is to live as an historical being of the last 100 or so years—means first, to have the possibility of experiencing the world, or portions of it, as if it or they raised self-referential questions. A self-referential question is one that raises the question of what something (actually) is. One of the reasons that World War I can mark the beginning of the modern century is the experience that many had, both during and after those events, not just of "how can this be happening" but even more of "what is it that is happening?" The First World War marked a turning point in the confidence Westerners were able to express in the world around them. The conflict revealed to an incredulous Europe that the course of political and social events had acquired a logic and power of their own. The epoch that had begun with the anticipation of the possibility that human beings might at last possess the capacity and knowledge to control and shape their own destinies ended with the insane frightfulness of Verdun and the Machiavellian idealism of Versailles. "Men had died," wrote Ezra Pound, "for an old bitch gone in the teeth, for a botched civilization."[11]

What was lost was the sense that human action could be judged by a standard external and transcendent to it. Call this the reality of skepticism. What was gained, however, was what modernity makes possible—a confrontation with the nature or essence of the being of some activity. It is in the nature of modern art, modern music, as well as of, I would argue with Rousseau, modern politics to raise the question of "Is *that* art [music, politics, etc . . .]? Rousseau can in important ways lay claim to being the first modern (Westerner) in that his work impresses upon his readers not only the problems and inadequacies of that which passes for human society but does so by raising the question of what a human society *is*. I italicize "is" in that sentence because I claim in the book that follows that it is Rousseau's intent to force us to ask what a human society actually is, or what would have to be the case for a society in which we lived to be in its nature human.[12] When there is a general will, Rousseau argues, it allows us to see things "as they are."[13]

Rousseau found himself surrounded not so much by misunderstanding, but by the wrong kind of understanding; it was a source of much frustration.[14] His situation resembles that which Nietzsche attributes to his character Zarathustra. When Zarathustra first comes into the town he goes to the market place and announces the arrival of the overman who will supplant the last men. The crowd responds: "Give us this last man. . . . Turn us into this last man. Then we shall make you a gift of the overman."[15] Zarathustra's problem—and Rousseau's—is not that he is not understood, but that the understanding that people have of him is incorrigibly wrong: it misses the essential. One would have to change the person for him or her to be gotten right. This is why Rousseau writes to persuade without convincing and opines that the legislator figure would, "so to speak, have to change human nature."[16]

If to read someone or some text as a modern means to read it as raising the question of what something in its nature is, it thus, secondly, means to read someone or some text in relation to the Enlightenment. We might think of the Enlightenment as the origin and development of the critical tradition, a tradition that found its classical formulation in Kant's philosophy. Kant sought to uncover the conditions that had to be the case for some human action (for instance, knowing) to be possible. The critical tradition—later to find its political and human expression in Marx's critique of political economy and Nietzsche and Freud's self-critiques—sought to unmask and set forth the hidden world that made the world that appeared to us to have the quality of being the case. The question of what something actually was, not in its appearance but in its being, or its essence, or its nature was a question that called for revealing that which had laid hidden.

Hence the question raised by someone who works from or inside the critical tradition is "what is the quality of the world that is hidden" from us. For Kant, this was the noumenal realm, that quality of existence that made knowledge and morality possible. The point of the noumenal realm was not so much to posit a realm of that which could not be known, but to show that human reason was not exhausted in the act of knowing. Knowing something that is can never be complete in itself.[17]

Hence to read as a modern means to open oneself up to that which is or has been hidden to—and by—us. It is this realization that stands behind Rousseau's notorious insistence (already in the *Discourse on the Arts and Sciences*, but in the rest of his work also) that he knows nothing. When someone claims, as do Rousseau and Socrates, that they know nothing, one should ask what it means to know nothing. Below, I read this question in Rousseau as signifying that what we need to be human does not (in the end) depend on knowing. It is not to be known in the way that we know the height of Pike's Peak.

A final implication of the above reflections concerns the status of the multiple interpretations of Rousseau. Rousseau has been blamed or praised from and for almost every political position. Part of what makes a thinker a great thinker is that almost any interpretation of him or her seems possible. I do not need to rehearse here the range of interpretations of Rousseau, nor those of Plato, Machiavelli, Nietzsche, Hegel, and so forth. Indeed, I am tempted to say that it is a mark of a great thinker that any interpretation seems licensed by his or her text. Likewise, significant doubts about the viability of all (or almost all?) of these interpretations have been raised.

The opposition is between "interpreting" (which seems open-ended) and reading. The point here and more generally in the *reading* of political theory is that one should not look to find what a text's "true" meaning is. One of the points made in different ways by authors like Roland Barthes and Michel Foucault is that part of what makes a text a text is that it is read by multiple readers, who are, in some sense each coauthors. This does not license a relativism of interpretations, if only because, as I have argued above, the point is not to interpret but to read. Thus we find Rousseau asking in the preface to his epistolary novel, *Julie* (the letters of which he notes on the title page have been "Collected and Published by J-J Rousseau"), "Have I done it all, and is the entire correspondence a fiction? People of the world, what does it matter to you? It is certainly a fiction to you. Any honest man must admit to the books he publishes. I name myself as the head of this collection, not to appropriate it to myself, but to answer to it."[18] The actuality of the book, and its actualization in a life, requires a response. Rousseau writes so that he also must respond to his texts, just as must any reader-author.

There is thus no correct interpretation of Rousseau, if one means by that that one gets Rousseau right once and for all. What Rousseau offers instead is the possibility of responding to his texts as one would respond to a person, by finding oneself in them, by thus standing beside oneself while reading them. Aristotle called the friend "another self": so it is with Rousseau's books.

La Jolla, California
January 2001

Notes

1. Tracy Strong (with C. N. Dugan), "'A Language More Vital Than Speech': Music Politics and Representation in Rousseau," in Patrick Riley ed. *Cambridge Companion to Rousseau* (Cambridge: Cambridge University Press, 2001).

2. Mark Twain, "A Fable" in *The Complete Short Stories of Mark Twain* (New York: Bantam, 1964), 602–604. I owe my first knowledge of this story to my ancient *Eidgenossenschaft* with Carey McWilliams.

3. Friedrich Nietzsche, *Ecce Homo, Why I Write Such Good Books 2* (New York: Vintage, 1969), 291.

4. On the transformation of texts into containers see Ivan Illych, *In the Vineyeard of the Text* (Chicago: University of Chicago Press, 1993), 57ff.

5. *Dialogues* 2 OC i 778. See the discussion below, 10–12. For a key to the citations see 164.

6. Hence the answer to Stanley Fish's notorious question "Is there a text in this classroom" is always "no," unless one has a very special sort of classroom, say something like an agora, or perhaps a bibulous symposium. See the discussion of Scripture in my "How to Write Scripture: Words and Authority in Thomas Hobbes," *Critical Inquiry* (Autumn, 1993) and "When Is a Text Not a Pretext?—A Reply to Professor Silver," *Critical Inquiry* (Autumn, 1993). One might also pay attention here to what Nietzsche writes: "What is meant by philology is, in a very broad sense, the art of reading well—of reading facts without falsifying them by interpretation. . . . " in *AntiChrist*, paragraph 52, Walter Kaufmann, ed. *The Portable Nietzsche* (New York: Viking, 1968), 635.

7. *ESOL* 4 OC v 383.

8. *SC* II 7 OC iii 383. "Bring others along" renders *entraîner,* which means both to pull along and to train or to coach. John Scott, in his excellent edition of Rousseau's musical writings, also calls attention to this link and notes that Rousseau may very well be responding to Diderot's *Letter on the Deaf and Dumb* where the latter avers that French is the language in which to "teach . . . enlighten . . . convince." See Jean Jacques Rousseau, *Essay on the Origin of Languages and Writings Related to Music,* John T. Scott, ed. and trans., *The Collected Writings of Rousseau,* volume 7 (New England Press, 2000), 569. I should note that Scott's edition, and this book, were both accomplished without reference to the fifth Pléiade volume of Rousseau's writings, although I have changed the references in my text to the writings that are in that volume.

9. Ludwig Wittgenstein, *Culture and Value* (Chicago: University of Chicago Press, 1984), 55; see p. 42: "The comparisons of the N[ew].T[estament]. leave room for as much depth of interpretation as you like. They are bottomless."

10. *Dialogues* 2 OC i 808. See similar remarks in Stanley Cavell, "The Availability of Wittgenstein's Later Philosophy," in *Must We Mean What We Say?* (New York: Scribners, 1969), 71.

11. The preceding paragraph draws purposively from the opening paragraph of chapter 2 of my *Friedrich Nietzsche and the Politics of Transfiguration,* Expanded Edition (Champaign: Illinois, 2000).

12. Pursuing this way of reading, Steven Affeldt has recently argued that one should read the (notorious) passage in Rousseau about "forcing to be free" as an inquiry into the qualities of freedom such that it can require something of us (that we *be* free). See his "The Force of Freedom—Rousseau on Forcing to Be Free," *Political Theory* XXVII, 3 (June, 1999), 299–333.

13. *SC* ii 6 OC iii 380.

14. See, e.g., the discussion below, 12.

15. Friedrich Nietzsche, *Thus Spoke Zarathustra,* prologue 5 (in W. Kaufmann, ed., *The Portable Nietzsche* [Vintage: New York, 1967], 130).

16. *SC* ii 7 OC iii 381.

17. See Stanley Cavell, *The Claim of Reason* (Oxford: Clarendon, 1979), 53–54.

18. *Julie or The New Heloise* preface OC ii 5.

Preface

As long as I can remember, I have been a Rousseauian. Some of it is education and upbringing. I, too, grew up in Geneva, and a secularization of Calvinism is probably an inevitable consequence of Genevan life. Some of it, as with Rousseau himself, comes from sharing the simultaneity of belonging and not belonging—the threat of one always brings the other—that is characteristic of modern Western life. Indeed, in Geneva, where the lake comes together and the water flow accelerates to reconstitute the Rhône river, there is an island that bears Jean-Jacques Rousseau's name. On the island there is a statue of Rousseau, seated, looking out over the lake. The geography of the canton is such that it surrounds the end of the lake like a doughnut with a bite out of it. As statue, Rousseau is seated in such a manner that he looks out in the only direction that does not look at his hometown. He was a person of that city, destined to look away from it when he was there.

Such is my background for this book. I come to it more immediately from an experience as a teacher that I found repeated in one political theory class after another. An accusation was made against Rousseau that his doctrine of the General Will presupposed that someone could know better than I did what was good for me. Most often, this question would be expanded—not just in discussion of Rousseau, but also with Plato, Wittgenstein, Hobbes, Marx—to the question as to what claim one might make to know what another person felt or thought. Typically—these are late adolescents, mind you, but the fact is not confined to adolescence—a good number of students would insistently deny that they ever could, ever would, "really know" what another person was thinking or feeling or meaning. Their stance was, I felt, a matter of ownership and control. What was to them an apparently irreducible fact—that their body was their own and not someone else's—carried the matter against all objection. (Women were less likely to make such a claim, and the rare woman who had been pregnant, to my memory, never did.)

On the face of it, this claim contradicted what I kept insisting to them was their everyday experience. But it was clear that I could not persuade them of what their ordinary experience was. Something needed protection and I found their anxieties impervious to what I insisted was common sense. Moreover, when pushed, it soon appeared that any aspect of life was potentially a source of paranoia. In fact, their claims seemed to find substantiation not only in the endless philosophical debates on "other minds" but in much modern literature—and not only in Kafka: Sociologists like Erving Goffmann gave them a world in which the everyday was ontologically threatening. It did no good to suggest to my students that they "really did know" what someone meant when they extended their hand to you on the street: For them only luck and statistics kept your head above your shoulders.

Two thoughts came to me as I lived and read in this world. The first was that there was some truth to these perceptions. By the late 1960s, public life had a way of breaking your heart. It was not even that officials lied: There seemed to be little relationship between what they said and what happened, as if their words were disconnected from the world. So my first thought was that there was something lacking in the experience of the world, the absence of which made that world a threatening presence.

The second thought was cousin to the first. It was that whatever was wrong with the world could not be set right simply by explaining to others that one could, really, truly, count on most things, without even thinking about them. Arguments were not enough against the kind of skepticism I encountered: What was lacking was the ability to allow oneself to be available to another and to oneself.

To allow oneself to be available—I shall have much to say about availability in this book. But there was a moment that those present will remember. During the troubles that shook Harvard University in the spring of 1969, one of the issues was the institution of a program in Black Studies. For most students and faculty, this was separate from the strike that had closed the campus down. A faculty meeting had been called to vote on the issue of Black Studies, and it appeared that, at best, approval of the program would be a near thing. I was, with a friend, involved in trying to negotiate a bridge between the Black Student Association and the faculty. Neither of us had the standing to speak credibly at a regular faculty meeting, let alone attend one. A senior professor had indicated that he was willing to help. We called him at 2:30 in the morning the day before the vote, when things were looking desperate to the students. Without complaint or question, he came from across town to a room in which were five highly suspicious black students (who knew him not, even by academic reputation), my friend (who knew him slightly), and myself (who had never met him, but had read his work). Before anything could be said, the man asked for time. For 45 minutes he made available to them not what he did, nor what his commitments were, nor even who he was, but what he was. It was not persuasion, but presence. The students heard a voice; having read the work, I saw the man. We emerged some hours later into the first morning sun. "Nature's first green is gold."

I tell this story because it informs the book that follows. I hope to have found here the way to talk about such moments in a way that makes sense. So the first thing this book is about is the availability of one human being to another human being.

It is also about politics, and it is about politics because politics rests, I argue with Rousseau, on a particular availability, that of the ordinary or the common. What the students in my classes lacked, I might say, was the availability of ordinary life. Their language in these discussions held it at a distance. With Rousseau, I take that situation to be a consequence of some aspects of modernity (that is, of the situation of the West in the period that loosely follows the French Revolution). Their claim is thus a social and political matter, before it is an epistemological one.

I also take the ordinary or commonalty to be the stuff of politics. There is a great deal of talk these days about the end of communism. If it has ended, what is the *it*, one might ask, that has ended? Part of what would have ended was the idea that one knew what it would be like to live a life that was not exploitative, that was not one of dominion. Communism was the dream that a life would be possible in which one did not have to say no to the human in another human. The stuff of politics, if there is to be politics, must start from the human, that is, not from the way in which I am *like* you, but from the way in which I *am* you and the way in which you are me.

Various answers have been given as to this commonalty: utility, pain and pleasure, rights, reason. Rousseau dug or tried to dig under these answers, to what one might call the nature or being of commonalty. I hope to have made some of his explorations available here.

As befits a book on commonalty, I have written this book pretty much by myself. Helene Keyssar has helped to make it better. I owe much prompting to the work of Jean Starobinski and Pierre Burgelin. I have argued with great profit with my student Frank Sposito, now completing his own account of some of these matters. Thanks to Morton Schoolman for inviting me to pursue it in the context of this series and for his editorial suggestions. I thank also the Juan March Foundation, its director, Leopoldo Calvo-Sotello, and the staff, as well as Victor Pérez-Díaz, for having provided an unexcelled work environment in the fall of 1992, which permitted me to finish much of the work. I thank Marcel Hénaff for his generous help.

The most important voice in the book, however, is not here to read it. It is ironic and appropriate that this book should in part be about the human importance of the presence of absence. Judith Nisse Shklar died suddenly as I started the full version of this text. She had seen a little of my first encounter with Rousseau many years ago. Then, as now, we found ourselves in disagreement. It is a sign of her greatness as a teacher and a friend—as a human being—that I have been consistently instructed by my disagreements with her, and this for almost 30 years. I will continue to be so. She showed that the discipline of the text was no barrier to matters of import. I grieve that she is no longer beside us to tell me what is wrong with this book, but her voice is on the margins of most pages. I dedicate it to the presence of her memory.

—Tracy B. Strong
Madrid and La Jolla, California

1

Jean-Jacques Rousseau and the Fear of the Author

Je tiens Jean-Jacques Rousseau.
> Supposedly said by David Hume after Rousseau agreed to visit
> England and the later cause for rupture of their relationship.

In speaking myself, I delighted, I delight still.
> *Fragments autobiographiques, OC* i 1174[1]

I t is the lot of any great thinker at the same time to permit and to resist all interpretations.[2] Rousseau is no exception. He has been associated with almost every school of thought and political movement of Western modernity.[3] These schools of thought cover the political spectrum that has been available to the West since roughly the time of the French Revolution, that is, since the Enlightenment found its institutional and ideological embodiment. Rousseau's progeny populate the range of modern experience.[4]

In the face of such diversity of judgment, the writer is tempted to throw up his (in my case) hands. My intention is certainly not that of Hume: I do not want in this book to hold Rousseau down. But Hume's apostrophe can teach a valuable lesson; the claim to hold Rousseau itself makes Rousseau escape you. I rather hope here to give a reading that suggests why it is that Rousseau has been read so divergently. Such a reading would locate and describe the space(s) in which Rousseau made himself available to readers, but it would also describe why readers have refused to encounter Rousseau as the being as which he hoped to be met.

There is a preliminary point. In general, it does not seem to me fruitful in discussing political theorists to try to get them "right." The characteristic of a "great thinker"—one whom might want to call a part of a "canon"—is that it makes little sense to argue that they were wrong about something. There is nothing easier than to identify Plato's mistakes, explain Hobbes's exaggerations, pinpoint Nietzsche's contradictions, as if these writers were some average college sophomore. What is denied by such an approach is that some texts have the quality of being part of our education as persons, of becoming and being part of our common sensibility; they are below, one might say, the level of assessment. I do not know the limits of "our" in that sentence, except to say that it includes those who find themselves in response to a text as well as those who resist being in response to a text. If the *Meditations* of Descartes find no ear in you, I might be able to show you how to hear them, to find them in yourself; but I might not, and requiring you to would be a lost exercise, no matter how clever you may be. I should note that not all such texts have been authored by one person. The King James Bible is an obvious case in point, as, more recently, are a motley of feminist texts. But all such texts have the quality of being part of the world by which we judge the world. They are, so to speak, the conditions of our seeing and grasping, not just what we grasp. In such a way "nature imitates art," as Oscar Wilde once said.

Along these lines, I cannot attempt to account for the diversity of opinions on Rousseau by suggesting that such and such an interpretation "gets him right"—or wrong. What I want to suggest is that Rousseau gives us—meaning at least the white, western, male, 19th- and 20th-century worlds, as well as all those who must find (part of) those worlds in themselves—our language for politics and personhood. He does not, of course, give us it all, complete. Subsequent to Rousseau, Kant, Hegel, Marx, the German and English and American romantics, as well as some others (even Nietzsche), extend, develop, resist, struggle against Rousseau's presence and his words. Others continue to do so today. Rousseau is not the whole story of modernity, but he is, in ways that others around and before him were not, *modern*. I want therefore to read Rousseau in such a way that our questions appear as his concern. This is not an anachronistic imposition of contemporary categories on other historical contexts, as if anyone could say just one thing. It is a claim that Rousseau is part of us (that pronoun again).

I shall resist here the temptation to define *modern*. Part of my claim is that what we mean by modern can be seen by looking at Rousseau. This is a very strong claim and it flies in the face of considerable scholarly opinion. It is possible to investigate "Rousseau and the Political Science of His Time," although even the title of Robert Dérathé's book should give pause as the notion of *science politique* did not come into use until 1770.[5] But it helps us to understand our times to see that Rousseau is at the basis of the political arguments we have had over the last two hundred years. I do not reject the fact that Rousseau wrote from and in the words and language of his time—what else can anyone do?—nor that we need to know what those words and language were. But he did, I hope to show, cast it anew.

Who, then, was this person? It is not that his life will explain his writing—so much, at least, New literary Criticism has taught. But as part of the importance of his writing will be its ability to allow us, the reader, to find the person in the author, and thus perhaps to find ourselves in that person, I must here say something about the life of that person. If I were writing about Hobbes, for instance, I would not, I think, find the question of who wrote his texts (what persona the author presented) to require my response.[6] This is not, I hope to show, the case with Rousseau. As I must therefore have reference in what follows to the person Jean-Jacques Rousseau, I must sketch out his life. In this presentation of his life, I am not concerned, I should say, with explicating his *Confessions,* as I take those to form a book written *about* Rousseau. What follows here is what might be left, so to speak, on the blotter.[7]

Jean-Jacques Rousseau: The Life

Jean-Jacques Rousseau was born in a house in the old aristocratic quarter of the free city-state of Geneva on the 28th day of June, 1712. His parents were members of the lower citizenry. In the political demography of Geneva, "citizens," as both his parents' families were, were a restricted and privileged group, entitled to participate not just in the political life of the city, but in its sovereign magistracy.[8] Effectively, however, political power was reserved for the *citoyens du haut*, the higher citizenry, and not to the social group of Rousseau's family.

The baby Rousseau was baptized into the Reformed Church of Geneva a week after his birth; his mother died from fever three days later ("My birth was my first misfortune"[9]) and Rousseau was raised first by his father, a watchmaker by trade and a reader by avocation. He shared his reading with his son, such that Rousseau recalled with pleasure reading novels with him at age six. His father was forced to leave Geneva after a quarrel with a captain of the militia (the offense that prompted Isaac Rousseau's ire was very slight) and the young Rousseau, now aged ten, was brought up in the household of cousins and an uncle. An experience of being spanked with his pants down is his first erotic memory and leaves him with a mild taste for sadomasochism. He is accused of having broken a comb. To his distress no one believes his denials; even 50 years later, he persists in the proclamation of his knowledge of his innocence.[10]

In 1728, Rousseau, wandering in the countryside on a Sunday and unhappy with his apprenticeship as an engraver, finds the city gates of Geneva closed for the night. This decides him to leave his home. After a few days of wandering around Savoy, he obtains from the *curé* of Confignon an introduction to Madame de Warens, a Swiss baroness converted to Catholicism and living in Annecy, some 60 miles south of Geneva. Maintained by various pensions from the Church, she is eager for him to convert to Catholicism and to that effect encourages him to enter a hospice in Turin. At that time he fancied himself, he was to write, as Madame de Warens's "piece of work (*ouvrage*), student, friend, almost lover."[11]

In Turin, he abjures his Protestant faith for Roman Catholicism and finds his way to employment as a lackey in town. While there, he steals a pink and silver ribbon and blames the theft on a maid. The two are called on the carpet and Rousseau remains mute to the maid's pleas to "return to himself." Eventually, because guilt cannot be ascertained, neither is punished. The memory stays with Rousseau for the rest of his life.[12]

Rousseau begins at this point a relationship with Madame de Warens, the first of many liaisons with women, most often older women.[13] He will always call her *maman*, and she him *petit*.[14] She encourages his autodidacticism, constantly placing books before him. He also becomes skillful enough in music to give lessons, at one point pretending to be a Parisian composer. In 1731, bearing letters of recommendation, he goes himself to the French capital to seek his fortune and reunion with his friend Madame de Warens. Though the city will draw him back again and again, he sees "only dirty stinking little streets, ugly black houses, an aura of uncleanliness, poverty, beggars. . . . " It leaves him, he claims, with a "secret disgust for life in the capital."[15] In 1737 he visits Montpellier and writes to a friend how magnificent residences alternate side by side with miserable hovels, "all of them unfriendly to strangers."[16] This is the first occasion in which social inequality explicitly strikes Rousseau as the most obvious quality of the world around him.

The next years are bound up with continued self-instruction in philosophy and history as well as with developing his musical skills. His autodidacticism is impressive; he develops a numerical system of musical notation interesting enough that he is asked to present it to the Academy of Sciences in Paris in 1742. He supports himself working for others, most notably as tutor to the two sons of the *prévôt-général* (the chief provost marshall) of Lyons and in 1743 as secretary to the French ambassador to Venice.

He leaves the diplomatic service, having quarreled with the ambassador, and is irresistibly drawn back to the vortex and magnetic pole of contemporary Europe—back to Paris. His musical and intellectual abilities, as well as his awkward and intense charm, are again sufficient to draw attention to him, including the attentions of Diderot, Condillac, Voltaire.[17] This is the salon society of the *lumières*: Once introduced, it is only necessary to make an impression to be asked back. Rousseau does, and is. At this point in his life, Rousseau is moving into theater. He had already in his early 20s written a number of plays, none of which had been produced. Now he composes more operas, writes more plays, and authors articles on music, political economy, and other topics for the *Encyclopédie* project being edited by Diderot and D'Alembert. In late 1749, on the way to visit Diderot in the Vincennes prison, he conceives of the idea of responding to the essay topic proposed by the Dijon Academy—"If the reestablishment of the sciences and the arts has contributed to the purification of morals"—with a "no." To his surprise, the essay is awarded first prize the next year.

The success—a *succès de scandale*—is great: Rebuttals pour in from various quarters, including an anonymous one from the King of Poland. Rousseau keeps the controversy going by a set of sharp responses to the most important ones. The years are full. Since 1745 he has been living with Thérèse Levasseur, the mostly uneducated daughter of a family of low social standing that had fallen on hard times. By 1751 they have had three children, all of whom have been given over to adoption. With the furor engendered by the Dijon essay, Rousseau is suddenly at the center of European intellectual life. In 1752 his opera on a village wise man, *Le devin du village*, is a major success and performed before the king at Fontainebleau. Louis XV is so taken with the music that he wants personally to award Rousseau a pension. Anxious about appearing clumsy before the king and needful of the assurance of his independence (Were he to accept the pension, "farewell truth, courage, liberty"), he excuses himself on the grounds of ill health and leaves Paris before the ceremony.[18]

Controversy surrounds all he does. He becomes involved with important arguments with the composer Jean-Philippe Rameau about music theory, especially about the most natural relation of words to music and rhythm and the suitability of the French language for a natural relation to singing. His position is controversial enough that the musicians of the Paris opera hang him in effigy. Indeed, passion ran so high that "I appeared," as he writes later, "as the enemy of the Nation. One would have thought that the fate of the monarchy was tied to that of opera."[19] During this time his closest friend is Denis Diderot, the editor and spirit behind the *Encyclopédie* project.

His entry into a second Dijon contest, the *Discourse on the Origin of Inequality*, is not awarded first prize, but his reputation is sufficient that its publication is an important intellectual event. His friendship with Diderot reaches its height, such that Diderot can write in the article *"Encyclopédie"* in the fifth volume of the *Encyclopédie* (1755) that "the most flattering esteem is that of an upright man. Oh, Rousseau, my dear and worthy friend, I never had the strength to hold back from acclaiming you."[20]

Diderot was to find the strength he felt he lacked. At this point, Rousseau begins a series of quarrels that are to break off most of his relations with French intellectual society. Over the next several years Grimm, Voltaire, Holbach, and even Diderot give up on him or are cast aside. The publication of *Julie or the New Heloise* in 1761, with its mixture of tabloid sexuality and philosophy, meets with an enormous success, but that of the *Social Contract* and the *Emile* in 1762 draws the attention of the political authorities. Rousseau's books are condemned and burned in Paris and Geneva. The rejection from Paris he would have expected, but that of his *patrie* was an excision of self. "What! condemned without being heard! . . . Genevans, if such is your freedom, I find it a little regrettable."[21] Qualifying what has happened as an "unimaginable revolution," he renounces his status as *bourgeois*: "I take leave of those who reside in my homeland: they can do me no more harm, and I can do them no good."[22]

Homeless, he is offered a place to reside by David Hume. It was an honest offer, which Rousseau accepted, but with which he was soon to find fault. By the middle of 1768, despite having been granted an annual pension of one hundred pounds sterling by George III (also pridefully rejected), Rousseau has angrily left England and Hume. His *Confessions* are finished; they are read before various audiences, including that of the prince of Sweden. Nothing seems excluded from his text: Rousseau seems to think that everything about him is important and that all must be told if he is to be seen for the "singular soul, strange, and to say it all, a man of paradoxes,"[23] that is, for the person he finds himself to be. The reader learns of his lies, his taste for sadomasochism, his ambivalent relation to masturbation, his affairs, the children given up for adoption, his quarrels. It is all scandalous enough that Madame d'Epinay (with whom Rousseau had had a liaison, as well as one with her sister-in-law) asks the police to forbid future readings. With its self-certainty and pride in every aspect of life (even that of which he is ashamed), the *Confessions* at times resembles Nietzsche's own autobiography, *Ecce Homo*, with its sections entitled "Why I write Such Good Books," "Why I am so Wise."[24]

He finally marries Thérèse, botanizes, writes, composes. He suffers from a variety of ailments, including a chronic painful occlusion of the urinary tract. In 1778, at the age of 66, he dies. In 1794 his remains will be moved by the authorities of the French revolution to the Pantheon in

Paris. He was to appear on revolutionary playing cards of republican
heroes as the Jack of Hearts.

The Author as Personality

The preceding is a sketch of the man with whom the range of the
political positions available to modernity has been associated. There is a
second preliminary aspect to this association of Rousseau and the political
spectrum, somewhat related to my first one. This man Rousseau is not
merely associated with a very wide range of political positions: He is often
blamed or praised for them, as if they were his personal fault and responsibility.[25] This is odd. There are few authors held personally to account for
their texts. Nasty things have been said about the Leviathan, but Thomas
Hobbes, the man, tends to be excused. Nor is it the case that the personal
approach in Rousseau's case should be understood as consequent to an
overly grandiose notion of the importance of ideas on the part of some
commentators. Rousseau, of whom it is often said that he is the only
political theorist we call by his first name (in part because he invites us
to), demands personal recognition by and in his writing. I want to claim
here that Rousseau in fact *sought* the kind of direct responsibility, the
transparency to his texts, that has led many writers to attack him personally. He wrote so as to require response of his readers, not (only) out of
his own narcissism, but for well-worked out philosophical and political
intentions.

The sense that Rousseau's books require a direct and unmediated
response is not an invention of only latter-day readers, often desirous of
placing blame for the political horrors of the 20th century.[26] Already in
Rousseau's time, his readers wrote to him and spoke of him to others as
if he were their personal friend.[27] His works produced fan mail, not just
learned responses. What is achieved by a writing that has such presence?
The encounter with a (real live) person demands a different quality of
response than that which I might call "intellectual," in that one cannot as
easily hold a person at distance in the way that one can hold a text. Indeed,
one can probably not hold a person *as a person* at distance at all. A person
is not wrong or right in the way an argument is; it is precisely Rousseau's

ability to achieve this kind of almost bodily presence to his readers that is at the root of his greatness and of the claims he makes on his readers.

Such reflections raise the question of why Rousseau would have developed—quite self-consciously—a new form of writing. It was a writing that, as a reader who had never met him in person effused, "penetrated my soul, fortified my heart, enlightened my mind. . . . Ever since I read your blessed book [*The New Héloise*] I have burned with the love of virtue. . . . Feeling has taken over once again."[28] But the effect was not limited to those of what I might call his "regular readers." The above response is not dissimilar to the famous one that Immanuel Kant had after reading the *Emile*: He was so struck by Rousseau's demonstration (his *show*ing) that morality required no special qualities on the part of a human being that he missed his afternoon walk, a walk so regular and part of his being that the burghers of Königsberg were said to set their watches by his passage.[29] As Rousseau would have hoped, Kant was so moved by Rousseau's writing that his life was changed. Responses such as these—and these are not the only ones—are similar to the reactions that a serious reader of the Bible might have reported in the 17th century. A reason for theologians to insist that the Bible was the *literal* word of God was that "interpretation" was a way of protecting oneself, of distancing oneself. The reading of the Gospels—if one could but receive them as they are, without trying to control them—can set the light of God burning in a person's heart, and give a certainty and assurance that cannot be gainsaid.[30]

The Bible, at least, is the word of God. The problem for this-worldly writers is that their writing is human, even all-too-human. It is, I should think, easier to acknowledge the transforming force of the word of God than that of the words of your neighbor. Rousseau's project may be thought to be an attempt at developing a form of writing that will do for (modern) human beings what Scripture did for them in earlier centuries. But to accomplish this he will have to make available a text that is experienced as if directly by the reader. It is probably easier to place a barrier between oneself and the written word than it is to place a barrier between oneself and another person, especially one who has the quality of not letting you avoid him or her. Thus, if Rousseau could write in such a way that the reader encountered him and not his words, as if the reader were speaking to one physically there, as if one were experiencing another person, the possibility would arise that one would not be able to avoid a response, that one could not "hide behind words."

In the fragment "On God and Revelation," Rousseau suggests that the human *esprit* might be able to perceive matter directly, without thought.[31] In fact, for a thought to be of import, it must do this. If "the idea that strikes the brain does not penetrate to [the] heart, it is nothing (*nulle*)."[32] Where is the heart? The temptation here is to see in this expression a sign of Rousseau's underweaned romanticism, a kind of mushy valorization of feeling over thought. But heart here is like Pascal: "*Le coeur a ses raisons que la raison ne connait point* (the heart has its reasons of which reason knows not)."[33] To penetrate to the heart means then to become part of the way a person thinks, reasons, acts, and feels, rather than to be entailed by those qualities. It is to become part of the constitution of a person rather than an acquired predicate. Why, without this, is it *nulle*? Because it remains unincorporated, unincarnate; it has not been made flesh and given actual existence in and as a human being. Rousseau seeks to be incarnated by his words as his readers. As shall be seen, this does not mean to control them but to free them as themselves.

What was Rousseau's sense of the intimacy demanded by the public? Who or what does he have his readers encounter? Rousseau thought that he himself, as himself, had not managed to be the subject of this encounter by those around him. Although he was "created to be the best friend who ever was," he laments that "the person who would be able to respond to me has yet to come."[34] He thus required multiple authorial selves. In the *Dialogues* entitled "Rousseau judges Jean-Jacques," Rousseau as author tries to come to grips with what he thinks has been both conspiracy and calumny directed against him. The dialogue is between two characters, an unnamed Frenchman and "Rousseau," a name chosen, it is said, in order to restore to the family name that "which the public has thought appropriate to take away from me."[35] The subject matter of the discourse, not present to the two interlocutors, is "Jean-Jacques." The Frenchman wants consistency: "You will have to put yourself into agreement with yourself."[36] But the Frenchman is wrong. If "Rousseau" does not precisely want, in Whitman's overused and rarely understood phrase,[37] to "contain multitudes," at the very least he must resist being identified as one person. Not so, then replies the character "Rousseau"; his disagreement with himself will only be a problem for those who want to *make* something of him.

The desire for definition is in fact a hidden form of narcissism on the part of those who would define their person, once and for all. One of the particularities of Rousseau's persona was that, like some modern movie star, not only did his following write to him, they also wanted portraits of him; many were commissioned. "Rousseau" (the character of the *Dialogues*) notes that "Jean-Jacques" has placed a quatrain under one of these portraits:

> Those knowing in the art of pretense
> Who give me such gentle features
> No matter how much you wish to portray me
> You will only have displayed yourselves.[38]

The desire for a hard-line etching of an other, the desire to know the one thing or person someone *is*, the need to tack *being* down—all these will lead only to a projection of oneself onto the object of one's desire. The encountering of another in a non-narcissistic manner, let me call it the "acknowledging" of an other,[39] would be an experience in which there was no discrepancy between what was said and what was meant. To know what a book means, one has to know, says Rousseau, what it is to know the person who wrote it.

At the end of the first dialogue, "Rousseau" indicates that he is going off to *see* Jean-Jacques, the Frenchman that he will now *read* Rousseau. The second dialogue begins with "So? have you read him?—So? have you seen him?" and the whole task of the book is to bring together the experience of the person with the quality of his texts: the word and the flesh. Indeed, Rousseau had so despaired of the possibility of doing this that he had initially decided to deposit the manuscripts of the *Dialogues* on the high altar at Notre Dame in Paris, complete with a dedication to God. He had, however, he recounts, found his way barred by a grillwork gate he had never before seen; the next day he gave the manuscript to the *philosophe* Condillac, a man for whom he had retained considerable esteem. Returning to Condillac's home two weeks later, expecting, he assures us, to have been at last seen as he was, Rousseau was again disappointed. Condillac said "nothing to me as to the effect that my writing had had on him, nor of what he thought about the author."[40] Although Condillac did agree to help with the publication of the manuscript and apparently accepted Rousseau's condition that it should not appear until "after the end of the present century," Rousseau concludes that Condillac is not the man for his words. Rousseau decides later on the spur of the moment to give a copy of the manuscript to a visiting young English admirer, Brooke Boothby, with similar conditions attached. Shortly thereafter he is filled with regret, convinced, in a semiparanoid suspicion, that Boothby is "linked to his adversaries." Rousseau's attempt to find someone who will recognize him for who and what he is continues by *billet circulaire*; he offers the manuscript to "any Frenchman who still loves justice and truth," only to find—not without a certain *Schadenfreude*—that no one will step forward to acknowledge him- or herself to be such an individual.[41]

What then was this man who wanted others to find him out for what he was, a man desperate to be heard? He is so anxious that no error be made that he adds a passage to his will insisting that an autopsy be made to show that his urinary occlusion was consequent to a prostate condition and not to venereal disease.[42] If even his body needs explanation, it is perhaps not surprising that he should not have confidence in the work of that body, in the books he has left behind him. The books do not lend themselves to be understood, he thinks, unless one understands their author. Contemporary men cannot, it appears, see that author for what he is, at least not without help. Precisely the reasons that he is misunderstood will be the reasons that he needs to make his presence available to his readers.

Why Confess?

For his book to be understood, Rousseau will need then to present himself as a person, a human being. What can this mean? How does a reader come by the knowledge of the human *person* "Rousseau"? The answer comes from the fact that he, Rousseau, has seen himself as he is. Whereas others cannot see the author of these books, he can: Whatever his despair at what others made of him, Rousseau never appeared to despair at what he made of himself. But how to make that vision available to others? His is not an achievement widely available; he is unnoticed, as it were, by others, perhaps not even visible to them. Rousseau begins his *Confessions* as follows:

Voici le seul portrait d'homme, peint exactement d'après nature et dans toute sa vérité, qui existe et qui probablement existera jamais. (Here, painted exactly from nature and in all its truth, is the only portrait of the human that exists and probably the only one that will ever exist.)[43]

Here is an accurate picture: Look at it. However, the portrait is "of the human (*d'homme*)" or "of man"; it is not "of *a* man."[44] Yet the *Confessions* is a book filled with details that pertain solely to the subject of its author. The paradox intended is that a book that is filled with singularities about one person is to be a portrait of that which is human. Why is it necessary for a reader to know what would have to be embarrassing details about Rousseau's life? Why, except to satisfy the narcissism of the author, would anyone care? Even more important, why do we (most readers) care?

Rousseau is not unaware that his book may be ill received, or even ignored. There is, apparently, a danger that people will simply reject the book. To counter it, Rousseau exhorts his readers "by my sufferings and your entrails, and in the name of the entire human race, not to annihilate a unique and useful work." (This is, I presume, what is meant by the appeal to a gut feeling.) The usefulness of this work, he goes on to say, is that it may allow at last the beginning of the study of the human being. For the *Confessions* is a "first work for comparison." This is an extraordinary claim: The *Confessions* will make it possible for others to see the human. At the beginning of the first book of the *Confessions*, Rousseau sets the subject of the book up as what I might call "the absolute other." He is to be the touchstone for the "innumerable crowd of my fellows (*mes semblables*)."[45] Who, or what, is the being who if portrayed accurately will make humanity available to itself, for the first time?

In a little talk written to preface the public readings of his *Confessions*, Rousseau writes that "due to a singularity of nature, [he] in no way resembles other men," who in any case have always been mistaken about him. How is this possible? Does not Rousseau have eyes, legs, blood, reason, happiness, sadness—all the elements of the catalogue that Shakespeare's Shylock uses to require that he not be treated as *Jew,* that is, that he be treated as humanly as a human can naturally expect to require?

What does it mean to claim that he "in no way resembles other men" and for the *Confessions still* to be painting a portrait of *homme*? The only possible sense such a claim can make, even allowing for hyperbole, is to say that he is *homme* and that no one else is (at least no one who will read his book). It is important to him that the details of his life be known to someone who will survive him, someone who "loves justice and truth."[46] Rousseau, it is clear, felt himself different from those around him, different to the point of being convinced that the lack of acceptance he met was both unfair and inevitable. Although he did not cease from railing against his fate, that fate is not to be alone but to have only himself for company. "Here I am alone on earth, now without brother, without neighbor, without friend, having only myself for society. The most sociable and loving of humans has by unanimous agreement been proscribed."[47] Rousseau is *homme* and he is "the most sociable." What has been proscribed, in one voice, by the whole world, is therefore the human understood as sociable.

It is important to note that the sense of being alone is not something Rousseau came to only at the end of his life when reality and his paranoia about persecution came close to coming together. In 1752 he identifies himself as a Prometheus who would also be a "citizen" (of Geneva, no less!), chained to a solitary rock for having brought light to humanity.[48] It is also important to realize that the opening of the *Rêveries* just cited ("Here I am alone . . .") is actually an indication that no human is as a human ever completely alone. One can, as Thoreau knew, always have oneself for company.[49] This means that the state of being human is also always an ecstatic state, that is, a condition of being besides oneself. The epigraph to the *Confessions* is *"intus et in cute,"* which translates as "interiorly and under the skin." The full text of the passage from Persius reads *"Ego te intus et in cute novi"* ("Myself interiorly to you and in a new skin"). Rousseau would have preferred, I think, to find other human beings (the *you*), but he could always find himself.

It is for this reason, one might note here, that he is at pains to establish his rejection of masturbation, "a dangerous supplement."[50] It is dangerous because it "fools nature" into giving the appearance of the other. It is (for males?) a way of dealing with the "alarms" produced by a first orgasm, an event Rousseau notes as "involuntary," as if another had taken over your body. Masturbation is, in other words, a means of controlling an original fear, the fear of not being your own person, of being controlled. But masturbation does not control that fear in a "natural" way. Whatever else Rousseau may mean by "natural" here, he means at least "having to do with others," as that is what masturbation is designed to avoid. If Rousseau was disappointed that he has "no more friends"—and the text allows only that he was so disappointed—it is important to remember that he did not move from his loneliness to assert a kind of solipsism. The acknowledgment of himself, in the *Confessions*, in his other works, in his life, means that he cannot despair of otherness: Otherness is part of being human.

The necessary presence of (himself as) the other in Rousseau's very sense of separateness is important. A standard reading of Rousseau asserts that there are two Rousseaus, the one a solitary individualist, the other an extreme collectivist. These two Rousseaus are seen either to contradict each other or to be consequent one to the other—as if, unable to have society, Rousseau retreated to the mountains and sulked.[51] From what I have just said this must be wrongheaded. Even when "alone," *especially* when "by oneself," one is not alone, for there is always the being one is "by." Rousseau thought humans not as singulars, nor even as "double," but as "composite."[52] So it would not be surprising that he thought himself so also.

The passage in which he asserts that humans are composite comes in a draft of the *Emile* ("we are not precisely double but composite"). In it, Rousseau works out an idea that he clearly does not yet have quite in hand. At the beginning of the paragraph he asserts that while we are all "double," with a natural self inside and a social spirit visible from without. He then realizes that this is misleading, for it is wrong to conclude that with the development of society "nothing is changed in us but appearance." We have been modified, and the result is that we are "peasants, Bourgeois, Kings, Noblemen, Populace, we are neither humans nor Citizens." The aim, for Rousseau, is clearly to be human *and* citizen, the first of which comes from a natural education and the second from a social education.[53] Rousseau explicitly leaves open here the question of whether or not these two educations resemble each other. What is important is that the individual who results from these happy educations (whom and which I shall examine in detail in chapter 4) is necessarily composed of different elements.

Thus it is not just the self that is several. The very *act* of presentation of the self will necessarily also be both transparent and multiple. In the notes he writes to himself to get the tone of his *Confessions* correct, Rousseau records the following:

It is a question of my portrait and not of a book. I am going to work, so
to speak, in a *camera obscura*, and will need no other art but that of exactly
tracing what I see.

The *Confessions* are not a book. They are rather a *camera obscura*, a
complex device of mirrors and reflectors that projected an image onto a
plate on which the artist etched the lines that appeared. This was indeed,
a *camera*, a room large enough for a person to enter. To this point, the
picture of himself that he gives us will be transparent. But whereas the
quality of *camera obscura* etchings was their singularity of line, Rousseau
will instead find multiplicity:

> I will not try to render [the image] uniform; I will always have that which
> comes to me and change it as I wish without care. I will say each thing as
> I feel it, without striving for it, without embarrassment, without worrying
> about *bigarrure* [being a motley, patchwork]. By giving myself over at
> the same time to the memory of received impression and of the present
> feeling, I will doubly paint the state of my soul.[54]

The doubleness that the *Confessions* require is precisely what will
permit him to paint the portrait of the person depicted by the *Confessions*.
"I am writing the life of a man who no longer exists, but whom I knew
well, a life no one but I have known. . . . This man is myself."[55]

Confession and Constancy

This last sentence denies any semblance of constancy to Jean-Jacques
Rousseau, even that of existence. "Rousseau" is not "uniform"; indeed,
he *is* no longer, although he was and still is a text, knowable. *Who* is it
that cries out to be seen for what he is? To what does *who* refer? What is
a being who/which has always been misunderstood? What does it mean
that *all* misread you?[56]

Again and again the process of growing up is associated by Rousseau
with reentering himself. It is as if most of the time most persons lived only
outside themselves, not with themselves, as if disembodiment were a constant threat. In *The New Heloise*, Edward writes to Saint-Preux that he has

"wished to philosophize before being able; [that he] took sentiment to be reason and was content to judge things by the impression they made on him."[57] Presumably such mistakes are the source of living outside oneself. The *Emile* is written, says its author, to effectuate "a return of man (*de l'homme*) to himself."[58]

"One should remember," writes Rousseau, "the moments of my life when I became someone else." It is, however, precisely "becoming someone else" that enables him to know himself. The purpose of knowing himself is not in the end *self*-knowledge. If he knows himself, by standing outside himself, he will be able to paint a portrait of himself as he is, as a human being. This portrait will then be available to others. It is a tempting mistake, but a mistake, to read Rousseau as proposing what might today be called a "politics of identity," even and especially when he appears the most self-absorbed.

Until now, he claims, all have misread him. But they have done more than simply misread *him*. The problem is greater than (just) that. "It is true that many think to know others, but they are wrong."[59] They do not know anyone else, they do not know that they do not know, and thus, most important, they cannot grasp the human in themselves or others. The intention of the *Confessions* is really quite extraordinary:

> To be able to know oneself well, the rule or the proof is to know well another than oneself. Without this, one will never be sure not to be mistaken. . . . *I want to make it possible that one may have at least one item for comparison, such that each person can know him or herself and another and that this other be me.*[60]

The purpose of the *Confessions* then is to make it possible for others to know themselves, an act that can be undertaken only with true knowledge of another. Rousseau is able to know himself, something that ordinarily could not be accomplished alone, because he is not alone; he is at least double or multiple. The authority of the *Confessions*, I might say, lies in the fact that it makes the slightest fact about Rousseau significant. What one encounters in reading the *Confessions* is meaning shining in every facet of Rousseau's existence. Their unity consists only in that he can tell their tale.

The political implications are democratic and egalitarian. If *everything* is meaningful, then meaning is available to all, for the events of the lives of each of us are at least as significant as the events in Rousseau's life, if only we are able to acknowledge them as such. The success of the project of the *Confessions* will thus be to annihilate the author of the book and to replace him/it with a human. The authority of the book comes from the fact that it makes its own author unnecessary, indeed that it succeeds in deauthorizing Rousseau and replacing him with a human like any other human.

Why must an "author" not be (a) human? One of the responses made to the *First Discourse* was to accuse Rousseau of contradiction: Here was a writer who appeared to rail against Arts and Letters and was nonetheless himself a successful composer and author. Rousseau was not insensitive to the criticism and went to some pains to show it wrong. In the preface added in 1752 for the first production of his youthful opera *Narcisse*, Rousseau notes that he was in his youth often tempted by the role of *auteur*. He has now, after much "reflection, . . . observation and time" been able to give up this temptation. The works that he has authored (his comedies, operas, verse, most especially) are like "illegitimate children whom one still caresses with pleasure all the while blushing to be their father and whom one sends off to seek their fortune without worrying much about what will become of them."[61] When he was an *auteur*, he was like a father who took no responsibility for that which was his.[62] Rousseau is quite clear that the desire to speak with an authorial voice, rather than a human one, was a temptation to which he had occasionally succumbed and from which he now thought he could claim to have freed himself. If Rousseau succeeds in this self-deauthorization he will have freed his readers from the author of the (his?) text.[63]

What can an "author" not do? Rousseau seems to think that the stance of author is a stance that avoids and makes it possible to avoid the encounter with the human and thus is unable to make the human available in modern times. The *Confessions* are a "tracing," hardly authored at all. The *Dialogues* call authorship into question. The reason that Rousseau casts himself almost as the transcriber of the vision in the woods that becomes the *First Discourse* is precisely to avoid being placed in the transcendentally privileged position of author. In that *Discourse*, in fact, he says he sought "to bring humans back to the common sense (*au sens commun*)." They had lost a sense that was common because they thought to know something; Rousseau's task was to show them that "they knew nothing."[64] I thus hear in Rousseau's statement of his intentions for the *Discourse* something like what Wittgenstein meant when he wrote:

> Where does our investigation get its importance from, since it seems to destroy everything interesting, that is all that is great and important?... What we are destroying is nothing but houses of cards and we are clearing up the ground of language on which they stand.[65]

Clearing the Ground:
The *First Discourse* and the Question of Philosophy

My discussion of authorship and confession brings me now naturally to Rousseau's first important "clearing up of the ground," the first piece of writing he presented to a public as himself. The *Discourse on the Arts and Sciences* is about what humans *can* claim to know and about the claims that they *do* make to know. It is thus about what a human can tell another human on the authority of the human alone. Rousseau's answer is as old as that of philosophy itself: that one knows nothing. Knowing that you know nothing is thus what human knowledge is, that is, it is knowledge that acknowledges its human origins as the conditions of its existence. This "knowing nothing" is as much about "nothing" (and our resistances to it) as it is about "knowing." It is what Cordelia knows.

I have said here that the intention of Rousseau in his texts is to require of the reader an acknowledgment of the human and that the human was conceived of as social and as "the common sense." To further investigate this, let me turn in a focused fashion to the *Discourse on the Arts and Sciences*.

The conditions of the writing of the *First Discourse* are well known.[66] In October 1749 the Academy in Dijon had announced a prize of a gold medallion valued at 30 *pistoles* (a respectable sum) for the best essay on the topic of "Has the reestablishment of the sciences and arts contributed to the purification of morals [*moeurs* meaning also mores]?" Rousseau, on his way to visit his friend Diderot in the Vincennes prison, happened to have with him a copy of the issue of the journal *Mercure* in which the Dijon prize essay was announced. "At the moment of reading this topic, I saw another universe and I became another man." The transfiguration came from his perception that he must answer the question in the negative. In other words, for Rousseau, the *refusal* of the claim that to be human requires the acquisition of knowledge is the source of his transformation into *homme*. Arriving at the prison, he confided his experience to Diderot, who encouraged him to proceed. "I did so and from this moment I was lost. All the rest of my life and all of my misfortunes are the inevitable consequence of having strayed for this moment."[67]

The theme was, it should be said, not entirely new to him. Around 1740 Rousseau had written a short play, *The Discovery of the New World*. It centered around the marriage of a Spanish officer in Columbus's fleet to an American Indian maiden. This was itself also not a new theme: Voltaire had used it to considerable effect in *Alzire*, a play Rousseau had seen a few years earlier. Two details particular to Rousseau stand out. In the prologue, "Destiny" announces to a self-congratulating "Europe" that it is inevitable that she (Europe) will bring her knowledge to the New World. This knowledge is at one point referred to as "chains"; to my ear the scene is at least ambivalent about the so-called European civilizing mission. For, at the end of the play, with the marriage now successfully set up, Columbus announces:

> Boast then of your supposed brilliance,
> Europe; in this savage climate
> One finds as much courage,
> One finds more virtue.[68]

This early effort is not a great work. But a similar tension and ambivalence becomes the structure and motivation for the *Discourse on the Arts and Sciences*. Rousseau, trained as an engraver, set great store by his frontispieces; typically, he gives his tension iconic expression in the engraving that serves as frontispiece. The picture, which, says Rousseau, "shows everything in the text," depicts Prometheus bringing fire to humanity, here represented by a young naked man on a pedestal. A satyr, attracted by the flame, rushes to embrace it; Rousseau cites Plutarch's version of the fable in which Prometheus warns of the fire's ability to hurt as well as to help. The satyr, importantly not human, is in Rousseau's account identified with "vulgar men who, seduced by the brilliance of Letters, have indeterminately given themselves over to its study."[69]

The *First Discourse* was published anonymously, with the author listed only as "a Citizen of Geneva." One of the manuscripts does not carry even that identification. That Rousseau chose not to put his name on the essay may have had something to do with the fact that he was not well known at the time, but it is even more likely to be consequent to the fact that the point of the essay is that one should not seek to be known. "A citizen of Geneva" should be enough for this theme: A citizen is inevitably a citizen of somewhere, but all that is needed to know what is known in this *Discourse* is that one be a citizen. Because the *Discourse* is about the human, it also appears that one need be a citizen to know the human as human, or at least that there is no contradiction between the two.

After an epigraph from Horace warning that "we are taken advantage of by the appearance of right," the author of the *Discourse* immediately identifies his position as that of "an honest man who knows nothing and esteems himself no less for it." Rousseau now reformulates the question of the Academy to include a third possibility that the restoration of arts and sciences has neither improved mores, nor been neutral, but may have corrupted them.

It is a "great and fine spectacle," Rousseau assures us, to see how in recent generations humans have by their own efforts somehow emerged from "nothingness (*du néant*)." What had been lost during the Middle Ages was a sense of the common (*sens commun*); this had been inadvertently restored to the West by the conquest of Constantinople. But arts and letters, as they reappeared, served simply to justify the chains that society and government impose: "happy slaves."[70] The reintroduction of antiquity cannot provide a model, Rousseau avers, as the societies whose mores are being reintroduced were corrupt, slavery based, easily vanquished, degenerate. To make the point clear, Rousseau ticks off Egypt, Greece, Troy, Rome, Constantinople, China. Following Montaigne ("Of Pedantry"), Rousseau mentions a few peoples who maintained virtue without letters: the Persians, the Scythians, the ancient Germans, and the early Romans, to which list he adds the contemporary Swiss.[71] The point is not that society is bad, but that the hold of society on its members is greater when the chains of society are covered over by the garlands of the arts. It appears then that one of the problems with the arts and sciences is that they keep people from recognizing how determined their own self is by the society in which they live. Thus

> There governs in our mores a vile and deceiving uniformity and all minds (*esprits*) seem to have been cast in the same mold: constantly, decorum (*politesse*) insists, propriety demands; constantly, one does what is done, never one's own genius. One no longer dares appear as what one is; and under this perpetual constraint, the humans who make up this herd called society, if put in the same circumstances, would do the same things.[72]

The only note of hope that Rousseau allows as the first part of his essay rises to a rhetorical climax is that things would be worse if humans were born learned.[73] The theme is not developed here but implies that, although each child is presently born into a corrupt society, the child is not born corrupt. It is conceivable that if one could keep the child from becoming *savant,* the gilded slavery of the arts and sciences could be avoided. Rousseau is thus led to turn in the second part of his *Discourse* to a consideration of the arts and sciences "in themselves," as opposed to the simple association of them with present-day corruption that he has been making.

In the first part of the *Discourse*, Rousseau explicitly associates himself by a long citation from the *Apology* with the philosophical stance of Socrates.[74] He immediately also joins the Athenian's name to that of Fabricius, a Roman known for his civic virtue. Rousseau's literary device is the prosopopoeia, an original speech invented by Rousseau for the Roman from a half dozen extant classical sources. He had first penned it after the inspiration on the Vincennes road. It is noteworthy that whereas the example of classical philosophical excellence is clear, no single ancient text serves for Rousseau as the model of civic virtue: He had to compose his own. The task of the *Discourse*—now *Rousseau's* text—is to bring together the Socrates who knows that he knows nothing and the model of civic virtue here attributed to Fabricius. In his reply to the critique of the *First Discourse* by the Abbé Raynal, Rousseau will indicate that if a reader took away from the *Discourse* only the words "virtue, truth . . . truth, virtue" that he (Rousseau) would have nothing more to say to such a person.[75] How is it possible to know that you know nothing [human truth] *and* to be a citizen [human, this worldly, virtuous]? Or in another way: What is the relation between Socratic knowledge and political virtue? Rousseau appears not to be satisfied with Socrates' apparent claim that "knowing that he knew nothing" was sufficient to make him the first citizen in Athens.

The die of Rousseau's life was indeed cast that day in Vincennes: The endeavor of joining the naturally human and civic virtue in one will occupy him until his death. The question of civic virtue will, however, occupy but little of the remainder of the *Discourse*. Rousseau inaugurates the next section by invoking the scene from the *Phaedrus* in which Socrates, outside the walls of the city for the only time in his philosophical career, tells Phaedrus of the Egyptian myth of Theuth bringing the sciences (especially writing) to an Egyptian king only to have them rejected.[76] Indeed, a bit later on, Rousseau will make reference to the "awful disorders" brought about by the invention of printing and the fact that such disorders have given permanence to the "dangerous dreamings of the Hobbes's and Spinozas."[77] In the next chapter, I will examine Rousseau's judgment on writing and books in more detail, but I can note here that his association of writing and books with the sciences means that both divert humans from that which is truly their own. They are gifts from a God that humans must refuse. Indeed, Rousseau proceeds with a short catalogue of how the various sciences each spring from one or another human vice, astronomy from superstition, rhetoric from ambition, and so forth, with ethics even emerging from human pride.[78]

What is wrong with the arts and sciences? Rousseau entertains a number of responses: They make humans lazy, make humans cowards, corrupt the taste and, most centrally, "introduce inequality between humans by means of the distinction of talents and the disparagement of the virtues."[79] But there is in fact nothing wrong with the arts and sciences *in themselves*, as Rousseau explicitly declares in his response to the King of Poland. The sciences allow one to participate in "the supreme intelligence . . . of the author of all things." The problem is that the sciences "are not made for human beings."[80]

Well, what can that mean? The expression, "the author of things" had found currency in the writings of Leibniz and Malebranche. It suggests that the universe has, by virtue of its creation by God, a moral quality in addition to or in conjunction with the quality of being divinely caused.[81] To participate in the "supreme intelligence," as Rousseau suggests the sciences permit, would thus be to know the moral quality that the universe has as universe. Such for Rousseau is the claim of "philosophers."

But this is precisely what he wants to resist about the claims of philosophy. Insofar as the sciences and the arts are claims to knowledge, indeed, most generally, insofar as philosophy is a claim to *special* knowledge, it will produce only foolishness and contradictions, an attempt to be God-like. Rousseau mocks the most famous philosophers of his period and the "lessons" they have produced.[82] Whatever it is that we should not have acquired from the arts and sciences, it is not something that might otherwise be taught to us. In the *Confessions*, Rousseau indicates that when he was reading these writers for the first time in 1736 he at first desired to try to reconcile their contradictions. At the time of the *First Discourse*, their contradictions become an indicator of what is wrong with what is generally called philosophy.[83] What is wrong with philosophers, it seems, is that they are not concerned with *human use*. By "use," Rousseau does not mean with being "practical." He means that one should look at how humans *use* various concepts to see what they *mean* as human words (I do not think that Rousseau thinks there are other kinds) and that philosophers, by denying this, by looking, for instance, for truth, also avoid the human. ("Let the use teach you the meaning," Wittgenstein tells us; *teach* is central.) In his reply to the King of Poland's intervention in the controversy, Rousseau was drawn to Saint Augustine. God can be worshiped in nature, says Rousseau, without having to understand nature as a philosopher might. In manuscript, he adds a sentence from Augustine that "God has not willed that we know these things but that we have the *use* of them."[84] By *use* here, I think that Rousseau means to point at what he thinks is wrong with philosophy and by extension to the forms of philosophy that are the arts and sciences. Use is, after all, the principle that will become the basis of Emile's education.[85] Philosophers seek to know, but they do not look and see. They find nothing in human use. Thus they are blinded by illusions of which it has been forgotten that they are illusions. "Will we always be the fool of words? will we never understand that studies, knowledge, learning and Philosophy are but vain simulacra erected by human pride."[86] The "natural state" of man, Rousseau goes on to say, is ignorance.

I read this to be a claim not so much about ignorance as one about the human, as if what we need to be human does not depend on *knowing*. It is not a matter, Rousseau insists again and again, of going back to live as savages with the bears, to "burn the libraries," and so forth.[87] It is not precisely that we have too much knowledge, but that what we have keeps us from *being*, from what Rousseau calls "living." Whatever virtue is human virtue is there in front of us and our knowledge constantly keeps us from seeing it. "All circumstances," says Rousseau, that lead humans to cultivate the sciences lead to corruption. The desire to know, when placed in a condition of inequality in which one person compares himself to another, becomes a form—reinforces the structures of domination—of inequality. Hence such persons are subject to and reflect the structures of society, structures of inequality, "from which are born all these abuses."[88] This is a society built around "those dreadful words *mine* and *thine*."[89] To escape this, one would have to be an extraordinary person (Rousseau cites Newton, Bacon, and Descartes) who because they create something *new*, a new language, are not subject to these dynamics.

The Language for the Human

It cannot be required of us that we be a Newton in order to be virtuous. Virtue must be commonly available. What kind of language is there—what would be the ordinary speech —for such philosophy as Rousseau would have? Rousseau's most extended consideration of language comes in the *Essay on the Origin of Languages*, a work that remained unpublished during his lifetime, although he came back to it again and again.[90] Rousseau's description there of an "original language" sounds very much like what he is trying to accomplish in his own writing:

> This language would have many synonyms . . . few adverbs and abstract words. . . . It would have many irregularities and anomalies; it would neglect grammatical analogy in favor of the euphony, variety, harmony and beauty of sounds. Instead of arguments it would have pithy sayings; it would persuade without convincing and depict without demonstrating.[91]

It is not, I think, an accident that Rousseau's conception of an original language and his sense of the (proper) task for philosophy resemble each other. The proper model for language appears to be that of music, more properly that of melody. Languages that are perfectly fixed and precise are "frigid," where the written word bears increasingly less relation to the spoken.[92] Music is in fact the most human of the arts, "precisely because it brings man closer to man and always gives us some idea about our own kind."[93] Music properly produces "moral effects when it [is] doubly the voice of nature."[94]

Why so? I think that Rousseau here privileges music precisely because it need not only, as must, say, painting, *represent* things that can be seen.[95] In other words, music has a much more tenuous relation to the world of physical objects than do the other arts and therefore it must operate by "substituting for the imperceptible image of the object, that of the motions[96] which that object's presence excites in the beholder's heart."[97] Music can thus "excite in a soul [of the listener] the very same sentiments" that the composer had. This means that to the degree that a language is like music, that it sings, it can give me the same experiences as it gives you, precisely because it is not (really) representational. Music is "doubly the voice of nature" because it makes nature available, as nature, without representing it. We see here the beginnings or rather another form of a theme that preoccupies Rousseau: the dangers and limits of representation. Words, especially written words, stand for something, and fix it once and for all.[98] Originally, music, like spoken language, does not.[99] It *is*.

Taken together, the *Essay on the Origin of Languages* and the *First Discourse* propose three central Rousseauian themes. The first is a claim about philosophy, to the effect that philosophy will never do anything living as long as it advances claims to knowledge. If we call what Rousseau thinks he does (real) philosophy, then philosophy should proceed by looking and seeing, by unmasking and unveiling, by making evident. *"Ce que j'ai montré* (that which I have shown)" is Rousseau's monstrously repeated claim. Philosophy is or should be about what human beings think about when they think about human things, that is, things they cannot help but think about because they are human beings. Such matters, Rousseau seems to be saying, appear to us; they are not summoned by acts of knowledge.[100]

Secondly, the *First Discourse* sets as a problem the relationship between a thought that would claim to know nothing and civic virtue. Can a philosophy that is Socratic be linked with civic virtue, with its necessary qualities and even prejudices of a particular time and place? Rousseau is explicit: Socrates is no model for our times: "Although Socrates and Minds of his stamp may be capable of acquiring virtue through reason, Mankind would have long ago ceased to be if its preservation had depended solely on the reasonings of those who make it up."[101] Socrates, I might say, was *heroically* ordinary, heroically human. But, for Rousseau, we can no longer require that the human correspond to an act of heroism: no Newtons, no Socrates. The reason is to him clear. Whatever made Socrates possible in Athens also required him to drink the hemlock. What is at least wrong with modern society is that it will not require from Rousseau what it required of Socrates, despite the fact that Socrates said "precisely the same things as" he. Something has happened in modern society that makes the example of Socrates no longer available. Modern society, that is, no longer cares enough to put Rousseau to death: Instead he is feted. "Give us this Rousseau"—the cry comes not only from Hume. No wonder Rousseau was afraid of the author.

How has this come about? A preliminary indication is that some of what is wrong with philosophy (the arts and sciences) has to do with the nature of any society based on inequality. It is clear that an approach other than that of the Greeks is necessary.[102]

Last, the only person who could truly speak such thoughts must be a person who does not speak for (in support of) him- or herself. One may think that Rousseau protests too much when he repeatedly avers that he has broken his silence only out of "love for humanity" and as "an isolated being who neither desires nor fears anything from anyone, who speaks to others for themselves and for himself . . . It is not J. J. Rousseau whom I wish to defend."[103] Well, then, who or what does he wish to defend? The short answer is "the truth."

Does Rousseau not then claim to *know* the truth? Is he not asserting himself as much as those he condemns? Suppose, however, that what Rousseau meant by the truth did not refer to something that one *knew*. Suppose it was an expression of his conviction of a human relation to the world, a relation ordinary and common to him because he shared in it, but which, being human where others were not, it was his responsibility to make available. Humans have the truth with them always, even unto the end. But it is not there to be known, at least not in the way the height of Mont Blanc can be known.

Rousseau typically expresses this matter by referring to his "feeling."
Feeling is a word he employs so as not to have to say *know*. (He almost
never uses the word *believe*.) In the *Emile*, *knowing* the truth is not held
to be a *human* quality. Speaking to a proponent of revelation, the voice of
humanity says:

> Apostle of truth, what have you to say to me of which I do not remain the
> judge?
> God himself has spoken, listen to His revelation.
> That is something else. God has spoken! That certainly is a big word. And
> to whom did he speak?
> He spoke to men.
> Why did I hear nothing of it?
> He charged other men to bring you his word (*parole*).
> I hear: it is men who are going to tell me what God has said. I would have
> preferred to have heard God himself; it wouldn't have cost him anything
> and I would have been protected from seduction.
> He assures you by guaranteeing the mission of his delegates.
> How so?
> By great acts (*des prodiges*).
> And where are the great acts?
> In books.
> And who made these books?
> Men.
> And who saw these great acts?
> Those who attest to them.
> What? always human testimony? Always people telling me what others have
> said! How many there are between me and God![104]

"How many there are between me and God!" This is the space in which
Rousseau wishes to live—the space of humans, between the isolate and
the divine. But what kind of claim can one make to speak from *inside* that
space without claiming an authority from *outside* the sphere, be it the
authority of God, of philosophy, of *lumières*? One cannot be a "apostle"
of truth. In two texts written in 1847,[105] Søren Kierkegaard raised the
question of the difference between one who brings forth something new
that is assimilated by the human race (a "genius") and one who brings

forth something new that, because of its paradoxicality, always remains a challenge to the human race (an "apostle"). Plato or Shakespeare would be examples of the genius, St. Paul of the apostle. The apostle has authority, and authority "comes from another place."[106] In these terms, Rousseau is caught in a strange paradox. He finds himself a singular being, like no others. In this, he is like Kierkegaard's apostle. But the message he brings is one that he thinks is available to all humans as humans: Although it appears as a paradox, it can be assimilated and no longer appear new. The politics in Rousseau's anxiety about authorship comes from the fact that Rousseau seeks to develop structures by which the novelty of his message could be generally received by all. Treated only as an apostle, he wanted to be seen as a genius.

"How many there are between me and God!" This is our home. With this last response Rousseau begins to refer to his thought as a "system," the trunk of which is real and solid although most readers see only branches. All the themes that have developed from my juxtaposition of the *Confessions* and the *First Discourse* are themes central to Rousseau's entire work. There are as many ways of reading Rousseau as there are ways of avoiding another human being. The panoply of interpretations are impositions of categories that seek to fix a person once and for all. No wonder Rousseau fled from Hume. What can be home for a human being?

2

Rousseau and the Experience of Others

I ask not for the great, the remote, the romantic. . . . I embrace the
common. I explore and sit at the feet of the familiar, the low, and you
may have the antique and future worlds. What would we really know the
meaning of?

> R. W. Emerson, *The American Scholar*

The natural is always the historical.

> Martin Heidegger, *What Is Called Thinking*

One of the intents of the *Discourse on the Arts and Sciences* was
to show that most if not all of what was called "civilization"
actually set obstacles in the way of ordinary, human, activity.
When Rousseau claimed that humans were naturally good, he meant at
least that all humans had, as part of being human, the capacity to act
morally.[1] This claim will, incidentally, be true (or false) regardless of what
Rousseau may understand the "content" of morality to be. It would establish only that whatever is meant by morality must have the capacity of

being accomplished by virtue of whatever makes individuals human. It is not just that civilization keeps us from our natural selves, but— Rousseau's analogy—like the statue of Glaucus that had been so eroded by sea water that it was no longer recognizable, "the human soul [has been] altered in society by a thousand constantly renewed forces."[2]

A thousand forces. This is not a "romantic" claim, at least as that term is often used. Rather, Rousseau wants to refer "moral" behavior to what humans beings are as commonly human. The problem with society as we generally experience it is that it not only keeps us from seeing what is human, but that it persuades us that what we do see is natural. At the end of the *First Discourse*, he contrasts the men of civilization with "vulgar men," with whom he identifies himself. *Vulgar* is designed to shock but it also carries the connotation of ordinary, everyday. Vulgar men do not have "great talents"; they are not "destined for glory"; they are to "remain in obscurity." "We," says Rousseau, do not "run after a reputation that will escape us." However, Rousseau continues, the principles of virtue are "engraved in all hearts." "True philosophy" would consist in "returning into oneself and listening to the voice of conscience."[3] I take this statement about true philosophy to be a claim about the relation of such philosophy to the *we* and the *vulgar*.

Whatever else this claim is, it is at least the claim that human beings are the source and definition of the human good and that the world in which we live makes it hard for us to act like ourselves. The *First Discourse* had established Rousseau's claim that humans were hard to see. In 1753 another announcement in *Mercure* informed its readers that the Dijon Academy had again proposed a prize topic. "*Quelle est la source de l'inégalité parmi les hommes et si elle est autorisée par la loi naturelle?* (What is the source of inequality between men and is it authorized by natural law?)"[4] The prize was again to be a gold medal with a value of 30 *pistoles*.

Citizen of Geneva

If the *First Discourse* had been published anonymously out of concern for the humanity of its authority, no such reticence was shown with Rousseau's response to the 1753 topic. He changed the title to "Discourse

on the Origins and the Foundations of Inequality between human beings"
and signed himself straightforwardly as "Jean-Jacques Rousseau, citizen
of Geneva." Three things are of note. First, Rousseau was rushing his
patriotism a bit. He did not complete the process of renouncing the
Catholicism he had assumed in 1728 until the first day of August 1754,
almost two months after the writing of the dedication and title page of his
essay. Without this second abjuration, he could not formally finalize his
reintegration to Protestant communion and Genevan citizenship. The
signature then designates, clearly, his own understanding of himself,
rather than his legal membership: "Citizen of Geneva" has become part
of what he was in the world.[5] Second, his signature also announces that
he is established, or must be understood as established, as a person,
separate from his *patrie*. The dedication is datelined not in Geneva but
from across the lake in the Savoyard town of Chambéry, as Rousseau
makes sure to note. Last, his transformation of the title changes the subject
of the essay. It places more emphasis on the nature and import of inequality (rather than simply on its source); in addition, the question of natural
law is simply left aside, as if the matter were a wrong track.[6]

It is in fact in this work that for the first time Rousseau assumes a full
voice as his own. The voice proved too much for the Academy: This essay
did not carry off the laurels, which went instead to an abbot named Talbert
who argued that inequality was a manifestation of God's will. In fact,
Rousseau's work almost neglected the requirements of the Academy:
Whereas the essays were to be of a length to be read in 45 minutes,
Rousseau produced a piece of some 112 pages (in the small type of the
Gallimard editions), and expanded its scope to speak of humankind, not
just humans. A question such as his, he avers in the opening pages of the
body proper of the essay, could only have been asked by humans with a
desire for the truth; some, he goes on to assert, even those who are *les
sages*, may not have understood their question nor what would count as
an answer.[7]

So "Jean-Jacques Rousseau, citizen of Geneva" will here show his
readers why his question is a better one: what it is about the experience
of persons that keeps them from being able naturally to be humans. This
is the project of the *Second Discourse* and it will require him to "mark the
moment when in the progression of things right succeeded to violence,
nature was subjected to law; and to explain by what linkage of wonders

the strong could resolve himself to serve the weak, and the people to purchase the idea of repose at the price of a true happiness."[8] "True happiness," I should note, is contrasted not only to repose, but also to the subjugation of nature to law and to the rich serving the weak.

What is this moment? Most succinctly, it is the moment of inequality, of political and moral inequality. Rousseau is concerned to show how it is that inequality has become the dominant, even the only, form in which society makes itself available to its members. Inequality is the structure of what we experience of history, that is, of the way in which the human past is present to and in humans. Thus when Rousseau seeks to investigate the "origin and foundations" of inequality, he is seeking to make available the way in which people like us experience society.

This is a different investigation from that of the human experience of society. How it is possible to experience political society as a human being is the question that will occupy Rousseau in the *Social Contract* and in the *Emile*. That concern is, I might say, a type of ontological question. The question of the *Second Discourse*—how living historical human beings experience the kind of society in which they live—is the focus of a historical anthropological question. That is the subject matter of Rousseau's essay.

It should be noted that Rousseau is not interested here in "natural *society*." In the first place, Rousseau is clear that society as we experience it is not "natural" to human beings. It depends on human actions, on the recognition of others, and most important, on the specific character of those interactions. Society *is* constructed for Rousseau; but it is constructed in a way such that it is only available to human beings in a manner that dehumanizes human beings. Thus, second, society is a convention that keeps its members from being human beings, and it keeps them from being human beings because it lacks what for Rousseau is the single human element that would make it real: It lacks commonalty. Rousseau's insistence that he is of the vulgar, his thankfulness that his father was in no ways remarkable as a citizen:[9] All such are claims that he has—that he *is*—the qualities necessary to make available in his life and work that which society presently lacks, that which is ordinary or common. It is clear that what is now the so-called experience of society is only a succumbing to pretense.[10] As Rousseau notes, "in every matter the false appearance of order is worse than a complete disorder."[11] I want here then to read the *Second Discourse* as an essay about pretense and lack; I want to read Rousseau as the thinker of what humans might experience when they actually experience society as human beings, that is, when one experiences society as life with others and with oneself.

What is the import of the *with* in the previous sentence? I will argue in some detail in the next chapter that Rousseau is the first philosopher of what humans have in common. His concern is not with the reasons that might lead people to join with each other to further their individual programs or interests, as arguably had been the case with Hobbes or with Locke. Nor is Rousseau's concern precisely with how all humans are alike—a pursuit of a common core or human nature, in the way that a Bentham might undertake. Indeed, Rousseau rejects the tacit assumption in writers like Hobbes and Locke that the reason for the transition from nature to society determines the legitimacy of social constraints. For Hobbes and Locke, it was the theorist's task to determine the most rational way of moving from nature to society; but for Rousseau, nature and society are different categories with no rational or necessary link between them. Thus if nature for Rousseau designates that which human beings are capable of doing as human beings, the common or the vulgar (or, in its volitional form, the general) designates what they experience when they experience the natural in each other.

What worries Rousseau about society as it is experienced in the contemporary world (his world and to a great degree still that of the West) is that the actuality of the common is no longer available to most persons. It is his claim that the actuality of the common, the actuality of my existence *as* your existence (and yours as mine), needs to be reclaimed. Put a different way: When I share something with you, it is not that we have possession of the same thing—in fact we precisely *don't*. Joint tenancy is not sharing. Indeed, we could not share anything, unless we were to acknowledge each other's separateness. Thus Rousseau's thought of the common will also have to be a thought of what makes and retains the difference between human beings. Rousseau cannot possibly think about the common unless he also thinks about difference. The nature of the space in which we are when we are in common is a space determined by the actuality of being different. What is the thought of this space? Thinking this thought is, I want to argue, what drives all of Rousseau's thought.

The Absence of the Thought of the Common

The *Second Discourse* is about lack. One might start by asking what keeps us from thinking the thought of the common, the thought made possible in a space in which I am in just the same way as are you. Why is this space not available? The short answer is inequality.

It is clear that the investigation of inequality is an investigation of that which keeps humans from thinking this thought, of that which keeps them from what a human experience of society is. (It is not that human beings do not live together, but they do so, as it were, in a lie: Why do they lie?)

By and in its multiple complexities, the structure of the *Second Discourse* already reflects the power of this lie.[12] An almost impermeable architecture keeps the reader in the book. After the title page and two subsequent engraved illustrations, the reader traverses the "Dedication to the Republic of Geneva." The dedication is signed by Rousseau with all the multiplicity of a citizen. He is "with the most profound respect, MOST MAGNIFICENT, VERY HONORED AND SOVEREIGN LORDS, your very humble and very obedient servant and co-citizen," at present living outside the city walls in the Catholic Savoyard town of Chambéry. (The capital letters are Rousseau's and are consonant with the scriptoral form of address he used for royalty when serving as secretary to the French ambassador to Venice.) Not content with making a walled city (and not its lords) the recipient of his essay, Rousseau now insists on moving outside any city. In an elaborate preface he moves out through another gateway with an invocation of the inscription over the entrance to the temple of Delphi. Self-knowledge—the Delphic injunction—will still not prove enough. After a citation from the Stoic poet Persius to "learn what the god has wished you to be, and as human what your place is in things,"[13] Rousseau restates his version of the Academy's question as being about inequality between persons, only to start not his essay but an exordium to the discourse proper with the claim that he must instead speak of "the human (*de l'homme*)."

What, or where, is the human when persons live in inequality? This, not the Academy's question, is the subject of Rousseau's *Discourse*, and he will keep the reader who has made his or her way through the entrance gates locked into this problem by a solid end-wall of 19 notes.[14] "All our learning keeps us in here," the text proclaims: Nothing, once in, can get out, and Rousseau wants to make sure that the reader has no reference point for society other than the ones that he, the author, finds available.

In order further to emphasize the closed nature of the world in which "man" is to be presently found, Rousseau will insist at the end of the *Discourse* that we have come full circle. At the beginning, in the "state of nature," humans found themselves all alike, undifferentiated by any quality that was their own. At the end, the undifferentiated returns in the equality of slavery: Rousseau explicitly calls it a circle; there is no way out of where we find ourselves.

But the end is not the same as the beginning, for in the process humans have gone through a final structural break. They develop self-consciousness, and thus each, while loosing any difference that he or she might have with an other, does not find it possible to recover the original stage of innocence of the beginning of the cycle. In case we miss it, he reminds us of our fall in the ninth footnote. *Self-knowledge is not enough:* Such we should have known when we pushed *beyond* the temple at Delphi. Humans are caught in a kind of *circulus vitiosus*, a compulsive repetition of nothingness, of the unhuman. That there is no way out is part of what characterizes persons as they presently experience themselves and others. Any self that beings such as us could know is not a human self. Darkness is our lot.

But the devise of Geneva is *post tenebras lux*. Into this darkness comes a light from the author. The play, we discover, is already in process: In a dramatic gesture that marks the final beginning of the *Discourse*, Rousseau pulls aside the curtain that has hidden humans from their history.

> Human: of whatever country you be, whatever be your opinions, listen: here is your history as I have thought to read it, not in the books of your fellows who are liars, but in Nature who never lies.[15]

This is to be a presentation of the history of what being human has come to mean—regardless of country or opinion. Rousseau is going to read it in nature, that is, he is merely going to transcribe what is there already. The position of the author of the *Second Discourse* is thus passive—this is not really *Rousseau's* argument, merely his presentation in a public forum of what he can read. Nature is to be approached literally, and literally approached. In this sense, as I noted in the previous chapter, nature occupies the same position for Rousseau that the Scripture had for an earlier, more theologically inclined, generation. Rousseau's project requires that the authorial self be transparent to its audience, such that "my heart would speak to [yours]."[16] For this to occur, two commands must be obeyed.

Looking Into Books

First, do not read "in the books." Rousseau's hostility to books appears often in his work. In the *Lettre à de Beaumont*, he emphasizes that as soon as "I was in the state to observe men I looked at their activity, I listened to them speak." He goes to recount how he saw, he sought, he found—but never in books where he also looked: "I consulted the authorities (*les Auteurs*)"—only to find charlatans."[17]

Why do books lie? "I hate books," the tutor proclaims in the *Emile*, "They teach one to speak of that about which one knows nothing."[18] But this seems to be only a claim that books mislead or are full of errors. Why do they *lie*? The answer comes, I think, in Rousseau's sense of the relation of most texts to a reader. As readers, we will find in a book what we want and will thus recover only the sense we have made to ourselves of ourselves back to ourselves.[19] Books make us judges in our own case, as it were; they represent our selves to ourselves, and hence give us a self-referential image of our selves, as any representation must.

Here, there is a clue in Rousseau's emphasis on seeing. His distress is with the fixed, much the same distress Emerson offers to his readers in "Experience." Emerson writes:

> Our love of the real draws us to permanence, but health of the body consists in circulation, and sanity of mind in variety or facility of association. We need change of objects. Dedication to one thought is quickly odious.[20]

For Rousseau, it is sight that keeps us, as it were, from becoming too fond of the "real." That which is heard or seen is not fixed, but exists only in the moment of its embodiment. Its actuality is transitory and to pretend otherwise is to insist one's own permanent control. Thus to obtain a "change of objects" in the vein that Emerson urges on us, Rousseau again and again emphasizes the importance of vision. The *Confessions* are a "portrait." The *Discourse on the Arts and Sciences* opens by presenting the reader with a "spectacle." In the *Social Contract*, the figure of the legislator is justified on the grounds that the people "wills the good, but does not always see it."[21] Rousseau is, he claims in a fragment entitled "My Portrait," "an observer, not a moralist," more of a "botanist" than a "physician."[22]

"All definitions [of Natural Law] that one finds in books," writes Rousseau in the *Discourse on the Origins of Inequality*, "aside from the fault of not agreeing, have also the fault of being drawn only from knowledge that humans do not naturally have."[23] The question must then be what kind of knowledge it is that humans do not naturally have. This turns out for Rousseau to be knowledge that derives from ideas rather than from images, from words rather than pictures.[24] In the *Essay on the Origin of Languages*, he indicates that "ancient history" was "filled with ways of addressing arguments to the eyes" and presented objects "before anything was said: . . . one speaks much better to the eyes than to the ears."[25]

From the beginning, the reason for the opposition to books is Rousseau's resistance to permanent definition. Books, or more accurately, writing does not "fix (or stabilize) language, [it] is precisely what alters it; it changes not its words but its genius; it substitutes precision for expressiveness."[26] What is wrong with precision is that it eliminates the human from the world. If the world is always more than we can make of it, then the desire to make it precise is a way of separating ourselves from the world. It is a form of domination. When in the *Essay on the Origin of Languages* Rousseau insists on the primordial expressive quality of language, it is precisely this fact that makes a language a human language. Books necessarily lie because their authors give permanence to that which is transitory. Rousseau, on the other hand, proclaims himself the "author of the only writing in this century that has carried into the soul of readers the persuasion that dictated them."[27] Note that even here the author is of strange status, because the writing was "dictated" to him by the writer's "persuasion."

Yet Rousseau writes books. The *Second Discourse*, a book on our "history," is therefore presumably a book that is not drawn from knowledge that humans do not naturally have, nor presumably a book that substitutes a false precision for expressiveness. But is it not his book? Again and again, Rousseau seeks to remove himself as the direct authorial presence. In 1751 there appeared from Rey's publishing firm in Amsterdam *Julie, ou la nouvelle Heloise,* "Letters of Two Lovers," which are said to have been "Collected and Published by J-J Rousseau." He asks in the preface: "Have I done it all, and is the entire correspondence a fiction? People of the world, what does it matter to you? It is certainly a fiction to you. Any honest man must admit to the books he publishes. I name myself as the head of this collection, not to appropriate it to myself, but to answer to it."[28] He (Rousseau) may be responsible to this text, but he is not the "author" of it, that is, he does not stand outside it. The author of the *Dialogues: Rousseau juge de Jean-Jacques* is multiply doubled and inserted into the text as the "Rousseau" who appears as a character and as the subject of the discussion who is referred to as "Jean-Jacques." That whole text is preceded by a lengthy discussion of the "subject, object and form of this writing" and followed by a "history of the preceding writing." Rousseau claims to be only the "editor" of the "Confessions of a Savoyard Priest" that appear in book four of the *Emile* and whose unorthodox religiosity was to cause him (Rousseau) such difficulties with the authorities.[29]

Why this repeated distancing of himself from "his" text? It is as if the texts are in fact not really his: He can show them but does not own them. For Rousseau, the privileged status and power of the position of the author was not only threatening, it may render impossible his goal to make the human available to his readers. I noted in the previous chapter the image of Rousseau tracing the image he sees in a *camera obscura*: It is that of an automatic recording of himself. This is the stance he takes again in this *Discourse*.

So it is inevitable that the second command for understanding how to read history is to "read in nature." It follows that the "Second Discourse" is a reading and that Rousseau, far from being an author, is really a reader. Reading is seeing what is in front of you, as it is. Thus he is going to simply tell us what he sees: "I see an animal less strong than others. . . I see him seating himself under an oak tree. . . . "[30] The task of/for the writer of the *Second Discourse* is to convert historical experience into a narrative picture, to make what he sees into a story such that it can be read by others. One might think today of a moving picture.[31]

Thus Rousseau will indicate that he reasons here on the "nature of things" and that one "should put facts aside for they have nothing to do with the matter."[32] This is what it means to read in nature and one of the explicit aims of the *Second Discourse* is to strip away from humans all that the passage of time has done to them so as to ask *what their being would be without time*. This is for others a process analogous to the one he will claim to have accomplished for himself in the *Confessions*. The *Discourse* is a book written to explore and deny historicity. It is thus that he can read in nature.

What Nature Is Not

But what kind of book is nature, such that one may read in it without risking the kind of representational fixity that is the source of so many errors? The first part of the answer is that nature is not human society as we presently experience it. In the opening section, Rousseau is quite clear that most of what other theorists have seen as "natural man," with whatever qualities they have supposedly found there, has been wrong. In fact "none of them has gotten back [to nature]."[33] The *philosophes*, writes Rousseau in a fragment on *The State of War*, "may very well know a bourgeois from Paris or London but they will never know the human."[34] To understand humans in a society of inequality we must first find out what qualities they might "naturally" have.

It is not just that previous thinkers did not go far enough: They did not go the right way. Here Rousseau differs from the other great theorists who precede him not only by his conclusions but by his method.[35] Take the much maligned paragraphs that Locke devotes to property. In the *Second Treatise on Government*, Locke spends considerable time developing a theory of property that rests on the naturalness of the relationship that each individual has to that which has become "his (or her) own." This relationship—the theory of property—has been much discussed. Locke has been accused (by C. B. Macpherson) or praised (by Leo Strauss) for fitting sheep's clothing on early individualistic capitalism; in this view property gives rise to politics. Others (Peter Laslett) have attempted to soften this portrait and have claimed that the discussion on property is a stricture against greed; far from being an early capitalist ideologue, Locke was merely a secular Calvinist, straitlaced in morals as well as in politics. More recently Locke has been praised (by Richard Ashcraft) for promoting a revolutionary theory of government, to which the argument about property is merely a side-payment.[36]

All this is probably true, but from Rousseau's standpoint, all variations on a similar theme. Locke is overly struck, Rousseau would say, by the substantive links between human beings and that which is not human—let us call it nature. For Locke, humans beings are nothing without activity, and that activity leads them to acquire characteristics in their interaction with that which is not human, with nature. Typically, for Locke, that activity and interaction leads to the imprinting on human energy (call this a blank slate) of the forms that exist in nature. So, when I pick up a plum, *it* becomes *me*, mine, property, still a plum, but now *my* plum, part of who I have become. For Locke humans have no naturally existing definition, no natural characteristics, but they have natural activities and thus make nature part of themselves.

Yet, Locke realizes, this slate that now has one mark on it—a plum—is threatened. I am threatened—for it is "I" who is at stake here—by the fact that there is no way for me to limit the corruption of time. Without such limitations, I will have no defined existence. So a limitation is drawn from the fact that I have acquired a characteristic. I could not extend myself and then let myself rot away over time: No more plums than I could eat, or barter. That no plums rotted would be the sign that the center held. This is Locke's response to what he sees as the threat of time to the self. For Locke, the slate with the plum mark on it is part of our interaction with nature: Thus we acquire property naturally. We need society to make nature safe. Not so for Rousseau.

For Locke human activity in the state of nature had the quality of producing that which was mine, property. This happened naturally—there was no other possibility. Rousseau shares Locke's focus on activity, but for him human activities have no necessary permanent consequences in time and thus cannot be said to have qualities. There never was anything to protect.

Rousseau is rather concerned to establish what he calls in the *Lettre à de Beaumont* a "genealogy" of how moral sentiments arise.[37] A genealogy understands developments as contingent and not as logically required by a law of development. (So one understands what it means that Nietzsche is the son of a clergyman but one does not necessarily understand Nietzsche *as* the son of a clergyman.) In the state of nature, as Rousseau sees it, the genealogy of the human is found in two "operations of the human soul . . . two principles prior to human reason": pity and *amour de soi-même* (self-love).[38] By pity, Rousseau means the capacity humans have of recognizing another human being as like oneself, rather than as a dog or a tree. Pity is "the pure movement of nature prior to all reflection."[39] Indeed, identification, prompted by suffering, is the central aspect.[40] In the *Essay on the Origin of Language* this thought is developed more fully. There Rousseau argues that pity would remain "inactive" without imagination to "set it in motion." Pity sets us in motion by

> transporting ourselves outside ourselves; by identifying with the suffering being . . . How could I suffer when I see another suffer, if I do not even know that he suffers, if I do not know what he and I have in common? Someone who has never reflected cannot be clement, or just, or pitying; any more than he can be wicked and vindictive. He who imagines nothing feels only himself; in the midst of mankind he is alone.[41]

To know what I have in common with someone else, I must be able to stand outside myself. Pity is the archetypical activity that makes the commonly human and the humanly common available. Nor can one experience the common (or the human) alone. Pity involves seeing someone else and seeing that one is like that other being. There is a theatrical presupposition to pity: It requires the witnessing of an action. It requires that I have differentiated myself from another whom I recognize as like myself. Nothing, however, follows from it, except that humans have the capacity to see that which is human as human.

It is also clear that pity is relatively ineffective in the state of nature—that is, in the state where humans have nothing in common. Pity generates nothing in common that has existence. Even sexuality and procreation are not sufficient to give definition. In state of nature interactions, fear generally comes to dominate and keeps people apart: "Man . . . was prepared to do to others all the ill he expected from them."[42] For pity to work, we must be transported outside ourselves, that is, acquire a relationship with ourselves.

I shall have some more to say on pity below, but it is important here to see it in the context of the other original human faculty. *Amour de soi-même* or self-love "interests us intensely in our well-being and our self-preservation."[43] Self-love, says Rousseau, is not precisely a "moral" faculty, as there is "original perversity in the human heart." However, as long as we are kept from relations with others, we will do no evil.[44] In the *Dialogues*, Rousseau indicates that the passions are the kinetic action-producing force in human beings, and that in an ideal world "the primitive passions . . . would only involve those objects that related to them."[45]

The object that is related to self-love is the self. Something will have gone wrong, for example, the self was no longer the object of this "primitive passion." However, when the self was the object of the passion, and this is combined with pity, what occurs is that *others are available to me just as I am available to myself.* This is what Rousseau means by "nature." Humans are naturally human when they find others in themselves as they find themselves. (It is, of course, not the case that one *automatically* finds oneself in oneself: I am an other mind for my own mind.)

We need differences. The natural passions will not naturally differentiate humans one from the other. For the (later) purposes of society, this is why Rousseau so strongly insists on the absence of any significant substantive differentiated qualities between humans in the state of nature. It should be noted that, as long as humans are not differentiated one from the other, they can have nothing in common. Locke's declaration that "God gave the world to men in common,"[46] can have no meaning for Rousseau, for in nature human beings do not conceive of themselves as different one from the other. They can thus have nothing in common.

In fact, in nature, because humans are not wicked, they are "relieved of having to be good."[47] In nature, beings are *nul*.[48] Individuals have no individual characteristics: Even the word *individual* is misleading. With no qualities and few passions, beings are "sufficient unto themselves."[49] Note Rousseau's language as he concludes (a conclusion that Voltaire annotated as that of "a very bad novel"[50]):

> Let us conclude that, wandering in the forests without industry, without speech, without settled abode, without war, and without ties, without any need of others of his kind and without any desire to harm them, perhaps even without ever recognizing any one of them individually, subject to

few passions and self-sufficient, centuries went by in all the crudeness of
the first ages; the species had already grown old and man remained ever
a child.[51]

Eight times *without*: Absence is central. There is literally nothing to
humans in the state of nature.[52] Thus the defining quality of the human
is not to be defined or fixed: This is what we know as humans. Any definition that we might have is therefore acquired. Thus the acquisition
of any substantive quality has the effect of differentiating one person
from another and of keeping others from being available to me as I am
to myself. The process of differentiation occurs as a consequence to
the encountering of obstacles to human self-preservation. Different
obstacles lead to different differences but the consequence of all of
them is that humans tend increasingly to think of themselves *in relation*
to others. First, the species distinguishes itself, but in doing so each
"was from afar preparing an individual claim to pre-eminence."[53]
Although not necessary, this process is inevitable. Even in *The New
Heloise*, Julie indicates that children depart "the state of nature almost
from birth."[54] We are what we become; thus we must be careful about
what we become.

There is a reason, however, that humans acquire the sense of mine and
thine, of superiority, and of domination—all those qualities that Rousseau
identifies at the opening of the second part of the *Discourse* as property.
This has to do with the flaws in the nature of the tie in the state of nature.
"If," and the qualifier is central, this

perfect independence and liberty with rule had stayed attached to ancient
innocence, it would have always had an essential vice, harmful to the progress
of our most excellent faculties, that is the fault of the ties of the parts that
constitute the whole. The earth would be covered with men between whom
there would be almost no communication.[55]

The consequence of this is that we would not be united; each would be
isolated; we would "live without feeling anything, we would die without
having lived."

Passions, and not needs, are the source of the first social institution,
language.[56] Language, in fact, distinguishes humans from animals, and
morals are only possible by virtue of language. Indeed, Rousseau seems

to indicate that no natural capacity that humans might have (of which pity is the foremost) can possibly be set in motion except by language.[57] I will have more to say on language later, but for now it is important to note that the vices and virtues that humans acquire in society have their quality because they relate humans to each other.[58]

So nature cannot automatically provide a standard for humans who have learned to differentiate themselves one from the other. Nature is not even developmentally related to civil society, as had been the case with Hobbes and Locke. The Englishmen had deemed civil society a natural or necessary response to the dangers and inconveniences of the state of nature. Not so for Rousseau. Responding to Monsieur Philopolis (Charles Bonnet, a Genevan naturalist who had attacked the *Discourse on the Origins of Inequality*) and the argument that anything that came from human faculties would have to be natural, Rousseau responded:

> Society is natural to the human species like old age is to the individual and peoples need Arts, Laws, Government as the old need crutches. The whole difference comes from the fact that the state of old age derives from the nature of the human being, whereas society derives from that of the human species, not directly as you assert, but only as I have shown *with the assistance of certain external circumstances that could have been or not have been* . . .[59]

There are several important claims in this sentence but central among them, I think, is that the existence of and need for civil and political society is the product of circumstances that did not have to be.[60] For the species, the natural is the product of accidents. We have grown old, but we did not have to. The explanation of this cannot come from isolating human nature, or by determining what is natural to humans. By chance or even, as it were, by mistake, we have lost that. In fact, there was literally nothing to have or to lose. Instead, any exploration must come from the abstraction of oneself from one's self, because that self is of the world we are seeking to re-form.

Once the aging process has been set in motion by various accidents, a "partial and moral existence is substituted for a physical and independent one."[61] Indeed, the more the natural life is eradicated the stronger and more durable will the acquired qualities be. This is not, however, a growth or an evolution.[62] It is a *dénaturation*.[63]

Growth is the exit from the state of being inconscient and innocent. In early times, however, there was no historical motion at all. Now the problem is that time moves too fast, faster than humans have been able to deal with. In the *Second Discourse*, for instance, no sooner has someone looked at another than he or she is ready to succumb to the notion of mine and thine. No sooner am I and are you set in distinction one from the other than we are susceptible to the blandishments of the rich to accept the idea of property. We simply are not equipped to think in a different manner. We have no thought to oppose to the thought of property.

Why not? Rousseau sees the same process at work in both the race and in individuals.[64] His solution will be the same in both—to slow down time.

> If you wish to put order and rule into the growing passions, extend the space during which they develop, so that they will have the time to order themselves as they come into being. Thus it will not be man that orders them, but nature itself.[65]

How does one slow down time? In the elaborate prefaces and introduction to the *Discourse on the Origins of Inequality*, the pursuit of the human had taken Rousseau beyond the Delphic imperative to know thyself. I can now ask what it means to put that imperative in a secondary place. For Rousseau, knowing oneself cannot be the basis of the human. When Rousseau reformulated the question set by the Academy of Dijon, he removed the question of whether or not inequality was "authorized by the law of nature." The reason, presumably, was that nothing can have the quality of being authorized before it is social.[66] Rousseau's intention here is to show that one can "be a human before being a philosopher."[67] That is, a human being must elaborate his or her understanding in a manner that does not implicitly or explicitly claim for it a privilege and an exemption from the world. Among other things, this will take one beyond the naturalist Buffon, whose emphasis on a too little-used supposed "interior sense" Rousseau still saw as part of the realm of flawed self-knowledge.[68]

If the quality of the human in nature is negativity, then the idea of human nature only makes positive sense in terms of the accomplishment of a complete denaturation and the translation of the negativities of the human into its actualized essence. Thus Rousseau explicitly denies that he is looking for the "man in the child." He seeks instead to think of that "which he was before becoming a man,"[69] that is, that which is not human. It is important to realize here that this accomplishment has its dark parallel in the procession of human history traced in the *Second Discourse*. There, in a circle, humans are returned to a second state of nature, a state in which they are again nothing, but in which their nothingness is now completely exterior. The problem for Rousseau, one might say, was to retain the original nothingness as a interior quality of the human itself.

How can denatured negativity make my self available to myself, others available to me, and myself to others? Why would it not become simply a form of solipsism? A stunning picture of the lure and possibility of this alternative is given at the end of Rousseau's playlet *Pygmalion*. Written in 1762 and set to music in 1770, it was performed without Rousseau's permission at the Paris opera in 1772. The story is standard: After despairing of the meaning of his talent, the sculptor Pygmalion finds that his marble statue of Galatea comes to life.

GALATEA [She touches herself and her first word is]: Me.

PYGMALION [ecstatic]: Me!

GALATEA [touching herself again]: It is me.

PYGMALION: Ravishing illusion which reaches unto my ears, ah! never leave my senses.

GALATEA [takes some steps and touches a piece of marble]: This is no longer me. [She touches him]: Ah! me again.

PYGMALION: Yes, dear and charming object: yes, master work fit for my hands, for my heart and for the gods. . . . It is you, you alone: I have given you all my being; I will only live through you.[70]

However attractive this possibility was to Rousseau (one thinks of his relations to Madame de Warens), this solipsistic view of commonalty is possible only in a play when an object a person has made comes to life. Rousseau, no matter how much he may have longed for this awful perfect community, knew enough to know that it was not one of human beings. That which is in common here has no commonalty at all. I cannot be human if the other for my being is a *thing*, even a living thing.

Looking at Rousseau's attitude toward society can make this clearer. Although society is a denaturation, humans owe to it "that which is most precious . . .: the morality of . . . actions and the love of virtue."[71] It is not just the only place where a person can "fulfill his duties," but in fact the only place where duties can exist. Society is the realm of obligation and such obligation will have to become part of the individual.

Loving Oneself

This theme haunts Rousseau. In 1740 or 1741, at about age 18, Rousseau writes a play entitled *Narcisse, or the lover of himself.*[72] It was not at that time produced. In the aftermath of the success of the *First Discourse* and with some retouching by Marivaux, it was first performed in 1752, on which occasion Rousseau wrote a preface for it. The play has the structure of a modified Roman comedy. Two couples are to get married. The woman in one couple, Lucinde, has been receiving *billets doux* from an unknown admirer, who, unknown to her, is in fact her fiancé, Léandre. Intrigued, she finds excuses to delay her marriage. Her brother, Valère, engaged to be married to Léandre's sister, Angélique, falls in love with a portrait of himself dressed as a woman, a portrait commissioned by Angélique. Not recognizing himself, he declares that he cannot marry until he has found the woman of the portrait. In Roman comedy, typically, each of the pairs of lovers find, then lose, and then find each other again; the second finding establishes social and institutional bonds, usually marriage.[73] Here the second finding and thus legitimated human society is threatened by the demand for a bond that cannot be: the solipsism of Valère's love of a self that he does not know to be himself. Because the other is himself, it cannot be an other, and cannot be loved. Neither love nor knowledge of others is possible alone. In society at least, as these characters are, one cannot love oneself without loving others. Solipsism would not threaten if Valère could recognize himself for who he is, at which point he would not love himself alone. Note that it is not simply the reflection of himself that leads to solipsism: The mirror in front of which he preens does not satisfy him. It is *not knowing* himself.[74] But to love himself, he would have not to be himself. Solipsism is thus to want oneself not as oneself.

At first his fiancée, Angélique, finds this enchanting. She uses terms that reflect the passions of the state of nature: "He has seen himself by my eyes."[75] But she is mistaken, she soon realizes, and as Valère persists in his solipsism, all relationships are threatened. The father of Valère and Lucinde finally threatens to disinherit his son, send his daughter to a nunnery, and marry his son's fiancée himself (Léandre is told that he will simply have to wait). All society will devolve to a patriarchal domination. Just prior to this, in a key exchange, the particular quality of the social dynamic is expressed as follows:

> VALÈRE: Go on. Remember that who loves nothing does not deserve to be loved.
> ANGÉLIQUE: It is even better to love nothing than to love oneself.[76]

Angélique's line could be Rousseau's motto. Others are necessary, *as others*. Because the presence of others is not (logically) necessary—this was the point of the first part of the *Second Discourse*—there is nothing about their presence as presence that will provide the basis for a nonsolipsistic situation. The problem that the *Social Contract* will later resolve is how to combine self-love with the knowledge of similarity and the actuality of difference.

In the *Second Discourse*, no such solution is seen, or even attempted. Society as humans presently experience it is in fact very much as if Valère had made the choice to pursue his distorted portrait. Here it is significant that the eventual marriages of the end of *Narcisse* are made possible by Valère freely choosing Angélique over the portrait *before he knows that it is a portrait of himself*. Self-knowledge is consequent to and does not precede the recognition of another. To encounter oneself is to encounter another.

The Self Encountering the Self and the Other

The most complex examination by Rousseau of the encounter of a self with the self and with others takes place in the *Dialogues*. In the introductory "Subject and Form of this Writing," Rousseau raises the question of how he is to talk of himself for others. If a man were properly honored for his achievements there would be no need. However, because he has been "disfigured," it will serve nothing to recount his achievements for they have not been—could not be—seen for what they were. "In such a case, a proud and disdainful silence would be more appropriate to him, and such would have been my preference; but it would not have accomplished my goal, and to accomplish it I necessarily had to say *by what eye, were I another, would I see a man such as I am.*"[77] The *Dialogues* thus establish the necessity and possibility of seeing another as an other.

The *Dialogues* were written over a period of years in the late 1760s and early 1770s, a period during which Rousseau became convinced that a plot to destroy his reputation had been formed by many of the leading figures of the Enlightenment (among them, Diderot, Grimm, d'Holbach, d'Alembert). A fragment in his correspondence allows a precise dating of this "discovery": November 9, 1768. I am not particularly concerned here with the truth of his claim. Like all paranoids, Rousseau had real problems also as well as reality problems.[78] What is clear is that the recognition of November 1768 was to Rousseau a lifting of a veil (he uses the word specifically), an experience like the one he had offered his readers at the beginning of the *Second Discourse*. If that text was to make clear *ton histoire* to humans, so the recognition that precipitated the *Dialogues* was to make clear the world in which he was living. The task of the *Dialogues* is to develop a way to see, to make available to others the "eye" with which Jean-Jacques Rousseau might actually be seen by others as what he was. How can he establish both his alterity and similarity? Or: Why can alterity and similarity be established only together?

Reading and Seeing

The task, as the beginning of the *Second Dialogue* makes clear, is to move from reading him to seeing him.[79] This has been difficult, for "Jean-Jacques" (the character in the *Dialogue*, who is the subject of the portrait the author of the dialogue wants to paint) has by his behavior encouraged misrepresentation. "Rousseau" says:

> I have seen him in a unique and almost incredible position, more alone in Paris than Robinson [Crusoe] in his island, sequestered from interaction (*commerce*) with humans by the crowd pressing to surround him and keeping

him from attaching himself to anyone. I have seen him voluntarily go along with his persecutors in order ceaselessly to render himself more isolated, and, while they worked without pause to keep him separate from others, he would distance himself more and more from others and from them.[80]

"Rousseau" has seen "Jean-Jacques" and throughout the second *Dialogue* "Rousseau" attempts to depict "Jean-Jacques" as he "really" is, admitting even that the *Confessions* failed in its intent at making the real "person available to the world."[81] This time, the portrait works. The word-picture drawn by "Rousseau" accords with the words of author as available in his books. But one could not see the reality of these words without having seen the author. While on a lengthy stay in the country between the time of the second and third *Dialogues*, the Frenchman reads the writings of "Jean-Jacques" and concludes that the author of these works is "the most hideous of all monsters and the horror of the human race." In demonstration of this, he has compiled a list of extracts from Rousseau's works that he now presents to "Rousseau." The Frenchman now can see in the works that Jean-Jacques is as he has been said by "Rousseau" to be. In what does this horror consist? Of that which makes Jean-Jacques a monster, the "only thing" that astonished the Frenchman is that "an isolated stranger, without parents, without support, holding to nothing on earth, and wanting to say all these things, could have believed he might do so with impunity."[82] The citations the Frenchman has pulled out almost all emphasize the fact that Jean-Jacques's contemporaries are caught in institutions that do damage to them as human beings and that they are unable to change. Indeed, perhaps change is itself impossible. The reason that Jean-Jacques is misunderstood is that society is such that humans no longer possess the categories to understand him.

> If you had not depicted your J-J, I would have believed that natural man no longer existed, but the striking relation of he whom you painted for me to the author whose books I have read leaves me no doubt that one was the other, although I have no other reason to believe it. . . . I may never love him, because that does not rest with me: but I will honor him because I want to be just, I believe him innocent, and I see him oppressed.

Thus, because the Frenchman now knows "Jean-Jacques" from "Rousseau's" portrait, "his books have accomplished the work that you had begun."[83] Authors cannot be known, but "Jean-Jacques" is not an author. Indeed, Rousseau was to note in his "Portrait" that "my book would rise up against me if I lie" (about himself), as if his authorship was so reduced that he had no power over the content of his portrait.[84]

The outcome of the *Dialogues*, after more than three hundred pages, is happy and ends with hope that "Jean-Jacques" may one day be available to a future readership. Furthermore, one has gained some idea why Rousseau is so misunderstood, so isolated, a Robinson Crusoe in the urban crowd. It is not that Rousseau is isolated because he is different, but because the society around him, indeed, all of modern society, is incapable of perceiving a human being as human. Why do they insist on making some thing of him and not just—the popular expression is significantly Heideggerian—let him be? This is the subject of the second part of the *Second Discourse*, to which I now return.

Nature and Denaturation

Here is what could have happened. During the process by which our denaturation made us into a "civil being," we might have acquired as, and in, our nature, the quality of being in common with others.

> Natural man is complete unto himself: he is the numerical unit, the absolute whole that has relation only to himself or to one like him. Civil man is only the fractional unit dependent on the denominator, and whose value is in his relation with the whole, which is the social body. The best social institutions are those that know best how to denature man, to take away his absolute existence to give him a relative one, and *to transport the I into the common unit*, such that each particular no longer believes itself to be one, but part of the unit and is only sensible in the whole.[85]

The "absolute existence" of natural man was indeed an existence defined by the absence of the in-common. But it was a condition of the species, but not of individuals. When we are launched willy-nilly into social existence both our reason and our passions develop from what had been at most the potentiality of the common.[86] Indeed, the condition of absolute existence has serious problems. In an important passage in the first version of the *Social Contract*, Rousseau writes:

> Thus the gentle voice of nature is no more an infallible guide for us, nor is the independence which we have received from it a desirable state. Peace and innocence have escaped us for ever before we had enjoyed their delights. . . . There is more. This perfect innocence and this liberty without rule (*règle*), had it remained joined to the ancient innocence would have always carried an essential vice, one harmful to the progress of our most excellent faculties, that is the fault in this linking of the parts that compose the whole.[87]

Yet here again it is a question of timing. In the *Letter to Philopolis*, after indicating that society is natural to humankind in the way that old age is to the individual, he goes on to affirm that "the state of society . . . has an ultimate limit which humans have it in their power to reach either sooner or later. . . . "[88] The danger is that humans will approach the "ultimate limit" too fast and will thus mistake the "miseries of a condition for the perfection of the species."

Rousseau's concern is then not just that human beings are unhappy, but that they confuse unhappiness with happiness. They embrace a condition they wrongly think to be one of virtue and perfection. What does it mean to tell people that the condition they call perfection is not one? Rousseau here inaugurates a problem that will extend throughout the 19th century. Nietzsche's Zarathustra will begin his teaching with an encounter with the "last men" who find desirable precisely what he is trying to dissuade them from. Zarathustra then comes to understand, as had Rousseau, that self-knowledge will not be enough, for the problem lies in the self that has knowledge of itself.

I should note here that this is not precisely the problem of false consciousness, at least as that question is usually understood. False consciousness implies that people can come to recognize their true needs, given appropriate circumstances. The "true" needs lie within, as it were, simply unseen. But with Rousseau (and Nietzsche), there is nothing interior that has not been seen. Because humans are human in virtue of their existence with others, they are the kinds of humans that that social existence gives them. Because there is no going back all that can be done is to think through the essence of their socialness.

This is Rousseau at his most illiberal, if by liberalism one means a political philosophy that holds that insofar as is possible all policies must be justified without reference to the particular qualities or virtues of the relevant persons. To the degree that a policy is or must be justified on the grounds that it makes me a better person—whatever *better* may mean here—to that degree liberals will want to reject that policy. As noted in the next chapter, Rousseau does share certain important characteristics with liberalism. But he is not a liberal in relation to the society in which he lives. The quality of relations in that society is such that they are no longer what he sees as "human" relations. Therefore the first politic task will be to make persons capable of humanity, either again or for the first time.[89] For Rousseau the real source of our evils is in life as we have experienced it itself and in the most characteristic of its propensities.[90] His cannot be a "liberalism of fear," because by the end of the *Second Discourse* it does not appear that individuals are human enough even to fear.[91] They are rather like the last men in the prologue to *Thus Spoke Zarathustra*.

So what has happened to make us incapable of humanity? To make the human unavailable? As humans become related to each other—here the concept of property is central—so also do they become what they are in relation to each other. With this change the availability of a state of absolute undifferentiated existence (and thus not subject to time) is no longer possible.[92] Thus:

> All attachment is a sign of insufficiency; if each of us had not need of others, they would never think to join together with them. Thus from our infirmity is born our frail happiness.[93]

But again, that which characterizes humans—their passions—only acquires its characteristics in interaction with others. In the *Second Discourse*, as long as there was no notion of mine and thine (no property), beings made no judgments about themselves or others and "their disputes rarely had bloody consequences."[94] From this it follows, I think, that to be human is to have a notion of mine and thine and to be able to make judgments about others. Our commonalty—the stuff of humanity—requires difference and there is no identity that is not that of difference. It will thus be the case that the particular quality of the concretization of relationships—institutions—will be inextricably bound up with identity.

Indeed, institutions are consequent to and coterminous with the existence of identity.

In a brilliant reading of Rousseau, Judith Shklar has struggled with the relationship between Rousseau's understanding of the soul and his understanding of politics.[95] Her conclusion—that there are several Rousseaus, and for good reason—is premised on the claim that Rousseau recognized that a politics that depended on identity would always be too weak to resist the temptations of power.[96] Although I will eventually dispute Shklar's conclusion, her premise is important. Why do people succumb? There is no reason, no cause: They succumb because there is nothing else they have available to them.

Consider: Human discontents do not derive from human passions, even though among the passions there is one that is "more dangerous," sexuality, which by its nature necessarily involves an other. Rousseau does give sex its due. Even early on, while the other passions are "little active," this one is "ardent, impetuous, . . . terrible and daring all dangers, reversing all obstacles." Every day humans "dispute their loves at the price of their blood."[97] Here one might expect that Rousseau would take the Aristotelian course of suggesting that sexuality and families constitute the original societies and that the structural source of institutions is in the family relationship. But he refuses this move, suggesting instead that primitive man "goes after it without any selection (*goût*) and any woman is good enough for him."[98]

The reason for not taking the Aristotelian move is, I think, that Rousseau is trying to avoid a developmental attitude toward the passions and human society. Instead he is after their "source . . . origin and principle."[99] This quality is the *amour de soi-même*. *Amour de soi-même* is almost always opposed to *amour propre*.[100] Both terms mean self-love, an important complication in that Rousseau also warns us that:

> One must not confuse *amour propre* with *amour de soi-même*: two passions very different by their nature and their consequences. The *amour de soi-même* is a natural feeling that leads any animal to watch to his own preservation and which, when directed in man by reason and modified by pity, produces humanity and virtue. *Amour propre* is only a relative feeling, artificial and born in society, which leads each individual to make more of his own case than that of others, which inspires in men all the evils that they do to one another, and which is the true source of honor.[101]

Rousseau goes on to say that in the state of nature *amour propre* does not exist because no individual has a point of view other than his or her own. Centrally: "Each man saw his own kind scarcely differently from the way he would view animals of another species." The recognition of difference—of mine and thine—thus depends for Rousseau on the recognition of similarity. Now we know that "the first look that [Emile] throws on those like him leads him to compare himself with them; and . . . This is the moment where *amour de soi-même* is changed into *amour propre.*"[102]

Rousseau's problem is how to allow for difference without that difference becoming a source of domination. The faculty of pity—the Savoyard Vicar's "divine instinct"—ensures that humans will recognize others as like them. Such human recognition is natural, or instinctive in that it preexists the emergence of reason. Reason will be socially helpful in that it is designed to control *amour propre*. ("Until the guide of *amour propre*, which is reason, can be born, it is important that a child do nothing in relation to others.") The problem lies in the manner that *amour propre* emerges.

I have said that the foundations of that which humans have in common are to be sought in the concomitance of pity and *amour de soi-même*. In the fourth book of the *Emile*, the pupil is at last ready to develop a moral being.[103] He has available two *sentiments relatifs*—structurally analogous to each other. The first is envy, the second pity. So as to encourage the second, Rousseau indicates that the child must now be exposed to suffering and death. The existence in common, the common existence, arises when we experience death and suffering: This is the groundwork of our common humanity, a humanity we cannot have in common until we have that experience.[104] Pity can, however, be inverted into envy and pride. (Rousseau is not alone here: Writers from Augustine to Montaigne to Nietzsche share this understanding.)

In society, pride will develop as soon as man "looks at himself." We are each the first other for ourself. Once I can look at myself, I can look at another. Should I see another, different, whether better off or not, envy, and thus domination, will result.[105] Rousseau is quick to suggest that time consolidated these judgments into categories, such that an individual would also judge "about those he did not perceive." There will here arise some "rare occasions where a common interest made him count on the assistance of those like him."[106] It is at this point that Rousseau tells the famous story of the stag hunt, a story often taken to show the importance of collective action. However, the point is to indicate that as long as mutuality depends only on the perception of interest, even "common" interest, it will not outlast the possibility of snatching a tempting stray rabbit for oneself, thereby ruining the common hunt. The stag hunt is about the fact that insofar as society depends only on common interest it will be transitory and ineffective as human society.

From such early mutuality, after many centuries, Rousseau's tale continues, the earliest societies were born, now around families. Note, however, that they were not born *from* families, but that families were born from mutuality. At this point, "all begins to change." Natural cataclysms (Rousseau was convinced by Buffon's argument about the role of earthquakes and floods in the civilizing process) reduce the size of the territory in which people live, cutting them off from random interaction with others and from open space; they are forced to interact more intensely. The species "continues to tame itself"; love and jealousy and quarrels are all born. As humans interact, sometimes in primitive festivals, "each begins to look at the other and want to be looked at himself." Here, in display and theater, in appearance, is born the first step toward inequality, whose emotions are vanity, disdain, shame, and envy.[107]

These pages are filled with two movements: that of revolution, cataclysm, and categorical change on the one hand; and, on the other, with beginnings, "as long as's," with development. Rousseau mixes the two because he wants to claim that apparently small, more or less expectable changes, things that happen—all these have consequences of enormous import, changing the very nature and texture of human existence. There is no single cause: Everything or anything can set off transformation. Indeed, the division of labor is not long in coming. "As soon as people perceived that it was useful for one to have more than he needed," all was lost. Natural divisions in talents now combine with social accumulation, and this becomes the structure of society.

> Here then are all our faculties now developed, memory and imagination has come into play, egotism is involved, reason has become active and the mind (*esprit*) practical; all arrive at the epitome of perfection of which they are capable. Here all the natural qualities are put into action, the rank and lot of each man established. . . . One's own advantage required that one show oneself as other than one was. Being and appearing became two different things, and from this distinction . . . come all the vices. . . .[108]

This situation gives rise to serious conflicts, by Rousseau's description worse than those Hobbes saw in nature because individuals have more to lose; finally the rich, feeling themselves in danger, conceive of political society. In an ironic parody of the Lockean social contract, Rousseau writes that this was

> the most ingenious project ever conceived by the human mind: to employ to one's own advantage the forces of those by whom one was attacked, to make defenders from one's adversaries, to inspire in them other maxims and to give to them institutions as favorable to oneself as natural right was disfavorable.[109]

It is the union of those who have, not of those who lack, that gives rise to what we call political society. In this form, political society is an illusion, a fake, an appearance. "All ran to their chains, thinking to preserve their liberty." The habit of dependency is soon acquired from its important advantages and a slow development appears. From the establishment of the law and right of property, we find the institutionalization of the magistrature. This power in turn becomes arbitrary such that the relation of rich and poor is changed first to that of powerful and weak, and finally to that of master and slave. This latter relation remains in place until "new revolutions completely dissolve the government or bring it closer to a legitimate institution."[110]

All of this follows, says Rousseau, inevitably from the "ardor in getting others to speak of oneself, from the furor of distinguishing oneself *which almost always takes us outside ourselves*."[111] Not *besides*, but *outside* our self. Dependency results, in other words, from the inability to allow differences between people to remain as differences. It results from the lack of commonalty, that is, of that quality of humans that permits them to have differences. It is precisely the need to live away from oneself that makes it impossible to live as a human self.

Rousseau now reaches a coda of disasters the end of which is that "all individuals (*particuliers*) return to a state of equality because they are null, and as the subjects have no other law than the will of the master, and the master no rule other than his passions, all ideas of the good and principles of justice vanish."[112] All this has happened because commonalty is not the structure of society.

The conclusion is disastrous: The logic of mine and thine has led to a vicious circle from which there is no apparent escape. As human development speeded up, humans were called on to confront occurrences for which they had not the epistemological tools. Now, however, they have been so shaped by the dialectic of master and slave that they have no being outside of that. Their chains are all they know. Is there another way?

Music and the Public Realm

I might go back to the moment at which people first started to compare themselves to each other. Rousseau is often mocked for a bucolic vision of rural life but country bliss is double-edged. Commentators point to his repeated use of the village festival, with its singing and dance and apparent *joie de vivre*.[113] Yet, as discussed above, it was such a festival that marked the moment when competition in song and dance eventually became the paradigm for social inequality. But festivals do not have to be like this, all presentation and show. It is also the case that Rousseau sometimes presents a different picture of such festivals. The core aspect of this other picture is what one might call its authentic musicality: I want here to look briefly at Rousseau's understanding of the relation of music to public life.

One development to avoid in human history was that of requiring that individuals be "philosophers before being humans." Rousseau means by this to point out that philosophy is consequent to the development of society and requires society to make it possible. Giving philosophy priority to or privilege over society is to require of it qualities that it cannot have. The secondary place of philosophy to experience finds exemplification in Rousseau's writings on music.[114]

Despite his repeated insistence it is easy to forget that Rousseau was first of all known as a musician. "Rousseau" says of "J-J" that "he was born for music. . . . He has discovered approaches that are clearer, easier, simpler and facilitate composition and performance. . . . I have seen no man as passionate about music as he. . . . "[115] This was no idle boast: D'Alembert confided the articles on music for the *Encyclopédie* to him.

Rousseau became, as noted previously, involved in a celebrated quarrel with Rameau about the relations of language and music.

In all of his writings on the subject, Rousseau is at pains to show that music and language develop coterminously. "Melody," he says, "is born with language."[116] Central here is Rousseau's insistence against Rameau that harmony was not basic. The reason for this has to do with the nature and possibility of commonalty. Language is what makes the world available in common. If language and music are of an original piece, the insistence that harmony was the basic quality of music would mean that each person or group would be singing (and legislating) differently, as it were, and that unity or commonalty would come only in the blend. This would not in fact be commonalty because the union would be different from each individual. No one, as it were, would be human.

Because the singing and speaking voices are of "absolutely the same nature," it would follow that strongly accentuated languages would be the most naturally musical. It is thus the case that music is at its best and most natural when in perfect sympathy with words and that words are their truest when the most flexibly musical. Here is how "Rousseau" praises Rousseau's opera *The Village Soothsayer* in the first *Dialogue*:

> What makes this opera approved by people of taste is the perfect accord of words and music, the tight bond of the parts that make it up, the exact togetherness of the whole which makes this work the most unified of any I know in its style. The musician has always thought, felt, spoken like the poet. . . .[117]

In antiquity, such a harmony of words and music was most evident in ancient Greece, where

> eloquence preceded reasoning, and men were orators and poets long before they were philosophers. . . . In the ancient festivals all was heroic and grand. The laws and songs carried the same designation in these happy times; they sounded in unison in all voices, passed through all hearts with the same pleasure, everything adored the first images of virtue, and innocence itself gave a gentler accent to the voice of pleasure.[118]

However, even in Greece, with the development of rationality forms became fixed, language became "colder and artificial." "The study of philosophy" plays a central role in this linguistic transformation. By cultivating "the art of convincing, that of moving people emotionally was lost. Plato himself, . . . jealous of Homer and Euripides, condemned one and could not imitate the other." With the conquest by Rome and the arrival of servitude, all was lost. "Greece in chains lost this celestial fire that burns only for free souls and could no longer find to praise tyrants the sublime tones with which it had erstwhile sung its heroes."[119] Latin is a "deaf and less musical" language than Greek.

A society that has a language for political life will value eloquence over the use of public force. The only form of speech appropriate to a people to whom it can be said "such is my pleasure" is a sermon and such people are taxed rather than assembled. In a society with no language for politics, no one can hear. In fact their language will have degenerated to the point that no one will be able to be heard in public.

Herodotus read his history to the people of Greece assembled out of doors, and he met with universal applause. Nowadays an academician who reads a paper in public session can hardly be heard at the back of the hall.[120]

This extraordinary analysis of Greece, complete with its Nietzschean condemnation of Plato, reveals a central quality that free society must have for Rousseau. There is to be no disjuncture between emotion and expression, between weeping and words, between meaning and saying. When the two are transparent to each other, there is no possibility to take the speaker as other than that person is. Furthermore, this experience of transparency only happens in a manner that makes it available in the same manner to any other person. The conditions of my freedom, as presented here musically, are the same conditions as that of yours.

What is important here is that those festivals in which words, music, and action came together provide the model of what commonalty is for Rousseau. In the *Letter to D'Alembert*, he footnotes a passage about free men with the following childhood memory. It is worth quoting at length in order to follow the development of the experience recounted.

The regiment of Saint-Gervais [i.e., the militia of one of Geneva's *quartiers*] had done its exercises, and, according to the custom, they supped by companies, most of those who formed them gathered after supper in the St. Gervais square and started dancing all together, officers and soldiers, around the fountain, to the basin of which the drummers, the fifers and the torch bearers had mounted. A dance of men, cheered by a long meal, would seem to present nothing very interesting to see; however, the harmony of five or six hundred men in uniform, holding one another by the hand and forming a long ribbon which round around, serpent-like, in cadence and without confusion, with countless turns and returns, countless sorts of figured evolutions, the excellence of the tunes which animated them, the sound of drums, the glare of torches, a certain military pomp in the midst of pleasure, all this created a very lively sensation what could not be experienced coldly. It was late; the women were all in bed; all of them got up. Soon the windows were full of female spectators who gave new zeal to the actors; they could no longer confine themselves to their windows and they came down; the wives came to their husbands, the servants brought wine; even the children, awakened by the noise, ran half-clothed amidst their fathers and mothers. The dance was suspended; now there were only embraces, laughs, toasts (*santés*), and caresses. There resulted from all this a general emotion that I could not describe by which, in universal gaiety, is quite naturally felt in the midst of all that is dear to us. My father, embracing me, was seized with trembling which I think I still feel and share. "Jean-Jacques," he said to me, "love your country. Do you see all these good Genevans? They are all friends; they are all brothers; joy and concord reign in their midst. You are a Genevan. . . . They wanted to pick up the dance again, but it was impossible. They did not know what they were doing any more; all heads were spinning with a drunkenness sweeter than that of wine. . . . I am well aware that this entertainment, which moved me so, would be without appeal for countless others; one must have eyes made for seeing it and a heart made for feeling it. No, the only pure joy and concord reign in their midst. You are a Genevan. . . ." They wanted to pick up the dance again, but it was impossible. They did not know what

Here we have a festival without invidiousness. This extraordinary description of what one might call the bacchanalia of the political contains a number of elements. First, the dance is both coordinated and formless: All work together as if all knew the same steps even though (perhaps because) the steps change all the time. This is not the coordination of Rameauian harmony, where each plays a different part and the whole is experienced only in the listener. Here each member performs the whole and hence, although requiring others, experiences the other as he or she experiences him- or herself. It is worth the reminder here that in the *Essay on the Origin of Languages* Rousseau indicates that music degenerates by "imposing new rules on itself," and by assuming a "fixed form," where the "rules of imitation were multiplied."[122]

Second, the name given to realization of this gaiety is that of the citizen ("You are a Genevan"). The unity achieved is the paradigm of citizenship: The joy is pure because it is unalloyed by that which it is not. If, as I have intimated before, citizenship is the pure form of humanness for Rousseau, this is because *it is all one can mean by nature in a world characterized by the knowledge of mine and thine.* "The only pure joy is public joy."

Third, women are brought into the festival body politic and out of their homes. They are no longer spectators; they cannot resist being swept up as participants.[123] Commonalty here transcends sexuality, at least for this moment. One should not be surprised that it does, because, as noted earlier, Rousseau had gone to considerable lengths to assure his readers that sexuality was not the basis of society.

Thus, fourth, the effect of the gaiety is to loose all sense of self-consciousness ("they did not know what they were doing") in the revelry of one's public identity. This is the true theater: life. In the *Letter to D'Alembert*, Rousseau had complained of the Frenchman's proposal to establish a theater in Geneva. But here one sees that Geneva, at its best, was itself a broad and universal theater. Rousseau does not so much want to keep theater out of life, but to experience life as theater. Molière makes this impossible when, as in *The Misanthrope,* he leaves us as an audience off the stage laughing at Alceste: This is the reason for Rousseau's attack. Molière gives the audience the pretense of being superior: His theater thus reinforces domination.[124]

Last, the quality of this experience is that it is "eternal," that is, is completely in the present. Time past does not effect, nor is it effected by the course through time. Rousseau, in his *Confessions*, presents himself as a person obsessed by his past: Crimes of his childhood, oversights and omissions of his youth haunt him and, as Marx and Joyce were to say in similar contexts, lie on him like a nightmare. The boldness of the *Confessions,* as I argued in the previous chapter, lies in the claim that by bringing his past into the present he will make himself available as an ordinary human being to those around him. The complete picture of a person is everything that person has been: No wonder humans are multiple beings. (All of us can be, have been, everything.)[125]

The quality of presence in the St. Gervais festival is thus an encounter with, a being-in, the world as it is, an encounter with its being and not its historicity. As Hannah Arendt, following Martin Heidegger, was to argue 175 years later, it is this experience that is at the source of human identity and of with being a people. The theatricalized political realm makes forgetting unnecessary: One can simply be what one is, naturally, as it were.

Alone, With Oneself

If that realm is lacking to us, fails us, or we fail it, as is the case for Rousseau in the modern world, are there other means that humans might adopt to retain their humanity, a kind of holding ground, *in extremis*? If our life be not theater, can life at least call up the possibility of theater, as it had in his childhood memory of Geneva? Rousseau experimented with the possibility in several places. He wrote two letters for the beginning of an epistolary sequel to the *Emile*, to be called *Emile et Sophie*. If all society and all others are corrupted, what is to be done? The issue is confronted in very stark terms. As the *Emile* ends, Emile and Sophie have gotten married. The tutor now takes his leave of them, a departure resisted by Emile. All apparently begins to fall apart. One of their children dies, as do Sophie's parents. The couple goes to Paris where Emile succumbs to the pleasures of the capital. Now unloved, Sophie takes up with another man and becomes pregnant. Emile leaves her and their son. He is taken prisoner by pirates while on a voyage to Italy and sold into slavery in Algiers. Brutalized, he is eventually put to work on a public building where, still cruelly oppressed, he decides to organize a strike of his fellow slaves. This action comes to the attention of the bey of Algiers to whom Emile explains that it would be only self-interested to treat his slaves better. He first becomes the personal slave to the bey and then, as the fragment breaks off, Emile has become the adviser to a good and fair ruler.

What is now the relation of Emile to what he has been? Is he caught in the other he became in Paris, "devoured" by the city?[126] Part of the thrust of this sequel is explicitly to reject the necessity that humans must be subject to time past. The extant part of the text takes the form of two letters that Emile writes to his (erstwhile) tutor, letters which he is not sure will ever be received. The *idea* of the tutor, that is, is now sufficient to Emile. Emile begins the second letter as follows:

> I have drunk the water of oblivion; the past is erased from my memory and the universe opens itself up before me. . . . In cutting the knots that tied me to my country, I extended my ties to the whole world, and I became all the more human as I ceased to be a Citizen.[127]

Rousseau, too, had given up his citizenship for a claim to humanity after the condemnation of the *Emile*. To give up citizenship in this context means to wish to appear unnoticed amid those who would otherwise be one's fellows. It is to be able to be at home everywhere, to have at least the appearance of citizenship. Emile goes on to describe journeys in which, because he "passes everywhere for a man of that country," he goes about unnoticed by all. But he is able to keep his own company. Emile says that because of what he is he is taken at his word as to what he says he is, thus "I was always in my own space (*j'étais toujours à ma place*)."[128] Even when a slave "the work of my hands was sold, but not my will, my understanding, my being, all that by which I was myself and not another."[129] However, the consequence of this is not that he ceases being a citizen—Emile is wrong about himself—but that he is ineluctably led back to a reintegration into a more or less just society, even at the risk of his life. He recreates at least part of a just polity. Emile will always seek out the other.

Rousseau himself takes the same stance. The *Reveries of a Solitary Walker*, written in the last two years of his life, start with this claim: "Thus I am here alone on earth, with no more brother, none near to me, no friend, no society but myself."[130]

Who am I then, when detached from them and everything else? he asks. He is like a man "fallen from another planet."[131] Yet even here, *Rousseau is his own society*—a situation he sees as "without precedent." His condition may be without precedent, but it is also a claim that dynamics of society do not require other bodies to continue to inform the humanity of a being. We can always be besides ourselves, and whatever Rousseau would have done as a citizen in Geneva, he can do as a citizen with himself. Being able to be besides oneself, to be in ecstasy, is the prerequisite and quality of the political life. The experience of others is the experience of myself. It is our grammar and thus our freedom.

Modern society, however, chains the present with its past and thus makes it impossible to live with others in the present. It turns he who (like Rousseau) can live with others into a completely strange being, a human among foreigners. Emile wrongly thinks he has "drunk the water of oblivion." But no one who had drunk of such water could remember that fact. What is it that allows one to forget? What is it that makes it unnecessary to forget?

3

The General Will and
the Scandal of Politics

The world is awakening to the idea of union, and these experiments show what it is thinking of. It is and will be magic. . . . But this union must be inward, and not one of covenants, and is to be reached by a reverse of the methods they [the New England reformers] use. The union is only perfect, when all uniters are isolated. It is the union of friends who live in different streets or towns.

R. W. Emerson, *The New England Reformers*

In truth, there are no more secrets to keep, nor truths to silence.

Rousseau, draft of a letter to the Archbishop Beaumont of Paris, upon the condemnation of the *Emile* as subversive (*OC* iv 1020)

The end of the *Discourse on the Origins of Inequality* described a scandalous situation. Political society as we experience it, Rousseau argued, traced its genealogy to inequality, that is, to the domination of one individual over another in terms of comparative

advantage. The specifically social form this took was that of the rationalization of private property to the advantage of the rich and powerful.
As such, inequality rested not only on illusion but on an illusion fostered
and promoted to destroy the moral and social equality of human beings.
It seemed as if we would have indeed to be philosophers before we
could be human, because the alternative was slavery.

At the end of the *Second Discourse*, it also appeared as if there were
nothing to be done. The term of the development of self and society was
a second state of nature in which all were equally subject to the domination of the ruler. Indeed, it might be more accurate to say "to the domination of rule," as not even the ruler rose above the general self-annihilation.

> *L'homme est né libre, et par-tout il est dans les fers. Tel se croit le maître*
> *des autres, qui ne laisse pas d'être plus esclave qu'eux.* The human being
> is born free, and everywhere is in chains. Such an individual believes
> himself the master of others and does not escape being more of a slave
> than they.[1]

Note: The chains are everywhere. It is no longer the case that some have
enslaved others but themselves remain free. "Freedom" is, in this situation, a matter of belief, part of the general illusion of social organization.
Masters are "more of a slave," presumably, because they do not know that
they are slaves. Rousseau makes the matter more precise in the *Emile*,
written around the same time. "Domination itself is servile when it is
connected with opinion, for you depend on the prejudices of those whom
you govern with prejudices. . . . To lead them as it pleases you, you have
to behave as it pleases them."[2]

The sequence in the "born free" passage is telling. Belief, opinion,
deference, domination: All individuals are bound up in illusory selves that
are defined by power relationships. Inequality makes illusion seem real
and makes us almost incapable of recollecting that illusion. Government
based purely on opinion gives us individuals whose very selves are shaped
by the terms of the relations of the society in which they already exist. It
is no longer their society: "Things are in the saddle and ride mankind,"
as Emerson remarked. The presence of the past, of time accumulated,
shapes humans inexorably. Worse yet, it is not just that we are defined in
terms of the society in which we live: We have no definition of our *own*

at all. At the end of the *Discourse on the Origins of Inequality*, Rousseau foresaw a series of stages in which society gradually emptied out the content from the structure of all historically defined human relations.

> Here is the last stage of inequality, and the ultimate point which closes the circle and meets the point from which we set out: Here all private individuals again become equal, because they are nothing. . . . Here everything reverts to the sole law of the stronger and consequently to a new state of nature.[3]

The Hobbesian state of war with its mistrust is the reality of our lives: On this Rousseau and Hobbes agree. But for Rousseau, such a state has come about and has become our nature. The same point is recalled in the *Social Contract* when Rousseau writes of the suffrage: "At the other extremity of the circle unanimity returns. This is when citizens have fallen into slavery and no longer have neither liberty or will."[4] Having liberty or will is to be one's own person; not to have them is to be a slave, not to have a self, not to be human.

Slavery is the threat. It is indeed for Rousseau inconceivable as part of a *human* society. It is an "absurd, . . . senseless" institution.[5] What is wrong with slavery is that slaves are unable to contract. Rousseau is at pains in this section of the *Social Contract* to show that no possible convention or contract can be possible between slaves or between slaves and nonslaves. The ability to contract is what makes an individual human. As Rousseau elaborates, what makes one human is the ability to consent to a social pact, that is, to become a citizen. Those who have "renounced their liberty [have given up their] human equality, have given up the rights of humanity, even its duties."[6] In the chapter on voting in the *Social Contract*, Rousseau writes that "the decision that the son of a slave is born a slave is the decision that he is not born human."[7] The insistence on the contractual basis of society is an insistence that there be individuals who are capable of contracting, as slaves are not, and that there be important social relations that are the proper subject of contract.

What is involved in Rousseau's claim here? From the end of the 16th century,[8] the idea of a social contract had been proposed as a formulation for understanding the nature of the political relationship. It had its historical origins in the controversies surrounding lay investiture, when theorists supporting the papacy, such as Manegold of Lautenbach, had argued that the emperor only held his office by virtue of a de facto contract with the people to provide for their security.[9] It acquired maturity with the development of Protestantism, where great emphasis was placed on the covenant between God and his people, arguing even that Adam was punished because he had broken his contract with God.[10]

The idea that society was to be understood as resting on a contract carried important implications. When applied to politics, as it was increasingly throughout the 17th century, it required three important claims. First, that no human being could be privileged in his (or her) access to the most important things, be these God or power. Second, whatever quality was required to be a participant in the contract had to be in principle available to all. It is not the case that this implies that character or ideas of the good were irrelevant (as liberalism would later emphasize), but that to the degree that such matters came into play all persons had to be capable of them.[11] Last, the idea of a contract implied that the status of government is always contingent, resting on no natural or necessary human quality.

The idea of the contract as the basis for society is thus first a claim about qualities central to human beings. The objections raised to the idea of a contract, however, focused on another issue, where there clearly seems to be a problem. If political society rested on a covenant or contract, when had this contract occurred, and between whom, and who was bound by it, and why? Most important, how would those who were bound by it know that they were so bound? The social contract appeared to make the force of social and political obligation too weak, because it was clear that humans had never actually agreed with each other. Locke, for instance, facing the problem of the obligation of foreigners to obey the law, suggested that walking on a highway in a foreign country was sufficient to subject one to the laws of the society even if not enough to make one a subject of that society.[12] Thus a tacit contract or consent would be sufficient to legitimate the keeping of public order.

Some years before Rousseau's writing, David Hume had faced this problem directly. He argued that the idea of a social contract as the legitimating basis of society was empty, in that it presupposed the very thing that it hoped to establish. Famously, Hume wrote, "In vain we are asked in what record the charter of our liberties is registered. It is not written on parchment, not yet on leaves or barks of trees."[13] Hume is perfectly willing to say that humans *consent* to the government they have; but he cannot say that they have voluntarily *contracted* to have it. His intention in this passage is not in fact just to denigrate the historical possibility of an original contract, but to assert that government cannot rest on anything like a contract (that is "on keeping our promises") unless, he says, we be "trained in a philosophical system."[14] He suggests that the community cannot be found that is based on keeping its promises, unless it would be a community that rests on a particular type of authority, that of special training and expertise.

Hume thinks, not unreasonably, that people will keep their promises only for reasons. In the context of collective benefits such as political society, the reasons will not, he fears, be apparent or forceful enough to most individuals, unless they be trained in philosophy. In these circumstances, contracts—that is, the acknowledgment of the claims of an other on oneself—are matters for experts, trained philosophers; and politics is, Hume knew, too important to be left to experts.

Hume has quite consciously attempted to take philosophy out of the question of political legitimacy. He did so for the best of reasons, a worry about the domination of experts and professionals, one might say. Furthermore, he knew that the kinds of justification that philosophy seemed to provide risked making people think they were entitled to more certainty in political matters than was possible. One needs then to moderate what Kant (and Burke) was later to lament as the danger of an unlimited "enthusiasm" in political matters.[15]

Hume was persuaded of this on grounds that derived from his epistemological skepticism. He was convinced that our knowledge of an other, and thus of what an other meant when he or she said "I promise," would only be secure if I could actually know the sentiments that other had in uttering those particular sentences. Because I could manifestly not have your sentiments, it followed for Hume that I would only be assured of them—that I would know that you mean what you say when you promise to obey the laws—in one of two ways. Either I might be trained and skilled in detecting your meanings—I might be a philosopher. Then I might know if you will keep your word. Or, if I were not so trained, if I were an ordinary person, then I could only rely on what ordinary people rely on, on the grooves of habit long worn into our social behavior. But the habit of social behavior was the habit of a particular social behavior, the habits, say, of Englishmen. Thus there was no universal legitimate basis for political society; there was only that basis that served to allow us to behave as, say, the English behave.

Thus, whereas opinion was to serve to delegitimate political society for Rousseau, for Hume opinion was its very essence. Hume was struck by this power of our historical identity and did all he could to foster that power. "Nothing is more surprising to those who consider human affairs with a philosophical eye than the easiness with which the many are governed by the few." He continues: "It is . . . on opinion only that government is founded, and this maxim extends to the most despotic and most military governments as well as to the most free and most popular."[16] He concludes this essay with a ringing endorsement to "cherish and encourage our ancient government as much as possible." The opinions that the English have are to be encouraged and each of the six volumes that Hume wrote on the *History of England* was designed to further that aim.[17]

This was, in the middle of the 18th century, strong stuff. Hume, whom Rousseau admired as an individual for having a "strong republican spirit,"[18] denied to government any legitimacy other than historical. Yet Rousseau's analysis of the historical quality of present-day governments, including that of England, had showed them to be based on fraud and illusion. Even if people had indeed consented, the consent was absurd, eventually a form of slavery.

The problem that Hume raised was that of the assurance that one could count on what one knew about another person. Hume, not unreasonably, thought the knowledge we have of others insufficient to be relied on. Here Hume's writing on politics created for Rousseau a scandal analogous to the one that Kant was to find Hume creating in epistemology. As with epistemology, the fact of the challenge was laid down openly. Hume formulated it in several different areas of social and political thought. When Hume wrote that "it was not irrational for me to prefer the destruction of the entire world to the merest scratching of my little finger,"[19] he was denying that rationality could settle moral decisions. Toward the beginning of the *Critique of Pure Reason*, Kant famously remarked that it was "destructive of philosophy" that no one had been able successfully to resolve the argument found in Hume as to the apparently purely contingent character of the relation between facts and understanding.[20]

The argument in the *Critique* is on the epistemological level, but it is clear that Hume also extended his understanding to other realms. Indeed, the purpose of Hume's social thought is to replace contingency with practice.[21]

Although Rousseau had almost certainly not read Hume's *Treatise* (a book, Hume wrote, that "fell deadborn from the press"), from the account in the *Confessions* he was clearly acquainted with Hume's thought. The extent is unclear despite his claim there to have read only part of the *History*. He possibly had read the political essays; he seems to have had acquaintance with the *Inquiry on Human Understanding*.[22] I would like to argue in this chapter that Rousseau's political thought should be thought of as a solution—or the attempt at a solution—to a stance that was, one might say, "destructive of political philosophy."

If political society as it is experienced in the contemporary world is illusion, then there was, under present theoretical circumstances, "nothing" for political philosophy to be about. Rousseau proclaims in the *Emile* that as there is no more *patrie* so also there are no more citizens. This is, it should be noted, a claim that because true political society has more or less disappeared from human experience, the citizenship that in earlier times was automatically available was itself also annihilated. For Rousseau, then, we no longer can learn citizenship from experience.

It is still possible to ask, however, what would have to be the case if citizenship were to be possible today for persons like ourselves with all the historical qualities that define us. It is to this matter that the *Social Contract* is aimed. The intention is to resolve the scandal in which Hume's skepticism had left political theory. Is there, Rousseau asks in the beginning of the book, "some legitimate and assured rule of administration, taking men as they are and laws as they might be."[23] A "rule of administration," Rousseau tells us elsewhere, will be what he calls its "constitution." He means by this that which makes society what it is. This equivalence between the "principles of political right" and the possibility of the existence of political society can be seen in the earlier titles Rousseau had entertained for his book. They included "The Constitution of the State," "The Formation of the Body Politic," "The Formation of the State," and "The Form of the Republic."[24] The book is about what constitutes the possibility of political society.

The "nothing" that passes for political society in the present refers, for Rousseau, not just to a society with a problematic tradition (this would still be something) but to a situation where each individual lives, as it were, outside him- or herself.

> The citizen, always active, sweats, scurries, constantly agonizes in search of still more strenuous occupations: he works to his death, even rushes towards it in order to be in a position to live. . . . The sociable man, always outside himself, only knows how to live in the opinion of others, and, so to speak, derives the sentiment of his own existence solely from their judgment.[25]

What is to be done? Obviously, humans should derive the "sentiment of [their] own existence" from their own judgment. But to achieve this what is precisely not to be done is to take off the chains that Rousseau has found everywhere. Our "own" will not be found by breaking all shackles. The task is rather, as he goes on to say, to "render them legitimate." "The gentle voice of nature is no longer for us an infallible guide, nor is the independence which we received from her a desirable state." Indeed, had by some chance this "liberty without rule" remained conjoined to our "ancient innocence," then the "earth would be covered with people between whom there would be almost no communication," human understanding would never develop, and we would "live without experience and die without having lived."[26] If contemporary society has made humans the nullity that they presently are, it will nonetheless only be in society that we now can be human beings. In a draft of the *Letter to the Archbishop de Beaumont,* Rousseau writes that he has "penetrated the secret of governments, . . . shown [that secret] to the peoples (*aux peuples*) not that they shake off the yoke, which is not possible for them, but that they become humans again from their slavery."[27]

Rousseau continues here in a revealing manner. The idea of "what it means to be human (*du genre humain*)," which one might have from this condition of deconstructed humanity, would give us, were we to conceive of it as a moral being, a "sentiment of common existence." In other words, to think of humanness is to think of common existence.[28]

This is the beginning of his answer to Hume. It will consist in understanding the equality among humans that was necessary for the contract to occur in terms of common human existence. The "social bond," writes Rousseau, is "that which is common" in all the various interests in society and it is "solely" on this that society may be governed.[29]

The Thought of the Common

What is common existence, such that it would be human? The root of common is the Indo-European *mei*, which denotes exchange and from which are derived a series of words in various Indo-European languages (among them the German *gemein*) designating the social. The word *common* carries with it a double meaning, each implied in the other. *Common*, in both French and English, refers to what we have in common, to what we share.[30] It also refers to that which is ordinary, everyday, even vulgar. In the Favre manuscript of the *Emile* Rousseau indicates that humans have a sixth sense "called the common sense (*sens commun*)." It is so called not because it is common to all persons, but because, he says, it is the outcome of the well-ordered use of the other senses. It instructs us in the "nature of things, by the collective participation (*concours*) of all of their appearance." This faculty exists only with reference to the world of the mind, that is, it consists in the ability to find relations between entities. It is not defined by a particular property but as the ability (sense) to see how two entities might respond to the same name.

Common has a complex and ancient history, in both English and French. History has parsed out several meanings to it: We have *common* as we use it when we speak of community, referring to that which humans have together as part of and as defining of a group. Thus "a lack of community" means a society of individuals who feel isolated from and like strangers to each other.

Common, however, also designates the ordinary, or vulgar. It is almost always pejorative when used this way and denotes an aristocratic superiority to that which is common. But it can become a badge of pride: One of the oldest English uses refers to free burghers as "the common" and it is of course from there that the English House of Commons drew its name. Pitt was, for instance, the "Great Commoner."

Most important here, however, is that these usages are all of equal antiquity. By the time the 13th century came to an end, Britons were speaking using *common* in all three of these senses. Derivatives cropped up everywhere: The *Oxford English Dictionary* spends nine pages on *common* and its cognates. The French lacked the extended institutional structure that corresponded to the commons, but the uses of *commun* were almost as variegated as they were in England. The *Le Robert* dictionary spends five pages on the word. In all of these senses, the reference is to a state of affairs based on equality, on the way that human beings are like each other. It is the ability to perceive the common that is at the root of the ability to have politics that rests on equality.

This is the subject matter most centrally of the *Social Contract*. The argument that Rousseau makes there is, in my reading, a claim that the common is only established in and by politics. Politics is thus for Rousseau, as it had been for Aristotle, constitutive of the human. The difference, however, is this: Whereas Aristotle had understood the human nature to be available to humans, for Rousseau, our nature or rather the conditions of our nature must be made. Politics thus precedes the human in Rousseau, rather than being coterminous with it. It is in politics that humanness, that is, the ability to experience the common in all of its senses, will take place.

Rousseau was attempting to make political philosophy again possible and, I shall argue, the key to his effort was the elaboration of a particular understanding of the human being that he called a "citizen".[31] Just as one *is* naturally not anything, so being a citizen is something one has to make. As such "citizen" does not, in my reading, designate only for Rousseau the member of a society or political system. It designates, more importantly, a being in whom the thought of the common is realized. The citizen is, in other words, someone who lives in the ordinary or common world, the only world that is a real human world.

For the thought of the common to be realized in one person that person must, says Rousseau, "so to speak, contract with himself." (So, as was seen, is the Rousseau of the *Rêveries* still a citizen, precisely because when alone he is with himself.) The formulation of the social pact is well known, but little understood.

> *Each of us puts in common his or her person and all his or her power under the supreme ordering* (direction) *of the general will; and we receive corporeally* (en corps) *each member as a part indivisible from the whole.* At that moment, instead of the particular self (*personne*) of each contractant, this act of association produces a moral and collective body composed of as many members as the assembly has voices, a body that receives from this same act its unity, its common ego (*moi*), its life and its will.[32]

This passage is not without its ambiguities. One reading would be that at the moment of the social pact the sum total of individuals is replaced by a collective being. Where there were many, now there is The One. This reading should give pause, however, if only because of the categories of Rousseau's musicology. This would be, as it were, the Rameauian harmonic approach. Another reading shows us that at the moment of the social pact we take into ourself, as our self, a self that is common or general, and that each individual engaged in the pact does exactly the same; each self has, one might say, the same melody. The social pact replaces in me the self that could individually compact with a self that is common. In this way, one would read the purpose of the social pact as the free realization of the humanly common. I have in some sense taken the others into me, as they have me into themselves.

I strongly favor the second reading. As such, my argument differs from a standard reading that Rousseau was mainly concerned to attack absolutism and late-feudal notions of monarchy. This reading, which gives a more or less "liberal" Rousseau, is certainly not wrong, for his argument clearly cuts against such notions. But this is not the focus of what preoccupies him. His concern is with what the word *common* means in phrases such as "the common people," "having something in common," our "common humanity." Common here is both ordinary, everyday, but also that which is our "portion" as human beings, the entitlement of our existence.[33] Liberalism may be one by-product of this understanding, but it is not Rousseau's thought. Indeed, the great variety of ambivalences displayed to Rousseau (from proto-totalitarian to anarchist) is consequent to not grasping this central pursuit.[34]

To approach this problem, consider a formulation of contemporary political theory. Some years ago William Connolly formulated the fact that politics has a claim on our life as follows:

> In our politics, people engage in acts of protest and civil disobedience; they also lobby, dissent, negotiate, blackmail, vote, engage in violence, and strike . . . [A]ny outsider who lacks our understanding of the distinctions among these actions could not possibly participate in or explain our political practices. To understand the political life of a community one must understand the conceptual system within which that life moves; and therefore those concepts that help to shape the fabric of our political practices necessarily enter into any rational account of them.[35]

In this account, the central and most problematic word is the first-person plural pronoun, *we*. What is its status? Does it mean we Americans, we democrats, we Westerners? If so then it must be *my* position as well, yet I am unaware of ever having assumed it for myself. On the other hand, with a little introspection and doubling my negatives, it seems to me not clear that it is not me.

Connolly's essay here generates but does not ask nor answer a, perhaps the, central political query. The question raised here is the question of what it means for me (or you) to acknowledge my (our) membership in a group to which I am not aware of ever having consented explicitly. This is the problem of citizenship, and of the claims on me that as citizen I am obliged to acknowledge. As such, it is a modern problem in that it proceeds from the realization that there is a question about who I am politically. No modern understanding of politics can start without recognizing the contemporary problematic nature of political membership. Were my position in the political realm to be clear (I am the Count of Poitou; I am Lord Anthony's serf) there would be no question. It is precisely the fact that there is a question that allows for democratic politics, as such politics requires that the question of citizenship never be settled.[36]

If there is a question, what is that question? As his political ideas come together, Rousseau speaks in terms that obscure the boundaries between the first person singular and the first person plural. Speaking in the *Rêveries* of the time at which his political thoughts were truthfully expressed, he writes: "Let *us* fix once and for all *my* opinions, *my* principles, and let *us* for the rest of *my* life be what *I* would have found *I* should be after having thought well about it."[37] The combination of the first persons singular and plural in what Rousseau calls a "project" is striking. I want to call this project that attempt to think the *we* in the *I*, that is, to think the idea of the common.

So the question here—the modern political question—is a question about what claim the common or the ordinary may be said to have on me—how is it available to what I am? Another way of putting it: To be a citizen is to be common, to experience the common, in common. Living in terms of others, devouring others (or being devoured by them), living in inequality, makes this impossible.

Look now in more detail at Rousseau's working out of the thought of the common. The *Social Contract* appeared in 1762. It was probably either a condensation or a piece of a projected longer work on *Political Institutions*, of which no clear trace remains. In general it was a book of which Rousseau was proud, praising it to Hume over *The New Heloise* and using it as a touchstone repeatedly in later works. The subtitle— *Principles of Political Right*—gives its scope and ambition. It is divided into four books, the first of which addresses questions of the nature of political society, the second those of the nature of sovereignty, the third the institutions of government, and the fourth, extraordinary structures designed to keep the government from becoming corrupted. The book was thought so politically dangerous that even Rousseau's supporter, the censor Malesherbes, was unable to authorize its importation to France from Rey's print shop in Amsterdam. It was ordered burned by the rulers of Paris and Geneva in June 1762 on the grounds that it contributed to political subversion.

The Nature of Political Society:
The General Will

As befits a book about the common, the *Social Contract* is a book bracketed by the first person singular. In French, it begins with the word *Je* (*"Je veux chercher si . . ."*) and ends with the word *moi* (*"j'aurois dû la fixer toujours plus près de moi"*). In between, Rousseau is concerned above all to understand how the person who might use this pronoun successfully, for example, a person who had received the education that Emile had, might with equal success use the first person plural. In the book itself, the first person plural is rarely used. When it is, however, it constitutes the establishment of a base line, a claim: "Will one never explain this word [force] to us?"[38] The common, I might say, is what occurs when no tension is experienced in movement between the first person singular and plural for the same activity.

As Rousseau comes to formulate the quality of the social compact in chapter 6, the reader is witness to a gradual change in pronouns. The problem is in the singular: "Find a form of association in which each defends with all the common force the person and good of each associate, and by which each person in joining him or herself to all nevertheless obeys only him or herself and remains as free as before." When Rousseau is led a page later to give a formal definition of the essence of the social compact, he has changed subjects. If the problem is in the singular, the solution is in the first person plural. This is evident as he returns to the formulation of the social pact.

> *Chacun de nous met en commun sa personne et toute sa puissance sous la suprême direction de la volonté générale; et nous recevons en corps chaque membre comme partie indivisible du tout.* [Each of us puts in common his or her person and all his or her power under the supreme ordering of the general will; and we receive as and in our body each member as a party indivisible from the whole.][39]

Whence this *we* that receives? In the act of association is created a moral body that has a number of aspects. It exists as, and only as, a "common me (*moi commun*)" and once was called, says Rousseau, a city, but now is a republic or a public person. Considered collectively, it is a State or a Sovereign or, on the international front, a Power (*puissance*). Considered in terms of each individual who makes it up, it is a people, a citizen, a subject. Differences between these terms are simply differences in perspective: They all designate the same entity. All of them are forms of the existence of the *moi commun*, that is, of the self that allows each person to designate him- or herself when using the pronoun *we*. Each, says Rousseau, "thinks only of himself in voting for all."[40] (Note: It is not thinking "of *all* in voting for *himself.*") Take the central concern of Rousseau's political philosophy to be how it is possible for an individual to use the first person plural pronoun *we* meaningfully. Why are *we* and inequality incompatible?

Rousseau's first realization then is that political legitimacy and legitimation cannot derive from, nor be understood as, analogy to the family, nor force, nor opinion, nor desire. He had made a similar point in the article on "Political Economy" for the *Encyclopédie* and had also, in fact, in the first version of the *Social Contract* included these discussions in a general chapter with the title "False Ideas of the Social Bond."[41] Instead, he argues, legitimacy must rest on the possession and exercise of one's own free will. As a faculty, will is of relatively recent origin. By and large the classical Greeks did not use the notion of acting willfully in the sense of acting freely.[42] Its first origins are in the Augustinian notion of human loves.[43] In Augustine, as in Hobbes, both of whom Rousseau knew well and admired, the will designates the capacity of humans to shape the world. Hobbes argued that the will was not to be understood as a "rational appetite" in the manner of the late middle ages.[44] He had, however linked it to a process that proceeded uninterruptedly from the actor to the act. The notion of freedom as part of the idea of the will was not completely present and probably required Protestantism and the notion of grace freely chosen to evolve. Rousseau, in his discussion of will, accepts Hobbes's first move, but rejects the second for a much more complex view.

An often rehearsed debate in Rousseau scholarship concerns the degree to which the general will is to be thought of as a collective or an individual faculty.[45] Yet if one insists that the central thought is that of the common, one is not forced to choose between these two readings. Rather they appear as poles of a misplaced dichotomy. For indeed, Rousseau insists, a civil association is *l'acte du monde le plus volontaire* (the most purely freely volitional act in any of the world).[46]

A free will thus makes society possible for Rousseau; indeed, humans have free will so that they may have society. Here Rousseau differs from other theorists often associated with him as part of the social contract tradition. For writers such as Locke and Pufendorf, society exists in order to ensure as much as possible of natural, presocial, liberty. Rousseau's concern is quite other. A free society is characterized by a free will common to all. This will, he is quite clear, is the "general" will, by which "all members of the State . . . are citizens and free"; and if this free will that is general were no longer to appear in majority decisions, it would mean that "which ever side won there would still be no freedom."[47]

The general will then has the common as its object and springs from a will that is common. It requires freedom for its expression and it is an expression of freedom. Rousseau here does continue in the line initiated by Augustine, for whom the will was also understood in terms of its object.[48] Rousseau distinguishes between a will whose object is particular and one whose object is general. Most interpreters have tended to read this distinction in terms of the character of the willer, with the first being individualistic and the second collectivistic.[49] But it is much more accurately understood as a distinction in terms of the object of the will, especially because the will is always for Rousseau the energy of freedom and morality. What is the general will then—a will to or of? Rousseau writes that the "general will, to be really such, must be general in its object as well as in its essence."[50]

Being "general . . ." in its essence means for Rousseau that if we were to judge of that "which is foreign to us we would have no true principle of equity." That which is foreign to us is that which is not common to us, that which we do not all have in the same manner. Being "general in its object" means that the only proper subject matter for the general will is the particular form of the commonalty, of *our* commonalty. As Bertrand de Jouvenel put it, the general will "is called general [not] because of the number of those in whom it appears, but in terms of its object."[51] Rousseau, himself, insists that "as long as several men consider themselves to be a single body, they only have one will, one that relates to the common conservation and to the general well-being."[52]

What is the general will such that it is general? A number of things are evident from what Rousseau says. It is not the same thing as everyone having the same opinion (which would be the "will of all"). It can be expressed and often is by a majority vote, but it is not determined by that vote. It is thus not the will of a "group." "There is often," writes Rousseau,

> a considerable difference between the will of all and the general will. This latter considers only the common interest; the former considers private interest and is only a sum of voluntary wills. But take away from these same wills the pluses and minuses that cancel each other out and the general will remains as the sum of the differences.[53]

Rousseau footnotes this passage with a citation from the *Considerations on Ancient and Modern Government of France* by the Marquis D'Argenson to the effect that any interest is formed by opposition to another. Rousseau then needs to determine what the interest of the general will is in opposition to in order for it to complete its task of canceling out the infinitesimal derivatives of each particular will.[54] He concludes that the interest of the general will is in opposition to the interest of each particular will. That is, the opposition is one of kind and not one of substance. The working out of this opposition in kind is the basis of the requirement of the "political art," that is, of politics as a human activity.

It is centrally important then to understand that the general will is something that each individual has, as an individual. It is as "collective" as "I" am and collective in the way I am. It is a will (one of the wills) of an individual, a will that one need not have (the members of the modern society at the end of the *Second Discourse* do not have it) but which anyone can have. In the *Political Economy*, he asserts that the common self is a "reciprocal sensibility and the internal correspondence of all the parts."[55] The common self, and by extension the general will, is the ability to participate in a certain kind of interaction. It is certainly not to be thought of as some kind of collective mind, unless one thinks that a sentence like "I am a citizen of Geneva" is an expression of a collective mind. Indeed, writes Rousseau, "each individual can, as a human being, have a particular will contrary or dissimilar to the general will he has as a citizen."[56] In fact the distinction between particular and general is a relative one, and depends on the perspective from which a particular entity is being viewed.

> Any political society is composed of other smaller societies, smaller and of different kinds, each with its own interests and maxims. But these societies which one notices because they have an external authorized shape are not the only ones that really exist in the state. All the particulars that an interest makes single make up other such societies, permanent or temporary, of which the strength is not less real for being less evident. . . .
> The will of these particular societies always has two relations: for the members of the association it is a general will; for the larger society it is a particular will which at first glance is often at right angles to the general and at second glance harmful to it.[57]

The general will is then the expression of my common self, that is, of the self that I find, as the same self, in myself and in others. From the previous citation, it is even clear that I can have several general wills in myself, depending on in how many social forms I find myself. (It is not clear that Rousseau thought this a happy state, however; see below.) But I can only have a general will that is my own as far as I am distinct from you. Far from being the expression of a single, unitary overarching collective consciousness, the general will is in fact the expression of the multiplicity and mutability of my being. It is, as Amelie Oksenberg Rorty has argued, precisely the qualities that make human beings divided or multiple that make humans capable of social life.[58] Indeed, in an early version of the *Emile* Rousseau had written that "we are not precisely double, but composite."[59] It had also been the burden of the *Discourse on the Origins of Inequality* to argue not just (as had Hume[60]) that there was no one true notion of the self, but rather that there were as many selves as there were interactions with others. For me to have a will that is general, I must be multiple, divided. Rousseau is not a theorist of the unified self.

The general will is then the will that resists the deconstruction of the self into the immediacy of power relations in modern society.[61] It resists that deconstruction by counterpoising it to the will of the common self, that is, to the will that makes me human in a time when God's definition of the human is not available. (Rousseau will report on the religion of an other in the *Emile*, not on his own). It is not thus quite a moral will à la Kant, even in the historicized reading of Kant that someone like Patrick Riley offers us.[62] The general will is the thought of the humanness of the human being, ontological rather than (merely) moral.

The general will, Rousseau indicates, cannot as general will have anything to say about that which is particular, that is, about that which is not common such that it would affect me in the way that I am socially and politically different from you. More concrete, the general will can say that there should be taxes, but it cannot say who should pay what amount. In this, Rousseau's understanding is importantly prescient of the fundamental move taken by John Rawls in *A Theory of Justice*. There Rawls will propose that political and social institutions be decided on, as it were, from behind a "veil of ignorance." He meant that each individual was to make a decision on the shape and form of the institution without knowing how it would affect him that is, if he (or she) would be richer or poorer, with more or less power, access to education, and so forth. Likewise, Rousseau writes that "if when an adequately informed people deliberates, the citizens were to have no communication among themselves, the general will would always result from the large number of small differences and the deliberation would be good."[63] Rousseau has proposed here a formulation to the classic problem of social cooperation known as the "Prisoner's Dilemma." In that game two prisoners are kept from communicating with each other. They are pressured to betray the other in return for a small reward; both do so and are convicted each of much graver crimes than they could otherwise have been, had they both remained silent. If, however, one combines a large number of players, then the game repeats itself, in the sense that each difference can be measured against the other.[64] What Rousseau argues here is that the combination of a large number of players and the lack of communication between them effectively induces each to think of himself as an other. Were there to be communication, the interaction of particular wills would produce a balancing of interests, rather than commonalty.

The general will designates what I see when I see myself in you, you in me, and me in myself. (I also thereby see you in you, at least in the way that you see yourself.) No point has been harder to grasp than this one about the general will. Most often it has been seen as the will of an anthropomorphized social body, on the model of Durkheim's "collective conscience." Yet Rousseau is quite specific: My will (any will) is general if and only if it has as its object that which is common to all concerned, that is, that which all concerned have in exactly the same way. In the sixth *Lettre écrite de la montagne*, written to answer the justification offered by the Genevan General Prosecutor, Jean-Robert Tronchin, for the Genevan decrees ordering the burning of the *Emile* and the *Social Contract*, Rousseau tries to reduce his thought on this matter to epigrammatic form: "Law, by its nature, may not have a particular and individual object."[65]

Law is the activity of the general will. When acting on the general will (when willing generally), I then encounter myself in others, that is, I encounter myself as what I share with others, as human. This is what is meant by political society. It is in political society only that I can encounter my humanity, what I have in common with others, because in the state of nature I was never actually in the acknowledged presence of an other. Not knowing an other, so also (in the state of nature) I had no being to know: The dialectic of particular and general interests noted above plays itself out here also on the level of self-knowledge. It is thus the case that the general will has the effect of freeing me from all dependency with others while nevertheless requiring of me acknowledgment of them.

The Seductor Narcissist

Why does independence require acknowledgment of others? What need I with them? Reasoning this theme fascinated, even obsessed Rousseau. In his *Pygmalion*, a part of which was explored in the previous chapter, one finds the sculptor lifting the sheet that veils his statue from him and then dreaming of a relation with Galatea like this: ". . . I adore myself in what I have made."

He goes to chip away some of the clothing on the grounds that the statue is "not naked enough." "Not naked enough": The mistake here is to try to remove that which keeps him from seeing his creation. After one more blow of the chisel, he realizes that the attempt to remove barriers to transparency is futile and he stops.

> Oh! that Pygmalion might die to live in Galatea! . . . Heavens, what am I saying! If I were she, I would not see her, I would not be he who loved her! No, that my Galatea live and that I not be her. Ah! that I always be another, to want always to be her, to see her, to love her, to be loved by her.[66]

"To be her, to see her, . . ." is a melding of subject and object. Why this insistence in Rousseau that at its best my encounter with others is an encounter with myself? From one reading it is sick—too great a narcissism. Rousseau's fascination with autoeroticism,[67] the constant youthful fear that pervades the *Confessions* of being seen when he had not shown himself, the insistence that no one can see him except himself: All this does not seem the material for a sound politics, indeed for politics at all.

But one should move slowly here. Certainly narcissism is part of Rousseau's persona, and the psychologizing temptation is almost too great to resist. One might look at this encountering of the other as the self more closely.

Some clue is given in the *Essay on the Origin of Languages*. There Rousseau suggests that the very act of encountering an other is itself already a threat. Passions, and not needs, are the source of interaction.[68] With the encounter of the other, fear and illusion are born as twins.

> A savage man, upon meeting others, will at first have been frightened. His fright will have made him see these men as larger and stronger than himself; he will have called them *Giants*. After much experience he will have recognized that, since these supposed Giants are neither bigger nor stronger than he, their stature did not fit the idea he had originally attached to the word Giant. He will therefore invent another name common both to them and to himself, for example the name *man*, and he will restrict the name *Giant* to the false object that had struck him during his illusion. That is how the figurative word arises before the proper (or literal) word does,

when passion holds our eyes spell-bound and the first idea which it presents to us is not that of the truth.[69]

Our first encounter with the other is one of fear. Fear keeps us from recognizing the other as a human like ourselves. Here language does not communicate: It expresses fear and keeps us from the other. We will only properly speak with the other when we have recognized it as like us.[70] We will, Rousseau indicates, overcome our fear of others, when we are able to call them by their "proper [or literal] name." To call something by its proper name is to see it as it is. When we are able to call others by the name of what they are, then we will no longer fear them. Hobbes had argued that the foundations of society are in fear, especially the fear of violent death. Indeed, he was so struck by the fact that many of those around him did not appear to fear death (they fought in the wars of religion, for instance) that he spent a good deal of time convincing people that they should really be afraid of death, the better for society to be built. Rousseau does not here want to use the fear of the other as the basis for commonalty, but he does not deny its reality. What we are told instead is that fear is not a necessary foundation for human interaction.

The perception of the other in myself and myself in the other had been made possible in the state of nature by pity and *amour de soi*. Fear is not the passion that will make pity stronger. How is this experience of the other possible? The hope in the *Social Contract* is that with "laws as they might be" and institutions that will make them concrete, the fear that one naturally has of others, a fear given a false solution by the illusions of modern society, will be replaced by the correct or literal use of words for others.[71] No more than his Calvinist forebears did Rousseau think that literalness could be achieved alone. Others were necessary to keep me literal, as it were: Alone, I could never know when I was self-servingly imposing myself on the text. Rousseau has in fact a much stronger appreciation of the importance and use of institutions than is often thought, certainly than is thought by commentators who find his psyche irresistible. A goal of his political thought is that of a "well-constituted state."[72] Being human requires institutions.

The institutions have a particular quality. They are to make human beings as little like their natural selves as is possible. In the *Emile*, Rousseau writes that "Good social institutions are those that know the best how to denature man, to take away from him his absolute existence and give him a relative one, and transport the self into the common unity."[73] What does *denature* mean here? In the second book of the *Social Contract*, Rousseau writes as follows: "It is agreed that each alienates through the social compact only that part of his power, of his goods, of his liberty whose use matters to the commonalty (*communauté*); but it must also be agreed that only the sovereign is judge of what is here important."[74] The exploration of what *denature* designates thus requires an investigation of sovereignty.

Sovereignty

The general will is Rousseau's formulation of the recognition of what it means to live as a human being, that is, to be capable of living with other human beings as human beings and as a human being (rather than as, say, a beast or a god). The second book of the *Social Contract* is an exploration of the way in which "laws" are established, that is, of sovereignty. "Laws" needs here to first be put in scare quotes in order to draw attention to the fact that Rousseau has an explicitly technical use of the term.

In the first version of the *Social Contract*, Rousseau had placed his discussion of law in the first book. As the book matured, he came to see that it required a separate and preliminary discussion of the sovereign as that which makes law possible. Already in the early version, however, he had recognized the centrality and novelty of his concept. Having proclaimed in the *Emile* that "this subject is completely new: the definition of the law is still to be made,"[75] he here boldly declares that what is called law is "properly only the conditions of civil association." The mood of this chapter is rhapsodic: It is "only to law that humans owe justice and liberty. . . . [Law] is the celestial voice which dictates to each citizen the precepts of public reason. . . . Without law an existing state (*l'état formé*) is only a body without soul for it is not enough that each be subject to the general will; one has to know it to follow it."[76]

Law is thus that which makes it possible to live generally by one's will. Rousseau describes a law like this:

When an entire people gives a law for the entire people (*statue sur tout le peuple*) it considers only itself. And if a relationship is thus formed, it is from one point of view a relationship of the entire object with the entire object from another point of view, without any division of the whole. Thus the matter for which a law is given (*sur laquelle on statue*) is general in the same way that is the will which gives the law. It is this act that I call a law.[77]

Law, in Rousseau's understanding, thus requires a people to be able to see itself as a people, to stand outside itself and, as itself, constitute itself. The object of a law is therefore always general, in the sense that the general will is general. It considers "the citizens in a body" and sees all actions in an general or common manner, that is, the same for you as they are for me. To act in such a manner is for Rousseau what is meant by sovereignty.

Sovereignty is how Rousseau legitimates the use of the first person plural. Rousseau moves as follows: The general will has as its aim the commonality of the political society. That which is common and in common is the essence of political society and is the basis for its ordering.[78] Sovereignty is the general will in action; thus, it cannot be alienated; as common being, it can only be present as itself because although power can be transmitted to or through another, the will cannot. I want to take these three claims in sequence.

What does it mean to be the general will in action? Let us think for a moment of the general will as similar to Wittgenstein's notion of grammar, or as what Stanley Cavell calls "categorical descriptives."[79] Such terms function both normatively and descriptively[80] and tell you (part of) what it is to engage in a particular activity. A grammar is that by which a language is possible but that has no existence except in and as part of a given language. Grammar, in Wittgenstein's sense, shows what is possible and appropriate to say in a particular time and place to a particular person. It is, in some sense, conventional. It is also, in some sense, not subject to my particular whim. But it is also not just always right, but rather the very determinant of what *right* means when applied to speech. It makes speech possible.

Following the terms of this analogy, one might then think of the sovereign as being for Rousseau the perfect user of the language of communalty, of the common tongue. The sovereign is that which does not make a mistake, because it is, as it were, grammar in action. The sovereign exists then only in the present as it can in no way "bind itself for the future."[81] For it to have existence in the present, it must do so by means of the doubleness that each individual can introduce into him- or herself. Each contracts "as it were," says Rousseau, with him- or herself. The most important thing to realize about this relationship of self seeing the self is that it is not guaranteed by anything, nor can it be. The essence of commonalty holds its right from the fact that it can claim no right, that is, it can claim no thing that is not itself.[82] Thus "the sovereign, by the mere fact of being, is always what it ought to be."[83] If what Rousseau calls the "sanctity" of the contract should be violated by any act that would be contrary to its being, then the contract would not be, and would hence carry no obligation. Indeed, the notion of obligation is inappropriate here as sovereignty collapses the time dimension of political society into the present.[84] Sovereignty, I might say, takes over the ambitions of the *Second Discourse*: It makes all our history always present to us, and thus frees us from history.

The sovereign, thus, for Rousseau is the citizens, that is, the individuals of a commonalty *when they are acting as members of that communality*, as citizens. "Indeed," he says, "each individual can as a human being have a particular will that is contrary or dissimilar to the general will which s/he has as citizen."[85] The social contract—what Rousseau often tellingly calls the "fundamental compact"—substitutes a legal and conventional equality for physical inequality[86] and it is precisely this conventional equality that is constitutive of and established by citizenship. There is no viable notion of citizenship without commonalty, thus none without equality. The conventional equality exists as, and only as, that which has been acknowledged as the common, of me as you.

Representation and Time

But why can such sovereignty not be alienated, nor even represented? Alienated would mean given over to someone else; represented would mean on loan, as it were. How can something be really mine, if I cannot give it away, or at least let it be borrowed?

The first thing to recall is that sovereignty does not exist over time, or even in time. Each moment of sovereignty is "absolute, independent of the preceding, and never does the sovereign act because he willed, but only because he wills."[87] This thought, given formulation in several places in Rousseau's drafts as he worked on the *Social Contract*, appears in final form as the extraordinary claim that "yesterday's law carries no obligations today."[88] In a gesture to the pragmatics of politics, Rousseau goes on to indicate that "consent is presumed from silence." However, what should not be missed here is that sovereignty and thus the being of political society is held to exist solely in the present tense. Not only can the future not be tied down, but it should not be named. Thus there is not, nor can there be, to speak precisely, "any kind of obligatory fundamental law for the body of the people, not even the social contract."

No "kind of . . . fundamental law"! Rousseau really means it when he says that political society is made possible and continues in its existence because of the free human will. Insofar as the idea obligation is a binding of the will to a future, Rousseau rejects the idea that political society rests on obligation. If I am obliged, I am available as a representation, I have represented myself to the future. The strictures that Rousseau places on the representation of sovereignty derive from the particular nontemporal quality of sovereignty. If something exists only in the present, then its only existence derives from the activity that it requires of those who engage it. Sovereignty is thus like a work of art in the sense that it exists only in the present. To represent it would be to give it a form that was fixed. Remember here the bacchanalia of politics Rousseau observed as a child in St. Gervais: The dancers of politics can only be told from the dance.

To pursue this matter further, I turn to Rousseau's other major consideration of representation. Rousseau thought the representation of sovereignty to be impossible. He feared representation in the theater for related reasons.

In a lengthy "Letter," Rousseau responded to the entry that the cosmopolitan aristocrat D'Alembert had written on "Geneva" for the *Encyclopédie*. In an article generally filled with praise for the city, D'Alembert had included—Rousseau thought at the coaching of Voltaire who wished to get his plays performed—a section complaining of the lack of theater in Geneva and had urged the Genevans to permit the establishment of one in order to "join the wisdom of Laecedemonia to the grace of Athens."

Rousseau's response has two foci. The first is on the audience. Rousseau argues that in the theater we (as audience) may have "pure" emotions at the spectacle in front of us, from which we are kept by the fourth wall of the stage, but that this is only because the emotions do not really affect us. In an important sense, they are not really ours. Thus one can afford to be upset or take pleasure in the spectacle for in theater "nothing is required" from the spectator. By "nothing is required," Rousseau means that our emotions (at the theater) have no life-consequences; it is, as it were, irresponsible to be an audience member, as if one were on holiday from one's everyday, common humanity.[89]

It is the concern with the commonness of the self that forms the basis of the second part of Rousseau's critique. Suppose we allow that an individual be affected by what he or she beholds on stage? How can we avoid this affecting him or her only in his or her individual separateness as opposed to what he or she has in common with others? Rousseau writes that although the emotions that occur in onstage characters are repeated in members of the audience, the goal of these emotions is not. Thus the audience will not and cannot retain a common goal, nor indeed any commonalty. The theater is the experience of all, I might say, but not the common experience. If this be true, the theater will indeed call the community and politics into question.

Here, in a discourse on theater, Rousseau repeats many of the same themes seen above. Representation makes the experience of the common impossible. Representation (on stage) requires interpretation of its audience, whereas a just political society was to be built from that which was so transparent in time and space that it could not be other than what it was. No matter what its subject, theater cannot be common. It cannot be the everyday—it is the perfected, immortal, transcendent particular self, precisely that self that wants to overlook the common, more like a god than a human being. I might note here in passing that in this matter as in previous ones, Nietzsche is again both Rousseau's great antagonist and his heir. It is the burden of the *Birth of Tragedy* to try to show that theater can induce precisely the ecstatic (*ek-stasis*: out of its place, besides oneself) present that Rousseau thought the defining quality of sovereignty, but necessarily absent in theater.[90] For Nietzsche, its presence in the theater made political life possible.

In the preface he wrote in 1752 for his comedy *Narcisse*, just after the success of the *Discourse on the Arts and Sciences*, Rousseau suggests in fact that theater is linked to philosophy and the arts and sciences in general in taking us away from the everyday and common in the desire to distinguish ourselves and stand out.[91] From such an approach, society can be built only on a networking of interdependencies and intersecting personal interests. In such a situation, Rousseau continues, "we must henceforth keep ourselves from being seen as we are."

It is true that in this situation, once we are in it, philosophy and theater can give us a simulacrum of virtue, in order to "keep us from the horror of ourselves were we to see ourselves discovered."[92] In these circumstances, representation can maintain perhaps the appearance of public virtue without that virtue being found in our hearts. Commonalty would be, to paraphrase Thoreau, a phrase on the lips of most people, but in the hearts of very few. For those who have no humanity, philosophy and theater can give them the clothing of the human, but it cannot make available the experience of oneself or another as human.

The choice then is between being a human being and not being. Being a human being is the result of a constitution and our only other choice is the existence of nonbeing. The reason for this is that the common—the *moi-common*—is what humans are as humans. Its existence is our essence. I should note here that this is not a claim that Rousseau is a, or falls on the side of, the "communitarian," to use a term from a currently fashionable debate. The *common* as I am using it for Rousseau has nothing to do with the thick self that modern communitarian theorists counterpoise to the "thin self" of liberalism. The common self is neither thick nor thin; it is simply ordinary and has the qualities that humans have as humans.

The problem with representation then, both in theater and in politics, is not just that it induces passivity into an audience but that some human qualities, perhaps precisely those qualities that mark the human, cannot be represented and be what they are. Just as you cannot on your own promise *for* me, nor unproblematically say for me that I am sorry, and just as Cordelia cannot "heave [her] heart into [her] throat" to speak truly the words her father requires of her, some acts must be my acts and cannot be given over. You can report my promises, but as yourself you cannot *make* them for me. I must presently perform those actions. Rousseau's political hostility to the idea of the representation of sovereignty is based on his understanding of what the nature of commonalty is.

Thus, in the third element of sovereignty, "power can be transmitted," but *will* cannot. Will, be it common or particular, must be my will. This, however, says only that institutions cannot be based on will alone, for will is something that exists only in the present and cannot bind itself for the future. In this third element of sovereignty, Rousseau points to that which is not sovereignty. There has to be more. This is government and the institutions of government, and it is to the consideration of this that he now turns.

Government

Sovereignty is a matter of what Rousseau calls "laws," and these laws establish the *forme,* one might say the frame, of political institutions, what Rousseau calls the government. This frame is at its best when it is "engraved" on the heart of each citizen.[93] How is the framework achieved, because unless a people has fortunately inherited virtuous traditions, they must come from somewhere? It is in this context that Rousseau considers the figure of the legislator.

The legislator, writes Rousseau, has nothing in common with the "human domain" (*l'empire human*). Some commentators see in the legislator a kind of superior being who, like Moses from the mountain, gives laws to humans and is obeyed because of his superiority. But such is not the case. The authority of the legislator, Rousseau indicates, is "nothing."[94] The legislator neither compels nor persuades humans of the validity of laws; instead, he must "persuade without convincing."[95] The phrase "persuade without convincing" had already been used in the *Essay on the Origin of Languages* in relation to the original language. I argued in chapter 1 that it described Rousseau's understanding of how philosophy might work in human fashion. Now, just as Newton "invented another language," so will the legislator give a grammar without his audience realizing that they receive it.

It is precisely the negative quality of the legislator that allows a reversal of the causal sequence between institutions and the human spirit. Instead of the spirit of commonalty emerging from institutions, the spirit of commonalty is infused into the hearts of humans and becomes part of their sensibility. For something to become part of what I am, I must not experience it as shaping me (e.g., be convinced by it) but rather experience it when I reflect on it as part of the way I shape my world (I must be persuaded of it, called out by it, that is, find it in me).[96] Thus the legislator is not only not part of political society (he has "lived all human passions but felt none of them"[97]), but he is not experienced as other by those in human society. This is not because he is devious or disguised, but because anything he might do is experienced as one of my acts. The legislator has no alterity and thus cannot establish relations of inequality. Each citizen, one might say, finds the acts of the legislator as part of himself. If this is a lie, it is a noble one.

What the legislator makes possible is the development of political institutions. The distinction of sovereignty and government is one of the earliest moves Rousseau makes in thinking about political society. Already in the "Political Economy" article he writes for the *Encyclopédie* in 1755, seven years before the *Social Contract*, one finds: "I beg of my readers carefully to distinguish political economy, which is my subject here and which I call government, from the supreme authority which I call sovereignty."[98] What Rousseau conveys with this distinction is that the general will, being general and sovereign, applies only to that which concern all equally, that is, in the same way and thus defines them as citizens. When Rousseau uses the term *law* he applies it to and only to such matters. Indeed, Rousseau occasionally wonders if laws even need to be publicly promulgated; he finally decides that they should be on the grounds that this will confirm each person in his or her mind.

But there is another realm, and that is the realm to which power applies, the realm of government. Rousseau is perfectly clear that all sorts of issues in any society not only will not come under the purview of the general will or the sovereign, but cannot because they are not general or common. "[A]s soon as it is a matter of fact or a particular right concerning a point that has not been regulated by a prior, general convention, the affair is in dispute. . . . [I]t would be ridiculous to want to turn to an express decision of the general will. . . . "[99] This is the realm not of law, but of administration. Administration is what government does.

In the chapter that starts Book 3, Rousseau begins with a warning that he does not know how to be clear for those who do not read him carefully.

Government is then defined as "an intermediate body established between the subjects and the sovereign for their mutual communication, and charged with the execution of the laws and the maintenance of liberty, civil as well as political." He goes on to indicate that government refers to the "legitimate exercise of executive power" and that the individual or body who exercises this power is called "prince."[100] The purpose of the *Social Contract* ("to seek a rule of legitimate and sure administration, taking men as they are and laws as they might be") refers to establishing the constitutional context of government by establishing a correct understanding of the sovereign (that to which the term *law* applies). The first two books of the *Social Contract* have established what would have to be the case for a legitimate government to be possible. Humans have manifested a political sensibility as an expression of what they are. Rousseau is now going to elaborate that possibility.

First, there can be no contract between the government and the citizenry. Indeed, Jean-Robert Tronchin, the General Prosecutor at Geneva in charge of bringing the case against the *Social Contract* and the *Emile*, had attacked Rousseau on precisely this point, arguing that this meant that there was no restraint on the populace as to what they could require of government.[101] Clearly, Tronchin was right. If the citizens are to be understood as sovereign, then contracting with any individual other than yourself is contracting with a "prince." You give that individual rights over you. But "it is absurd and contradictory that the Sovereign give itself a superior; then obliging oneself to obey a master would be to put oneself back into a state of total liberty (*en pleine liberté*)."[102]

From this it follows that Rousseau does not reject representative *government*. He does reject representative *sovereignty* as a *contradictio in adjecto* that is all the more dangerous as people believe they could have it. No critique of Rousseau is more standard than that he rejected representation. Even perceptive modern-day Rousseauists take up this critique and attempt to develop it in theories of "strong democracy."[103] Yet from what has been said here, it should be clear that Rousseau is required by his theory to reject only representative sovereignty, not representative government.

A better grasp of this can be had with an exploration of the relation of sovereignty and government, something that forms the focus of Book 3 of the *Social Contract*. To "express [himself] with fewer words," Rousseau elects to "borrow the vocabulary of geometry" even though he is "not unaware that geometric precision does not exist in moral questions."[104] His concern is the "proportion" of state, that is, the kind of relationship that should exist between the sovereign (as understood above as the being of community) and the government. Thus he suggests, first:

$$\frac{\text{sovereign}}{\text{government}} = \frac{\text{government}}{\text{state (people as subjects)}}$$

The sovereign is by definition equal to one (as common it must be unitary). The state is equal to the number of subjects. Thus Rousseau indicates that the sovereign should be to the government as the government is to the state (that is, the people considered as subjects). "Pushed to the absurd," as he remarks, this means that, second:

$$\text{government}^2 = \text{sovereign} \times \text{state}$$

Thus—Rousseau has his tongue more or less explicitly in his cheek here—because the sovereign equals one (is unity) the government should be equal to the square root of the number of subjects. Thus, third:

$$\text{government} = \sqrt{\text{sovereign} \times \text{state}} = \sqrt{\text{subject}}$$

Despite the playfulness, which I cannot help but read as written with Hobbes's love of geometry in mind, this discussion—which Rousseau warns the reader to read carefully—is intricate and important to Rousseau's understanding of the nature of the political. It is worth spending some time on. The making of laws—what Rousseau calls the legislative power—belongs to the people. Law is Rousseau's designation for pronouncements that partake of the general will; a law must be general in its object and common to all in its nature. Some body, however, has to bring the laws into being. The sovereign makes the laws concrete but because, as Rousseau says, the instantiation of a law can only take place in a particular and singular set of circumstances if it is to have existence at all (e.g., law: There will be inequalities of income; instantiation: 20% of the populace will make 50% of the income). A body is needed to "put the general will to work."[105] This body is what Rousseau call the government.

The government exists therefore between the people and the sovereign, in the sense that it makes specific the possibilities that are the sovereign will. It is the words used with that grammar, if you will. The sovereign can only enact laws (in Rousseau's sense); the *people* is the repository of the commonalty that makes possible and is embodied by the laws. The *government* thus should stand in what Rousseau call a "continuous proportion" to the other two members and is, he indicates, their proportional mean. A continuous proportion is an 18th-century technical term for a proportion in which the denominator of the first relationship is identical to the numerator of the second. Thus $A/B = B/C$.[106] An example of a continuous proportion would be $1/100 = 100/10000$. The (people as) sovereign is always unitary, the people (here given as 10000 subjects) are as many as they are. For the proportion to hold, the government has to (in this case) equal 100.

It does not really mean anything to say, by itself, that the government should equal 100. But what Rousseau is interested in is the relative strength of the government to the size of the state. The following implications are worth noting. First, if the size of the state should go up (the number of subjects increase) then to maintain the balance it is clear that the size of the government should become stronger. That is, for Rousseau the larger a state is, the stronger must the government be for it to be capable of justice.[107]

Second, to the degree then that the government is disproportionately strong in relation to the state, and, indeed, to the degree that it is strong at all, there will be a tendency for the government to usurp sovereignty to itself. This was in fact what had happened in Geneva, where the *Petit Conseil* of the high bourgeois families had over the course of the 18th century abrogated sovereign power to itself. (Rousseau's claim that the *Social Contract* is drawn from the model of Genevan institutions is thus ironically true). To remedy this danger, Rousseau proceeds to deduce a version of the division of powers from his understanding of the relation of the sovereign to the government. Should the government be too strong for the size of a state, it should be divided.[108] The division of the government will reduce its strength against the sovereign, while maintaining it against the state. Most important here, Rousseau indicates that the form and shape of the government is in no way determined independently of the particular conditions that happen to pertain. "There can be as many different governments in nature as there are states different in size."[109]

Rousseau is thus entirely flexible on the kind of government—monarchy, aristocracy, democracy, mixed or tempered—that is available and wishes only to adopt the form that best maintains the proportion of state. The key words in this entire discussion are the danger of *distance* and need for *liaison*. A *liaison* is a link, but it is also the ingredient that binds a dish together. It is what overcomes distance and distance is the space in which a particular will can exceed its proper goals and usurp the common. The overcoming of distance takes place through the constant and continuing exercise of will, in that the will provides a continuous presence for all parties.

How does this work? Optimally, as long as those united together consider themselves to be "one body" there will be one will that they will each have and that will be that of commonalty. The sovereign will then have only to make a few laws.[110] (Indeed, "the most vicious of peoples . . . is that with the most laws."[111]) The possibility that the sovereign might be silent in general is not a problem. Because the sovereign is the commonalty of the *we,* it exists as long as the *we* exists. In such circumstances, "tacit consent is presumed from [popular] silence," Rousseau notes.

The existence of the sovereign, then, is not dependent on the sovereign constantly being in action. Will is for Rousseau a state of being, not an action. Thus, "the sovereign is taken constantly to affirm (and confirm) all laws that it does not abrogate. All that he has declared once to will, he wills it always, unless he revokes it." I am what I am as long as I am. Resting the state on will ensures the continuous presence of commonalty. As will cannot be represented, "it is the same, or it is other."[112]

Representation is then much more complex in Rousseau than is normally thought. In 1955 John Rawls wrote an article entitled "Two Concepts of Rules" in which he distinguished on the one hand constitutive rules, those rules that made it possible for something to be done, and, on the other hand, rules that told you what to do when.[113] The distinction is Rousseauian, for Rousseau's hostility to representation is only in terms of what he calls fundamental—what Rawls, following Kant, calls constitutive—laws. Rousseau admits the possibility and even necessity of representation in relation to the *government,* that is, in relation to those rules that tell you what to do when. Indeed this is not the area of citizenship in that it concerns that which affects us differently, not in our communalty.

It is thus the nature of the sovereign act, as opposed to that of the administrative or governmental act, that makes it impossible that the first be represented and possible that the second can and even should be. The sovereign act has the particular quality of being perfectly and completely free, "the freest act in the world."[114] To be perfectly free, and thus ensure that the political society that results from the activity of sovereignty retain the quality of freedom, it cannot be confined by form. It must remain will, existing only in the present. The argument against representative sovereignty is consequent to Rousseau's understanding that the political life must be *one's own* life and that no life that is shaped by structures that have duration in time and extension in space can possibly be one's own.

Such a person is what Rousseau calls a citizen. This self is political, that is, it is a self in which is manifest the "essence of the body politic [which] is . . . the agreement of obedience and liberty, and . . . these words of subject and sovereign are identical correlations the idea of which is brought together in the single word, Citizen."[115] It is, of course, perfectly possible and perhaps the most natural thing in the world to think that one is free without actually being so. "The English people thinks itself to be free; it is greatly mistaken. It is only so during the election of members of Parliament; as soon as they are elected, it is enslaved, it is nothing."[116] This mistake, one should note, does not consist in taking on the *wrong* quality. It consists in *loosing* a quality, that is, in becoming "nothing," which is what one is when one is not a citizen. A page later, Rousseau will write that if a people gives itself (so-called) sovereign representatives, "it is no more."

Administration or government then is not a matter of will. It is rather the consequence of the fundamental laws which determine its form.[117] Inside this form there can be representation, as long as that representation does not destroy the being that has been created in the sovereign.

The threat of representation is then not just that I will be betrayed by the representatives and that my interests will not be served, but rather that the representatives will serve my interests and that I will let them. In this case, a body (the government) whose existence is "borrowed and subordinate" will take over, as it were, the living body of the citizen and that "I" will no longer *be*.[118] The self that is the citizen will literally go out of existence.

It is for this reason that Rousseau wants to create an "excessive dependence" on fundamental laws, that is, on those laws that give one being as a citizen.

The Threat of Corruption

The introduction of government was necessary to give the common self a concrete existence. Yet the government too had to have a "real life" if it were to "answer to the end for which it is instituted." This raises the difficulty of how one will "order in the whole this subordinate whole, such that it does not alter the general constitution in affirming its own, . . . such that, in a word, it be always ready to sacrifice the government [i.e., itself] to the people and not the people to the government."[119] One saw previously that the government is in constant danger of being out of proportion with the state and the sovereign. These concerns form the focus of Book 4, a book that explores the threats of and resistances to the possibility of corruption, of living together not as humans.

Political virtue cannot be recognized simply by its expression. Unanimity, for instance, is the sign of one of two possible conditions. Either it testifies to a healthy state, in which the general will appears naturally, by itself one might almost say, or it is a sign of complete servitude, where "citizens . . . have neither liberty nor will."[120] In this case, the speech of deliberation is replaced by adoration or curses. But why does the common presence of sovereignty loose its actuality?

If it is possible to determine the principles of political right, it is apparently not possible to give lawlike causes for decline. Corruption has a thousand different sources and can be dealt with only on a case-by-case basis. Thus Rousseau's discussion here notably changes tone. Whereas in the first three books the argument about political right has been more or less formal, now the discussion becomes historical and by examples. Displaying a good deal of historical erudition, Rousseau looks to more or less successful republics of which Geneva, Venice, and Rome are his three prime examples. They serve as touchstones to determine what institutional devices those states employed in order to keep their liaison in good working order.

A notable premise to his discussion is his tacit insistence that no institution should be exempt from change. He notes, for instance, that Cicero had argued[121] that the introduction of the secret ballot was a sign of and contributor to corruption. Whereas one might have expected Rousseau, with all his emphasis on the public quality of political life, to approve, instead he says that "although I feel here the authority that the judgment of Cicero must have, I cannot be of his opinion. On the contrary, I think that the loss of the State was accelerated by not having made enough of such changes."[122] Rousseau can accept the argument Machiavelli introduced into political theory that change was the dominant quality of politics because by the general will he has elaborated an understanding of present commonalty. It is on this reverberation that everything else must rest. The most striking quality, however, to his discussion is his insistence of the ultimate dependence even of social mores on a political system structured on the basis of the general will and commonalty. An institution such as the Roman practice of popular censure can serve in the end only to maintain good social mores, never to reestablish them.

> The opinions of a people are born from its constitution; although the Law does not regulate mores, legislation does give birth to them. When laws weaken, mores degenerate.[123]

A great deal here rests on the claim that Rousseau makes for the common. Most, perhaps all, humans can experience the common only in a rightly principled political order. There is not only no opposition between that which is common or general and institutions, the former requires the latter, although it is not found in them. Humans have, in the end, nothing to protect them from dehumanization except the life in this order. This is not, I repeat again, a preference by Rousseau for living in community. Whatever the word *community* actually means, it is a word I have avoided using in my discussion of Rousseau. His argument is that living a life that enables the common, that is, the human, although not itself a structured or rule-governed life, is not possible without such structures or rules. That which is most truly excellent about human beings, excellent in the sense of a defining virtue, is available to all human beings, should they but enable themselves to find it. The previous chapter showed some reasons why human beings might refuse the availability of the human: For Rousseau they refuse themselves.

It is worth noting how little importance mortality plays for human beings when they live centrally in the present, as Rousseau thinks they can. In my discussion of the first encounter with the "Giant" other, I noted Rousseau's differences with Hobbes. Mortality for Hobbes was the central fact of human existence. Fear of it gave leverage to political legitimacy. Not so for Rousseau: Death, insofar as it makes an appearance in the *Social Contract*, is to be welcomed as part of the life in common. The criminal condemned to die for his crimes is to look on his lot as chosen by himself in the act of citizenship. Not for Rousseau is Hobbes's placement of the fear of violent death at the center of human experience. In fact, one can say that one major point of Rousseau's political teaching is to remove death from a privileged place. It is clear, for instance, that if "true" religion ("the religion of humans, that is Christianity, not the Christianity of today, but that of the Gospels. . . . holy, sublime, truthful. . . . "[124]) should be established in a well-ordered state, it would duplicate the dynamics of that society and extend them even beyond death. But this implies that religion will not change the dynamics of political society: Extending the common beyond the grave does not seem to be very important or problematic to Rousseau, and it certainly carries no implications for the common in this world. Religion can be useful to have, but his discussion of it is tucked away amidst other institutions that may be of help against the curdling of the social tie.

Why this emphasis on the general, on commonalty? Why not simply abandon it as unnecessary at best, dangerous at worse? The question requires us to think about whether Rousseau's argument for the actuality of the vision of the *Social Contract* is designed to make humans somehow better—that is, is a moral imperative—or whether he thinks it an expression of what it means to be human for those who have had the history we have, the history he has unveiled in the *Discourse on the Origins of Inequality*. If political life is the life of common involvements, of what humans have in common, of what is common, the vision of the *Social Contract* is designed to express Rousseau's conviction that we are in common with each other. The *Social Contract* shows us, I think, not what humans are capable of: It is not an ethical imperative, unless being as a human is a moral imperative. Rather it shows what it would mean to make the human available to beings such as we are, whose history has been that of the nonhuman.

4

The Education of an Ordinary Man

We are born twice . . . once to live and once to exist.

Emile[1]

It [is] possible for me to do one thing today and another tomorrow, to hunt in the morning, fish in the afternoon, rear cattle in the evening, criticize after dinner, just as I have a mind, without ever becoming a hunter, fisherman, shepherd or critical critic.

Karl Marx, *The German Ideology*

The availability of the ordinary, the common, is thus the greatest in political society, in the society of the social contract. But it is also the case that such a society appears to have no actual existence; nor does it seem possible that it can. The problem here, I should note, is not precisely that the world of the *Social Contract* seems improbable, but that it is not available to contemporary individuals. What then is the fate for our world of the everyday, the human—how can one be *un homme?* How would one have to be in order to be

104

available to the world of the common? What would make the ordinary critical?

The precondition—that is, what allows the possibility—of being human is that we are first a child. Already in the *First Discourse* Rousseau had noted that humanity would have been long lost had it been born learned.[2] Indeed, the "human race would have perished if humans had not started by being a child." Only humans have children; only humans are children for so long. But if one cannot be a human except for having been a child, it is also clear that there is nothing about being a child that will automatically make one a human being. The inhuman society of inequality, where all is domination and slavery, makes that clear. So particular attention must be paid to how one is a child. This is the subject of the *Emile*.

The *Emile* and the *Social Contract* were both published in 1762 and Rousseau had worked on them in parallel for the preceding several years. In the *Social Contract*, one of the prerequisites for political society was that the laws of the sovereign be engraved in human hearts, that is, that they be part of the human sensibility rather than something of which human sensibility was convinced. The enabling solution to this matter in the *Social Contract* had been the figure of the legislator. Yet the process by which the legislator made the laws available to us as our own had been only pointed at toward the end of Book 2. The description of what the legislator accomplishes is unsatisfactory, not only in that we do not know how he effectuates a new human nature, but also in that we do not know what the accomplishment of that transformation would look like. It is in the *Emile* that Rousseau gives us a full portrait of the how and why. Were the legislator to have accomplished his task, he would have accomplished something like what Rousseau sets out in this book and, indeed, the *Emile* ends with a description of the principles of political right that is a summary of the *Social Contract*.[3]

How is it possible to be the sort of being who can experience the common in him- or herself? This is the subject matter of the *Emile*. The purpose of the education that Emile receives, I want to argue, is to make Emile capable of experiencing the world as it is, without becoming determined by it. To make it possible for Emile to become an ordinary person: That is the task. Indeed, says Rousseau, as humans are all equal in the natural order their "common vocation is the human condition."

Following out Rousseau's Protestant usage, I might say that their life-project, that by which they are defined, is to act as humans. Rousseau's focus is the human condition and the task of the educator is to make his pupil capable of "living the human life."[4] Rousseau will explicitly contrast his endeavor with that of Locke, who sought to make a "gentleman."[5] Rousseau seeks the human itself. Thus the aim of the education Emile receives is to make him capable of living as a human in political society.

We see no such possibility around us at present. That which passes as the usual "human" being, *l'homme de nos jours*, is "always in contradiction with himself, always adrift between his leanings and his duties and will never be either man or citizen." He will be of no good to himself nor to others. It will be one of "these men of our time, a Frenchman, an Englishman, a Bourgeois; it will be nothing."[6] Note that Rousseau will not even allow this being designation by a human pronoun: instead the "men of our time" are "it," and that "it" is "nothing." The language Rousseau uses about such entities is that of passive pointless motion: They are "pulled along," "forced," subject to differing impulses, fought against, "floating," "unable to agree with [them]selves."[7]

The *Emile* is a book for moderns—those who have available to them only a society of inequality such that they cannot see in the world around them a common life and thus cannot learn such a life from experience. In the past, Rousseau goes on to say, public instruction, that is, instruction in being a person who lived in the presence of others, in public, was possible. Plato's *Republic* serves for him as the archetype of this kind of instruction; it is thus not a book about politics but of education about and for the person who can live with others. But the situation has changed. Today, "public institutions are no more and can no more exist." Indeed, Rousseau avers, the very words of *citizen* and *patrie* no longer have meaning in our world: We are going to have to learn all over again how to use them properly. Elsewhere Rousseau indicates that in some insulated parts of Europe, Corsica, and perhaps Poland, it is still possible to use the words for political society meaningfully, but such is no longer the case in societies dominated by relations of inequality.[8] If public institutions are no more, we cannot learn the meaning of words like *patrie* and *citizen* by observing them in the world, in the manner, say, that the young Rousseau had been shown politics in the festivals of St. Gervais. Because the words are now only misused, public education is no longer possible. The meaning will no longer show us the use, in Wittgenstein's phrase, because these words are so seldom used. The motivation behind the *Emile* is thus Rousseau's understanding that moderns can no longer work from models. Not only are the Greeks not a model, but the model of what they did is not a model. Plato, Rousseau says, was able to hold up a model of the life in common in the *Republic* because there was a reasonable chance that his audience would be able to see it. But Rousseau despairs of the faculty of sight in contemporary times. We will have to learn how to see the world as it is before we can learn anything from the world.

Instead of *public* education, we are left then with "domestic education, that is, that of nature." Rousseau immediately asks what will a person brought up for himself alone become for others; he then intimates that it may be possible to unite the two forms of education (public and natural/domestic) into one, and that such will be the task of his book. We cannot under present circumstances teach someone to become at the same time a man and a citizen. Such was possible only with public education. We must rather first teach the pupil how to be human, and that will make citizenship possible. Thus the book is not, as some have argued, simply a text on how to survive as a moral being in a corrupt world.[9] Emile is to be both human and capable of citizenship.

To accomplish this will be to repair the depredations inflicted on humans by their own kind. The *Emile* begins: "All is well as it leaves the hands of the author of things [*des choses*—that which is]." As the first chapter showed, "the author of things" carried for Rousseau the implication of morality that it had for Leibniz and Malebranche. However, our condition is that of one who has taken leave of the author of things, that is, taken leave of the situation in which morality and actuality were conjoined. Rousseau, incidentally, says that when all leaves the hand of the author of things, it is *bien* (well) and not *bon*, which would be "good" and carry a stronger moral connotation. The immediate catalogue of what happens to "everything" when it takes its leave from the author of things is terrifying: Strange fruits are grafted onto existing trees; dogs, horses, and slaves are castrated. In fact, the destructive strength of society as it now exists is such that even were the young sapling to escape these mutilations it would not survive but be trampled in the midst of the path of existence.

The plot of the book is on the surface simple. It is the account of the education at the hands of a tutor of the young boy Emile, from his infancy

until his marriage. The child is healthy, breast-fed, but without the significant presence in early life of anyone other than the tutor.[10] Rousseau had
himself served as a tutor for the children of the Mably family in 1740 and
had written two long memoranda developing his ideas on education in
conjunction with his service then. In these projects he paid more detailed
attention to curricular matters than to the formation of a human being.
The book Rousseau now publishes—the *Emile*—is rather *about* education. That is, it is about what it means to learn as a human being, not just
the content of what one might learn.

As in his other books, Rousseau insists on a limited authorial presence.
The *Emile* grew, he says, of its own accord, despite his intentions. Like
his other books, it is the product of observation: This is what he has
"seen," even though he does "not see as do other men."[11] Rousseau
proposes that we study our pupils, rather than teach them; as the tutor has
observed Emile, so also will Rousseau have the reader watch and study
an education, that of the young Emile, who has been consigned to a tutor
by his mother from his earliest age. The reader thus watches more than
either the tutor or Emile. The tutor speaks in the first person singular and
the reader will clearly read Rousseau and Jean-Jacques in his character.
Yet the strategy of the book is part of its educational intent. Part of the
educational ploy of the tutor is to set up the situations that young Emile
will encounter in such a way as to make it obvious what the "natural" and
successful thing to do is. However, the reader of the book is, as Rousseau
intended, in the position of watching the *mise en scène*: We are backstage
and see the machinery. As readers, we are thus in the position of the author,
with whom we must associate ourselves and thus have an epistemologically superior position to the tutor and to Emile. But then the author is not
telling us anything, merely showing us what he sees.

The position of the reader is important. It is sometimes said, generally
as criticism, that the tutor manipulates Emile or, more accurately, manipulates the context that provides the pupil his cues. So he does. But the
reader of the book knows this. So the question that needs to be asked is
what Rousseau intends the effect of this knowledge to be on the reader.

The first thing to notice is that the tutor's presence to Emile is one of
absence. Never is the tutor to allow Emile to know that he is shaping the
world in which Emile lives. The negativity of the tutor is to be contrasted
with the directness on which Rousseau insists in the terms of the relation

of Emile to the world. Most important, the tutor is not to give nor tell Emile, nor instruct him into, understandings of what is in the world: Such would be to represent and thus to formulate and fix the world for Emile and thus keep the world from ever being Emile's world. Rousseau's consistent hostility to certain uses of representation thus reappears pedagogically. Emile is not to encounter "signs," but the object itself. The sign would preoccupy the student and make him "forget that which is represented (*la chose réprésentée*)."[12] So it is the very absence of the tutor that makes possible the presence of the world.

The role of the tutor has often been compared to that of God (in the *Second Discourse*) and to the legislator in the *Social Contract*.[13] The purpose of this comparison is sometimes to point out that the education that is supposed to make Emile an autonomous being is in fact highly, evenly totalitarianly, controlled.[14] There is an importance to the parallel, but also a real difference. To start with, God is absent from the world of the *Second Discourse*. Indeed, Rousseau more or less explicitly brackets God in order to indicate that the world as the human encounters it in the *Second Discourse* is already here and given.[15] So God is absent from modern society as we experience it. So also, I argued, was the legislator's presence in political society one of absence.

Modern society, the regime of inequality, is the world that Emile would encounter were he not educated properly. A premise of the *Emile* is that modern society is already here and given. But for Emile to become part of this world would be a disaster: The point is for him not to encounter that world, or, more accurately, not encounter it all at once. For this to be possible someone or something must remove that world from Emile and make it accessible only as it is available to the changes in the growing child. It is thus not quite right to say that the tutor manipulates Emile. In fact the tutor, although by his absence somewhat like God, has an active absence (which God does not) and this is what allows the world to become directly available to Emile as it really, naturally, is. The world is only naturally available when it is available to the capacities humans have, and Rousseau knew, these capacities come into existence neither automatically nor all at once. The absence surrounding the tutor is logically essential if Emile is to encounter a human world, one that is his own, instead of the illusory modern one. The point of the tutor's so-called manipulations is to keep Emile from being shaped by that which is not him, but it is not precisely to manipulate *him*. All mediation must be, will be, Emile's own.

The complexity with which Rousseau always addressed authorship must thus constantly be present throughout the work. The book is a collection of observations, of things he has seen in his subject, that is, seen in a being that can be taught. It is no more (or less) systematic than is "the march of nature" and, indeed, all Rousseau is doing here (he claims) is giving us an account of his observations of nature. It is true, he avers, that he "does not see as do other persons."[16] But all the book is an exact transcription of his sentiments. In fact, if at times he appears to affirm a proposition, it is "not to impose myself on the reader, but to speak what I think." The truth of what the book contains will thus be a matter of the reader finding for him- or herself what Rousseau has seen, of seeing as he sees, what he sees. A judgment on Rousseau's opinions will in fact also be a judgment on Rousseau, but it is right that he be at stake here for what is at stake is "the happiness or unhappiness of the human race."[17]

Education and the Philosopher

It is in this spirit, I would argue, that Rousseau understands the role of philosophy. At one point after a long disquisition on lying and reasoning, the tutor insists: "Readers, always remember that he who speaks to you is neither a wise man (*savant*) nor a philosopher, but a simple man, a friend of truth, nonpartisan, without a system."[18] To some extent, this is the voice of Rousseau, the author of the *Emile*, a man who appears as "editor" of other books, as a portraitist. But it is also, and more immediately, the voice of the tutor, who, to maintain his absence from Emile, will constantly structure the pupil's experience and repeatedly keep from him the source of things that happen to him in order to make him think that they have no source. The reader of the *Emile* sees the tutor engaged in these performances; the reader is thus also the student of the pupil in this book, for the reader is educated in what an education requires. Rousseau indicates, somewhat disingenuously, that he did not intend the *Emile* to be a "how to do it" book. (It is the case, however, that after reading the *Emile* many women did breast-feed their children, refrained from swaddling them, and followed other advice from Rousseau's pedagogy.) Instead, the *Emile* was a book, says Rousseau, "presented to wise individuals (*aux sages*), and not a method for fathers and mothers. . . . If sometimes I seem to address myself to them, it is either to be better heard, or to express myself more succinctly."[19] Even though the book was written in response to the request of a mother, she "knows how to think" and "is capable of philosophy (*elle a de la philosophie*) and knows the human heart."[20]

The *Emile* is a book not written by a *savant* but it is intended for *les sages*. One might say that it is a book written for those who do not need to be philosophers (they are *sages*) by someone whose philosophy keeps him from claiming that he is a philosopher. In other words, the *Emile* is (also) a book of philosophy or rather is written for those who might be capable of (some understanding of) philosophy. For Rousseau, to be truly a philosopher is to be *capable* of philosophy. The fact that the tutor is not a philosopher means that the reader is in effect put in the place of being a philosopher him- or herself, or rather that as we watch the tutor at work we are in the position of being capable of philosophy. To follow the tutor's method is one thing, to understand what education is to humanity is another.

The point of the *Emile* is explicit: It is to develop a "man nourished in the order of nature but brought up for society."[21] Such a person would be *only* human, which means that his life will consist in "seeing his place and holding to it." His "place," however, is not to be defined as a social role, for it will be "no thing" (*il ne sera rien*).[22] To be human is not to be any (one) thing: The force of the *Emile* should make the reader understand the natural as the human, or more accurately make the natural available as the human. To be human is to be not defined.

To fashion a being that is human, we must first know what it was before it was a human being. It is a child, asserts Rousseau. It has been remarked, not without a certain plausibility, that Rousseau "invented" childhood.[23] That is, he gave children a status that was not that of a grown-up in miniature. But the major thrust of what Rousseau says about education was not to glorify the separateness of childhood; it was to suggest that children, like humans in the state of nature, are born without qualities.

We are born feeble; we require abilities; we are born deprived of everything, we need assistance; we are born stupid, we need judgement. All that we do not have at birth and which we need when grown is given to us by education.[24]

At birth we lack the capacity for action, for other persons, and for informed will. Rousseau's key move, the one that legitimates his designation as the inventor of childhood, is to argue that the acquisition of human qualities is both multiple and serial. Rousseau's is not, as it sometimes thought, a purely developmental vision. He is not (quite) Piaget or Kohlberg before their time. What happens in the *Emile* is not developmental, if by that term one has reference more or less solely to ontogenetic differentiation. What happens in the *Emile* is much more like what the Soviet psychologists L. S. Vygotsky and A. R. Luria refer to as "zones of proximal development." Here the child learns by encountering zones that are at the limit of competence, in which what the child already knows how to do can be extended. To be avoided are situations in which a child encounters some activity with which he or she was simply unable to make natural contact. In that case the child would learn incorrectly or simply withdraw from developing in that arena. The tutor in Rousseau plays the role, one might say, of the purveyor of zones of proximal development. It is his function to bring the child into contact with activities it has not previously undertaken but that it could now undertake.[25] Then "once the effort has been successfully made the child has gained in strength, and as soon as he can use it in life, the principle becomes engrained."[26]

Different qualities thus require different faculties. There is no one thing that makes one a human being, a grown-up. Furthermore, as the various qualities of the human are separate from each other, they have to be acquired in a fairly precise developmental sequence. One of the major functions of the tutor is to extend the amount of time of education to a sufficient length that the child is able to grow up in stages. The major problem with contemporary education, indicates Rousseau, is that it occurs too rapidly. Even more than the tutor manipulates the child's environment, does he reduce the number of stimuli to which the child must respond, in order to allow the child to develop the capacities to distinguish one from the other. One zone of proximal development at a time is what this narration requires.

The purpose of an education is then to acquire the several abilities needed to deal with the several kinds of stimuli that the child will encounter. It is to make sure that the child is able to know what to do when, to know what behavior is appropriate to a particular situation. I might contrast such a state to that of neurosis, understood as the repeated unwilling use of inappropriate behavior or activity in a given situation, of not knowing what to do when. Knowing what to do when is both the manners and realization of philosophy. It is when one has learned when it is appropriate to use a word that one is able to use that word naturally.[27] So it is indeed the purpose of the education of Emile to make him into a natural human being, that is, one who can mean what he says in the variety of circumstances that compose a life. Emile's education is neither more conventional nor more natural than learning a language is.

The Stages of a Life: Feeling

What are the stages through which Emile must pass? Rousseau's claim in his introduction that the book "grew of itself" is designed to point out that these are the natural stages of a human being. The book is as structured as a life naturally is.

Overall, the *Emile* is composed of five books. Each is prefaced by a carefully chosen engraving that serves as both epigraph and icon to the pages that follow. The first three books form a unit in that in them attachment to other humans is systematically kept to a minimum: It is to objects that Emile must first learn relations. In these three books objects are manipulable in the sense that there is little necessity that any one of them be encountered. The tutor's main role, as noted above, is to slow down the rate at which Emile encounters both himself and that which is not himself.

In the first book, spread over the ages from birth to about two, the child's main contact with the world is through sensation. Here Rousseau is a sensationalist, like Locke. Sensation allows one to determine one's relation with the world through pain and pleasure.[28] But present social institutions already interfere with this minimal level: Children are swaddled tightly, the head is kept to one side by a bridle designed to ensure they do not choke on their vomit: "It would seem that one is afraid that they might seem to be alive."[29] The lack of freedom in its first years turns a child so contained into a "slave and tyrant."[30] Dominated, the child becomes a dominator. Education, will it or not, is from birth: The child will learn something in any case. Against contemporary practice, the point of this initial period should be to allow the child as much liberty of movement as possible. This does not imply that the child should be protected. Rousseau wants to make sure that it encounters the world in terms both of pleasure and of pain and spends several paragraphs discussing the temperature of bath water and why one should aim at eventually bathing the child in cold water. Reducing Sophocles to the minutiae of bourgeois life, Rousseau claims because it is the lot of man to suffer at all ages of his life, he would do well to learn suffering from purely physical discomfort. Because it will be his lot to suffer, the attempt to keep him from suffering (by picking him up whenever he cries, for instance) will give him the habit and experience of being able to command, to get his own way: Allowing suffering will avoid at least this early experience of domination.[31]

The aim will always be to keep abilities and needs in equilibrium. Indeed, Rousseau indicates that "a sensible being" in such an equilibrium would be "an absolutely happy being."[32] That is, if one is able to do what one wants and to want what one is able to do—the condition of justice in the *Republic*, it might be noted—then one will be at home in the world. Because during this first period the needs of the child exceed the child's ability to fulfill those needs, and because those needs (hunger and fears) can by and large not be avoided, the aim of the education should now be to make the child as insensitive as possible to the world he is encountering. Rousseau in no ways counsels leaving a child alone; we are only not to allow it to avoid the encounter with pain. The engraving that Rousseau chooses to head this section of the book is that of Thetis plunging her child Achilles into the Styx to render him invulnerable.

The image is not chosen accidentally. Famously, the mother holds on to baby Achilles's heel. But for now, the point in this first book is to ensure that the child does not become habituated to any particular pattern of expectation. The "preparation of liberty" requires delaying for as long as possible that any habit become part of what the child is becoming. If sleep and food are too regular, then the child will want them from habit, and not from need. To want something from habit is not to be free.

> The only habit that one should allow the child to acquire is that of not acquiring any. He should not be carried more on one arm than another; nor should one offer him one hand more than another. . . . [33]

Regularity is routine is definition. A defined self is a self that controls the world in its image and can in turn be controlled. Rousseau is not a theorist of the unified self, of the single identity. Indeed, he is quite the opposite. "Being oneself" can only mean being no one set person or thing, a temptation that is always easily available. Thus the task is to keep Emile from being some particular thing. Only in this way, Rousseau asserts, will we keep the child always master of himself such that, as soon as he has a will, it will be his will that he does. There seems to be a paradox here but it is an important one. The child is to be brought up always engaged in his own acts. At the same time this child is to be naturally perfect, without sin, one might almost say. The idea of nature here then means that I will be transparent to my acts, that my words and deeds will be my own. Thus it would "be very inappropriate that the child have more words than ideas, that he know how to say more things than he can think."[34] The quality of this nature is liberty, the freedom of my will.[35] Because, however, there was no will in the state of nature nor in earliest childhood (merely its possibility) one has to think of this nature (freedom) as a second natural state. Indeed, as Rousseau says, "there is more."

The "author of things" does not provide only for the needs that he gives us but also for those that we give ourselves; it is so as always to place desire besides need that he causes our tastes to change and brings changes to our manners of living. The further we are from the state of nature, the more we lose our natural tastes; or rather, habit makes for us a second nature that we substitute for the first to such an extent that none of us recognize it any more.[36] Rousseau's point seems to be that if we have only the needs that the author of things has given us, then we will develop new needs that are as simple and as much ours as were those. Change we must: The question is what changes, how, and when.

The Stages of a Life: Control and Morality

The next book takes Emile from age 2 until 12 or 13, the "most dangerous interval in a child's life."[37] The engraving that now serves to locate the education iconically is one of the satyr Chiron teaching the young Achilles how to run. Emile, as young hero, will in this book learn how to come into contact with the world and to gain control over his physical body. The acquisition of language is the acquisition of control. It permits specification, here of pains, such that it will now be the fault of others if the child still cries after having said that he was hurting. With language, others become involved in you.

Combined with the extension of the child's abilities, the development of language furthers "the well-being of freedom."[38] Freedom is always in the *Emile* something learned: If Emile is to live as a human being in the modern world he will have to learn how to be free. Now Emile becomes conscious of himself as an ego; memory extends this consciousness to all that he has encountered. This is, Rousseau indicates, the true beginning of the life of an individual, and Emile can from this point on be considered as a moral being.

The aim of education at this time is negative: to put as little as possible into Emile's head. Rousseau even indicates that if one could arrive at age 12 with the child knowing nothing, one would have "accomplished a prodigious education." As always, the emphasis on negativity is important: It is as if Rousseau were scared that Emile is at constant risk of living in a world that is not his own. For the world to be one's own, the activities that one engages in have to also be one's own, hence the worry about the too rapid acquisition of words and their consequent misuse. For words to be meaningful, one must use them correctly. They must be one's own words, not someone else's. This means that one must be able to use words in a world in which they work, a world in which and of which one has experience. One must not require activities of the student beyond those of which he is capable; this means that the world in which they are used must not exceed the grasp of the young student. For those activities to be one's own, one must own them; thus Emile must acquire some understanding of the nature of ownership. The idea of ownership is necessary to the achievement of a fit between words and the world. What is it for something to be "one's own"?

To achieve an understanding of what it means for something to be one's own, the tutor allows Emile to plant some beans. Every day Emile comes to tend them and, as they grow, comes to see "something of his person in them." Then one day, Emile arrives to find that the beans have been torn out. His distress knows no bounds until he finds out that he had planted his beans in the melon patch of the local gardener, whose melons have been overrun by Emile's hyperactive beans. From the exchange that follows, Emile learns not only that ownership comes naturally from the experience of mixing one's labor with nature, but also that ownership is only possible if arrangements are worked out so that others' ownership is respected. This is an important moment: For the first time Emile has acquired a natural usage of a term that involves other human beings. Human terms have their origin and their natural status in human activity.

The door that has been opened is, however, Pandoran: With the experience of the beans we have moved into the moral world and "the door is open to vice." To keep the child moving through this difficult time, Rousseau proposes as the form of education a kind of open field remarkably similar to that he had thought the characteristic of the politics of commonalty. Just as sovereignty had no permanent definition, the tutor is to "govern without precepts and to do all by doing nothing."[39] This and only this will leave the child in freedom. The instructor is to make sure that the pupil encounters nothing: There is to be no domination to resist and thus no occasion in which one would define oneself dialectically. The lessons Emile receives are not to be experienced as lessons: This means that what is taught by the tutor must not have the quality of a lesson, of coming from the outside. The authority of the tutor, says Rousseau, consists in making sure the child neither obeys nor commands.[40]

It is worth noting here that the story of the beans duplicates to a considerable degree Locke's understanding of property. When a person wandering in the woods picks up a plum or acorn, something of him- or herself becomes part of that acorn, as does the acorn become part of its new owner. Locke had eventually generated the need for political society out of the desirability of maintaining the unalienated relation between person and possession. This moves too fast for Rousseau, but the lesson on ownership is a start. The difference lies in the fact that property generated a need for Locke, whereas for Rousseau it gives rise to an ability.

So a human education will not use anything but the child's experience. Rousseau is quite clear that adults are often wrong as to what a child's experience might be (as, indeed, they are about their own). Care must then be given to make sure that the child actually has the experiences one thinks he or she does. Rousseau spends a few pages going through La Fontaine's verse fable about the crow who, in responding to the fox's flattery, lets fall from his beak the cheese the fox desires. Rousseau's tone here is that of the mode seen in the *Letter to D'Alembert*, a kind of mildly annoying Tom Sawyerish *faux naif* smart. He finds everything about La Fontaine's charming fable to be off, unconfirmed by the experience of the child: Animals don't speak; one should neither flatter nor swear (as does the fox); the goodness of the crow is confused with stupidity; and so forth. "None of us is enough of a philosopher to know how to put himself in the place of a child," proclaims the tutor.

Is the ability to put oneself in the place of a child the mark of an adequate philosophy? It may be necessary for philosophy so that one will not take as necessary and natural qualities that persons have genealogically acquired. In fact, Rousseau, in his reading of the fable, claims precisely to have placed himself in the place of a child, with the aim of recovering for his readers the ordinary moral use of the words that the fable has erased. The point is not, I think, to reduce the fable to nonsense by tearing it apart with naivete. It is rather to raise the question of the distance between the everyday use of the words and the hidden presuppositions that La Fontaine's usage requires. Whatever may be the laudable morality of La Fontaine's intentions, it is the text that is read. It is in the words that form the text by which meaning will be found. "Children almost always find in fables a moral opposite to that intended by the author."[41] Rousseau's deep concern here is that the meanings that words assume derive from the ability to grasp the intended context and that the ability is itself also learned. Some contexts—that of theater, for example—almost always necessarily overwhelm their words. It is a matter both of having the proper context and of being able to grasp it that is necessary in a human education. Indeed, reminded by his discussion of La Fontaine that the senses themselves need education, Rousseau proceeds with a long discussion of meat eating, smell, and so forth.

The Stages of a Life: Appearance and Convention

The subject of Book 3 is the world of adolescence. The weakness of a human being comes, Rousseau indicates, from the "inequality that exists between his strength and his desires."[42] From the age of about 12 or 13 to 15, the abilities of the child are greater than the needs of the child. That is, the child has more capacities than he has knowledge of what will satisfy them. In the previous zone of development, the external world was judged by its utility and objects were as they appeared, without mystery. Now the focus is still on objects and utility, but the pupil is taught to see through appearance. An experience with magnets that suddenly seem not to work leads to the understanding of polarity. The lessons here (astronomy, maps, and so forth) all serve to put Emile in control of the world in which he lives and moves about.

The book, famously, that Rousseau proposes to Emile is *Robinson Crusoe*, a book about how to be of society by oneself. The engraving that condenses all of this is that of Hermes inscribing the sciences on a stone pillar to protect them from a flood. The book and the engraving complement each other. Emile expands his world to the universe, always with the intent of "bringing ourselves back to ourselves."[43] The effect is to lay the groundwork for political society, a groundwork that requires the acceptance of a "conventional equality." A conventional equality is the presupposition that humans can identify a common relation to things (in this case property, but later political society). Money is for Rousseau an example of conventional equality in relation to things: It permits different persons to judge things in the same manner. The idea of fair exchange requires the idea of commonalty. Money is not a mere convenience as Locke had pretended; it is a step toward commonalty and a politics.

Important here is the fact that the groundwork of political society is being laid in Emile, even before he enters into relations with others. Having something as one's own presupposes equality—equality with others, and, one might say, with oneself without which one would slave and enslave. The word *homme* now begins to make its appearance along with the word *citoyen*.[44] Whereas Emile had previously only had sensations, he now has ideas and judgments.

Emile is now 15 and has no sense of social relations. But he is everything "one could be at his age." That is, if he were anything other than he is, that would be an illusion. He lives content, happy, and free. What does it mean to say that one cannot have an idea of social relations, a true idea, at age 15?

The Stages of a Life: Knowing Others

Book 4 sees a "second birth." The first one had been "to exist," the new one is "to live." "Life," Rousseau informs the reader, not only goes by extremely fast but is limited to the portion of our existence in which we are able to enjoy interaction with others. A human life has the quality of enjoying interaction with others. By Rousseau's analysis, the first and last quarters of our existence are lost to human life as we do not know how to enjoy the first and cannot enjoy the last. Of the remaining half, three quarters of it are taken up with labor, suffering, sleep, "troubles of that kind."[45] Human "life" is thus limited to one eighth of human existence. This is not much and it is clear that it must be special to Rousseau. The first 15 years of Emile's life have been spent making it possible that he will be able to live rather than merely exist.

Two related things happen to Emile as he turns his 16th year. The first is puberty and its consequent attraction toward the opposite sex. Attraction is undifferentiated in its nature but, as Emile is moving into society, his attraction to the opposite sex will be also an attraction to a particular member of that sex. As a result, Emile begins to make tacit and unself-conscious judgments that so-and-so is prettier, smarter, in brief, has more of some quality than does another. Love is the result of a judgment and judgments are the result of comparisons. "When love comes from nature, it is the rule and the brake of its inclinations."[46]

With genital eroticism, however, (re)appears the danger of domination. This is the second development. Reciprocity becomes a necessary part of the child's life, as there will be no love that is not returned and can be no love of this kind of oneself. In pity, the child has the tools for reciprocity, as pity was the sentiment that enabled him to see himself in relation to another. The suffering between the inevitabilities of birth and death that Rousseau sees as the human lot makes pity possible. Rousseau recalls here the gist of his analysis in the *Second Discourse*: "To become sensitive and pitying the child must know that there are beings similar to him, who suffer what he has suffered, who feel the pains that he has felt, and other of whom he may have the idea that they feel also."[47]

With this claim, it is possible here to extend the import of Rousseau's understanding of pity and to complete the analysis of his response to Hume that I started in the preceding chapter. Pity, I might say, is the faculty that permits acknowledgment of other minds. Hume had raised important skeptical questions as to whether or not it was possible actually to have knowledge of what others were (really) thinking or feeling. His doubts were based on a claim that to know (e.g.) a pain required that one have it, and that it was manifestly true that I could not have your pain. From this, it followed for Hume that assured knowledge of others was not possible and that one could only rely on the knowledge that experience accumulated.

For the first three books of the *Emile*, Emile has not needed to know others, and has in fact systematically been kept from such knowledge. He now must know others, if only for the species to survive. Rousseau must thus show that knowledge of others is possible without that generating relations of domination and subordination; if a person stands in relation to his or her feelings and thoughts in the manner that he or she stands toward private property, then all interaction between persons could only be in the realm of *amour propre*, that is, of "domination and comparison."[48]

Being able to be besides oneself means to find oneself in another and to recognize that another may also find him- or herself in one's own self. It is, as Rousseau says here in the *Emile*, to be "transported outside of oneself."[49] In this manner, Rousseau could have claimed, as did Stanley Cavell two hundred years later, that "I know your pain the way I know mine."[50] It is this quality that Rousseau seeks to foster at this point in Emile.

As always, the danger is that knowledge of others proceed too quickly. The presence of an other is a new phenomenon for Emile: The tutor had been defined only by his absence and was thus never encountered. The prolonged absence of the other now makes it be possible for Emile to do what has not been publicly possible in human history as it has come down to be part of us.

> Extend the space during which [the passions] develop so that they have the time to order themselves as they are born. In this manner it will not be man who orders them, but nature.[51]

The task here is to bring into existence the human. Rousseau is quite clear that being human—living—is something achieved and not gained naturally (in the sense of automatically). Indeed, he plays the word *nature* double as when he claims that "although shame (*pudeur*) is natural to the human species, children do not naturally have it."[52] So also one might say that being human is natural to individuals, but that individuals are not naturally human. It is pity that, if properly directed, makes the human possible as a form of life.

Pity was the capacity to see yourself in another. The restrictions Rousseau now tellingly places on pity consist in ensuring that commonalty be its focus. Thus, first, one should not in one's heart put oneself in the place of those who are happier than oneself, only in that of those who are worse off. Were one to put oneself in the place of those better off, one would not, says Rousseau, really be doing so, but only "appropriating for oneself a portion of what they have." Envy makes pity impossible; situations that tend to produce envy must therefore be avoided.[53] In order to "carry a young man to humanity," one must ensure that his "path to happiness be on the tracks of no one's." Envy, and thus appropriation of that which is not one's own, will be avoided by avoidance.

The second maxim for the orientation of pity requires that one experience in another only those evils from which one is not oneself exempt. Rousseau's examples are telling:

> Why are kings without pity for their subjects? because they expect never to be human. Why are the rich so hard to the poor? because they are not afraid of becoming such.

Kings are *not human*, and they do not even feel this as a lack. The Turks, in fact, are more human than are the Europeans because their form of government is so arbitrary that anyone might one day find himself at the bottom of the heap. When is a person not a human being? When, it seems, that he is a king, or rich, or a noble—when he is *defined*. Anyone, for Rousseau, is in danger of being a Lear, of losing humanity in the attractions and requirements of one's role.

Last, Rousseau gives as his third maxim that pity is to be had or not had, but cannot be measured. It is only a quality and one cannot therefore compare oneself to someone else in terms of amount. It is not how much you suffer that matters, but that I am able to make your suffering available to me. As soon as one starts to note "how much he suffers," asserts Rousseau, one will soon begin to "harden" oneself by saying "he is not suffering all that much." It is the ability to experience as others experience that creates the common, a fragile commonalty that will always be eroded by quantification.[54]

> In a word, teach your child to love all humans . . . to place himself in no class, but to find himself in all. . . . Human, do not dishonor the human.[55]

It is important to note here that the love of the human can only be achieved by putting oneself in the place of actual other humans. It is not a relation to humanity, nor one to those so distant in time and space that it would deny one's own corporeality. Although the human relationship is in principle possible with any (human) being, it will occur only with those with whom one has some proximity. What enables Emile to exercise pity is that he apprehends the *human* in the other, "what is common to all, whatever age, whatever rank, whatever nation they may be in."[56] But it is also the case that just as Emile had learned by doing, so here he will learn by seeing. We "enter at last the moral order . . . by seeing that justice and goodness are not only abstract words . . . but actual feelings."[57] Pity is universal in potentiality, but only exists parochially.[58]

Thus the claim that man is naturally good is not for Rousseau a claim that humans are good *by* nature, but that they are so *in* nature, that is, when they find themselves in others and others in themselves. In fact, this is what *good* means as a human quality. Nature is others: It is something that humans are in constant danger of losing. It will not remain in existence without careful structure, a reason for paying as much attention to the institutions of political society as Rousseau had in the *Social Contract*.

> I would that the societies of a young man be so chosen that he thought well of those who lived with him, and that he was so well taught to know the world that he thought badly of all that was done there. May he know that humans are naturally good, may he feel it, may he judge his neighbor (*voisin*) by himself. But may he see how society depraves and perverts humans, may he find in their prejudices the source of all their vices. May he be led to esteem each individual, but may he disdain the multitude; may

he see that all men wear more or less the same mask, but know also that there are faces more beautiful than the mask that covers them.[59]

Book 4 has as its general goal to enable Emile to understand and properly to use the word *to be*. This had taken place in the sphere of pity. The acknowledgment of other minds, the possibility of which was essential to keep Emile from falling under the domination of *amour propre*, required from Emile an act that is not simply that of bodily observation. It is also an act of thought, and once thinking is "begun, [humans] do not easily stop doing so." It is in the ability to be beside one's body that reflection and true philosophy develop. Once an abstracted idea has been had, how do we put a term to it? Rousseau goes straight to the end: "How do we know of God?" It is no surprise that the engraving that Rousseau selects for this book is that of Orpheus revealing religion to humans.[60]

The Premise of Human Criticism

In his *Critique of Hegel's "Philosophy of Right,"* Marx had noted that the criticism of religion was the premise of all criticism.[61] It was that premise because, if left without critique, religion made impossible an understanding of the human. Religion did so because it posed an impossible requirement for true knowledge of an other: Such knowledge was to be like the knowledge of God. Because knowledge of God was not possible, or at best ineffable, so also was knowledge of other human beings.

Only now does Rousseau think his pupil able to begin to deal with such questions, for it is "especially in questions of religion that opinion triumphs."[62] Because this is a matter with which Emile can have no direct bodily contact, Rousseau must doubly distance the matter. Religion is central as a paradigm of a relation to others, but it cannot be the object of experience. Rousseau marks this by transcribing a report of an encounter with a Savoyard priest made to him by a "man who is better than he." What is recounted here, Rousseau assures us, "really happened to the author of this paper that I here transcribe."[63] Rousseau thus establishes the truthfulness of the report of what the priest will say by showing that it is something that he (Rousseau) can have found in another person. The report itself has the quality of truthfulness, although he has yet to say anything about what the report is about. Furthermore, by being a report, this portion of the text can be lifted, so to speak, out of its context. The time for Emile to deal with these matters is now, but the report is, or might be, available to anyone at (almost) any time. We can find religion in ourselves, it appears, without having to solve the question of whether or not religion is "true," of whether or not God exists. It is important that in doing so we are not fooling ourselves: Rousseau feels no need to decide if religion is true; he seeks its truthfulness.[64] Emile, with neither father, nor mother, nor country, will at least be able to approach religion without worrying about sharing that of his ancestors.

In this introductory report, a young man, of the age at which Emile finds himself now and of the age at which Rousseau ran away from home, gives up his Calvinist religion in order to be taken in by a Catholic hospice and then, regretting the change, wants to leave the place to which he has come. He is not allowed to do so and is kept a prisoner there, no doubt with the hope of reinforcing his newly acquired Catholicism. Knowing that forced religion is worse than no religion at all, a traveling Savoyard priest takes concern for him and becomes his instructor in virtue. At this point, the narrator of the story drops the third person and tells the reader that the young man is actually the same *I* as the *I* of the tutor. The identity is complicated, however, by the fact that although Rousseau did run away and did abandon his Catholicism, the Savoyard priest character is, as Rousseau tells us in the *Confessions*, a composite of two priests whom he met at that time.[65] Nor is Rousseau simply the tutor. Religion, it appears, is part of the education to and of the human, but it is an education that cannot be accomplished without giving up all claims to authorship. Toward the end of the introductory account the young man confesses himself to the priest, who, in turn, explicitly confesses himself to the young man in the "Profession of Faith of the Savoyard Priest."

It is clear, as Judith Shklar has written, that the principles contained in the "Profession of Faith" are fairly close but not identical to those that Rousseau himself espoused.[66] But this does not resolve the question of their status in the character of Emile. The doubling of the author is an indication that this is to be something the truthfulness of which could be found in a spirit, and indeed it is to such openness that the priest begins by appealing. One subsequently learns, however, that the principles to which he is confessing are what is left after all of those he received from others had fallen away. They are, in other words, his own principles and their authority consists in the fact that he finds them unadulterated by other representations in himself. Belief in these matters, indicates the priest, is not a question of argument: Each philosopher or theologian spoke in his own voice, but without resonance in the priest. These beliefs are thus presumably what any human being would find in himself as human beliefs. To determine what is his own, the priest proposes to consult his "inner light," that is, that which "had immediate interest (*ce qui m'intéressait immédiatement*)" for him.

Inner light is the answer to the question of why these are the principles that are left after the others had fallen away. Here it is easy to be led astray by the apparent soft romanticism of Rousseau's language. But inner light is (only) another way of saying that in matters of religion as in matters of social relationships the foundation must be what I can find myself in and what I can find in myself. Emerson, some 50 years later, put it like this:

> Truly speaking, it is not instruction, but provocation that I can receive from another soul. What he announces I must find true in me, or reject.[67]

The ability to hear the voice of one's inner light, says Rousseau, is to give sense to the word *to be*.[68] Rousseau's point, as expressed here by the priest but widely repeated elsewhere, is the primacy of what he calls the "sentiments," or "feelings."[69] But feelings here means something like I "find in myself." For Rousseau, to be valid, any claim about the world must penetrate past logic and become evident as part of what we are.[70] If it does not, it will be only a "cold argument that will determine . . . opinions, not . . . actions."[71] It is for this reason that Rousseau must be concerned with education in the way he is in the *Emile*, for his fear, as seen at the end of chapter 2, is that humans will become or have become incapable of acknowledging such feelings. Emile is to be trained to be capable of finding truth in his feelings.

This is *conscience*, the "divine instinct" that forms the subject of the priest's most famous expostulation. It is for Emile what pity was to the species in the *Second Discourse*.

Conscience, conscience! divine instinct, immortal and heavenly voice, sure guide of a being who is limited and ignorant but also intelligent and free; infallible judge of good and evil, which renders humans like God.[72]

"Instinct . . . voice . . . guide . . . judge": The progression is important. Conscience makes our ideas available to us as our own ideas. It both gives us the world and the terms by which to make sense of it, somewhat as does our grammar. It gives us a standard that is *our* standard. By conscience we are able to stop doing philosophy and can be "humans before being knowledgeable." The real question, however, is not so much what conscience is but whether or not a person has it, or is able to consult it. Conscience may speak to all hearts, "but why do so few hear it?"

Well! it is that it speaks the voice of nature, which all has made us forget.[73]

Conscience is "timid," "afraid," "suffocated." In a telling sentence, Rousseau notes that "fanaticism counterfeits it and dictates crime in its name."

She no longer speaks to us; she no longer answers to us and after such a lengthy disdain it will take as much to call it back as it did to banish it.[74]

Conscience is thus subject to historical change and even loss, just as the human had been. Indeed, in *The New Heloise*, Rousseau is explicit: "Conscience changes and modifies itself imperceptibly in each century and in each people, in each individual even depending on the inconsistency and variety of prejudices."[75] The point, once again, is that nothing is more natural to present-day persons than not to have access to nature.

If the basic position of the priest is close to that of Rousseau, the rhetoric of the "profession" is other than that usual to Rousseau. Rousseau generally wants us more to "look and see" rather than to think. Although the priest proclaims that he does not want to philosophize, only to help the young man "consult [his] heart,"[76] he clearly has philosophy on the mind. The style is pedagogical-philosophical: He is reasoning with his readers. Indeed, much of the material in the "profession" is drawn from the *Lettres morales* that Rousseau sent to Madame de Houdetot during the time of his crush on her. Those letters have the tone of an older man who cannot be a lover, but who hopes nevertheless to win favor by the passion and brilliance of his instruction. The concern of the *Lettres morales* is to show that one must end where Descartes only (and illegitimately) began (with the *cogito ergo sum*) because as a starting point Cartesianism has been overcome, first, in Newton's demonstration that extension is not the essence of matter and, second, in Locke's proof that thought is not the essence of the soul.[77] So also the priest moves from his soul to his thought; so, apparently, should philosophy move.

The reason for the difference in style is, I think, to make it clear to the reader that inner light is not something that one can naturally see. To some important degree, it is the possibility of the condition of seeing and all Rousseau can do is present that possibility in such a manner that his readers would take it seriously and as a claim about the possibility of seeing. As the young interlocutor of the priest responds at the finish of the exposition:

> For me also to be sincere, I wish to consult with myself. "Inner feeling" is what is to lead me to your example, and you have yourself taught me that after having for a long time imposed silence on that feeling, it is not a matter of a moment to call it back. . . . If having really consulted myself, I remain as convinced as you, you will be my last apostle [i.e., I will need to hear no more].[78]

Thus, although the priest speaks the language of philosophy, he speaks it "with vehemence; he was seized by emotion (*ému*) as was I also. I thought to have heard the divine Orpheus sing the first hymns."[79] The orphic priest has tried to give philosophy the presence of music. This is, as the voice of the narrator announces when it comes back in, "an example of the manner one might reason with one's student without straying from the method that I have tried to establish."[80]

This is only half the story of religion, at least of the story that is told to humans as humans. The priest now goes on to talk of revelation, the scriptures, dogma, and so forth—all matters that cannot be grasped unless the listener is capable of the inner light that would ground them. After this point, the discourse of the priest will only be a matter of "good faith." The substance of what follows is, to modern readers at least, unexceptional. There is astonishment at the impact the New Testament has on its readers and the suggestion that when Plato speaks of those who would rather suffer injustice than commit, he is describing the character that was also found in Christ. The priest also deals with human authority and the prejudices of particular countries.[81] All religions should be respected: "The essence of worship is in the heart."[82]

Here the priest asserts in relation to religion a point similar to that Rousseau had made in the *First Discourse* against philosophy. The religion described up to the break in the argument is natural, common to all those who believe, perhaps the very expression of what it would mean to believe. Beyond that, any claim will require extraordinary means. These means could not be those of human authority, for "*as no person is of a different species than I, all that a person naturally knows I can also know.*"[83] As the extraordinary investigation develops, Rousseau is forced to invent a dialogue between and an "Inspired Person" and a "Reasoner."[84]

I have already looked at this dialogue in the first chapter in conjunction with the discussion of the proper use for philosophy. Now, having examined the place of religion in a human life, I can extend that analysis. The dialogue is explicitly said to take place in the "roughness of ordinary language." The exchange becomes heated, but the conclusion by the Reasoner is significant. (It is worth noting that Rousseau had entertained other names for these characters. The "Inspired" was successively "Missionary," "Prophet," and "Apostle." The "Reasoner" was "Theist," and "The Human"—*L'homme.*)[85] That conclusion is that nothing that depends on revelation can have a possible claim to be available to others in a legitimate manner, for the truth of revelation will always depend not on another person but on the authority of another's belief.[86] If God speaks to me (in revelation), then I will be convinced of the eternal truth, but it will not properly be *my* truth because it is not human. For something to be mine, it must also have the quality of being ours. I will not be able to make a nonhuman truth available to you without doing damage to you (and, therefore, to myself).

With the possibility established of consulting his self, Emile is ready to complete the process of becoming a man. Book 4, which begins with the announcement of Emile's puberty, has as prefatory engraving a depiction of Orpheus teaching the worship of the Gods to humans. But the book begins and ends with reference to Ulysses. In the first reference, Emile is warned not to loosen the winds from the bags that contain them lest he be pushed where he does not want to go. In the second, Emile is threatened with the comparison to Ulysses, who begs to be released from the mast to go and join the sirens. Emile, however, now has a self that he can control. With conscience, he experiences what he is and thus is able to stand outside himself. Able to tie himself to his own mast, as it were, Emile is now coming to his 20th year. He is ready to specify the other to whom he will be attracted: a person of the opposite sex. The rest of Book 4 is taken up with the education of Emile's sexuality.

Sex and the Other

"Tell him about it," says Rousseau—openly and frankly, even though French is a language in which the "obscene" is always too easily available. Make him want chastity, something that he will only be able honestly to want if he knows about sex. Warn him that he will not be himself if he follows not his will but yields to his passions. The realm of the erotic is that of two lessons, which Emile learns simultaneously. One is about sex: It is desirable and one risks losing oneself by yielding to passions. The second lesson, and in many ways the most important, is about authority. Emile, as the tutor pictures him, will first respond by wanting the tutor to take explicit control of his (Emile's) life.[87] This is the first recognition of and desire for external authority. Politics draws from the erotic and begins, Rousseau says, in the desire to be controlled for one's own good.[88] It is important to note that the tutor transforms the desire for authority that is now dominant in Emile into a self-imposed "contract."[89] The desire to be ruled must be transformed into a common relationship. The tutor is now thus concerned with the shape of Emile's will; he will no longer need to determine the circumstances of Emile's body.

Above, I suggested that the picture of the tutor as controlling Emile was misleading. The tutor's presence to Emile is absence. This will be the case here also; indeed, the tutor will now be doubly absent. The tutor is now worried about Emile's will, not just his actions. To work with the will, he ensures that Emile's will draw him toward what he, Emile, is not. Emile is warned to go slowly before making promises to the tutor to stay away from sex. When he finally does promise continence, the tutor structures matters so that Emile will spend the next part of his life constructing for himself a picture of his destined mate. She is not to be perfect, but to have the faults that would complement those Emile has; she will be named Sophie—wisdom. Wisdom is thus to be joined to will. Sophie's traits are to be defined as the negative complement of those that now characterize Emile. Might he be forward?—she will be modest. Will he perhaps give himself airs?—she will be simple.[90] Sophie is to be constructed in Emile's mind as what he is not, in order to keep him from becoming what he is not. Sophie is not what Emile lacks, as if to make up a more perfect male being. She is simply not Emile, so that Emile can be what he is.

Emile is ready for human society, as *un aimable étranger* (an agreeable outsider) to that society. The description of Emile's reception into the company of others—"At first his singularities will be excused by saying 'he will change.' Afterwards one will be accustomed to his ways, and seeing that he does not change, one will say 'he is like that.'"[91]—seems to be very close to the way that Rousseau imagined himself to have appeared in Paris, and perhaps not without some reason. Tellingly, as Emile "likes human beings because they are of his kind (*ses semblables*), he will particularly like those that are the most like him."[92] While looking for Sophie, he will acquire taste, learn not to like money too much, and learn most to enjoy those pleasures that are "pure because they are common to all humans."[93]

Emile's desires and pleasures are human desires and pleasures. The time has thus come to find Sophie.[94] But she cannot be in Paris. So Emile must leave existing society: There is, as it were, no possibility of an other for a human being in modern society.

Farewell, Paris, famous city, city of noise, of smoke and of mud, where women no longer believe in honor, nor men in virtue. Farewell, Paris: we seek love, happiness, innocence; we will ever be far enough away from you.[95]

The Stages of a Life: Sex, Politics, and Virtue

The entrance of Emile into society, his attraction to and desire for the opposite sex, as well as his eventual marriage are all bound up together for Rousseau. Book 5 resolves all of these questions in the context of Emile learning to be able to be a citizen. Openness to the realm of politics

is part of a good relation between the sexes and the relation to the opposite
sex ensures that politics will be virtuous.

First, Sophie must be found. To know where we will find her, we must
know what she is (for women, like all humans, are what they are because
of where they are). As Rousseau describes the process at the beginning of
Book 5, she is to be found, that is, she is to be recognized, by virtue of
the fact that she is a sexually differentiated being, *not male*. Rousseau
asserts that the *only* difference between men and women as men and
women is sexuality. "All they have in common is of the species."[96]
Sexuality is the realm of relations and differences, but it cannot be that of
the common. Sexuality will therefore pose fundamental problems in
relation to Rousseau's political project as I have tried to set it out in the
previous two chapters. It is a necessary quality for the perpetuation of the
species, but it is not a *human* quality as Rousseau understands that term.

Indeed, the terms of the sexual relation are precisely those of inequality
and dissimulation. The man is supposed to act willfully and powerfully
(*"qu'il veuille et puisse"*). But he can only do so if the woman plays hard
to get and yields. "The stronger appears as the master and in effect
depends on the weaker." This is said to be an "invariable law of nature,"
deriving from the fact that woman can more easily "arouse desires than
satisfy them." Indeed, male sexuality is a union of *amour propre* and
desire, made possible by the woman.[97] Nature wants woman to rule:
"l'empire des femmes." According to Rousseau, sexuality is, in fact, the
continuous being of women, at least during their youthful childbearing
years, whereas "the male is only male at certain moments."[98] So as long
as women are brought up to dissemble, they are the stronger; were they
brought up as males are, they would lose their superiority.

Rousseau's entire discussion of the relation between the sexes thus takes
place under a double warning: It is a relation of inequality and it is one of
illusion in which those who appear weakest are in fact stronger. In such a
relation, however, it is nevertheless possible to have an *"honnête-femme."*

Now this is peculiar, in that Rousseau appears to be claiming that if a
woman is honest, she dissimulates. In what, however, does the strength of
women in relation to men consist? It consists, Rousseau says, in the fact
that women must both *have* certain qualities and *appear* to have those
qualities. The following tortuous paragraph is typical and worth giving at
length.

Man and woman are made for each other, but their mutual dependency is not equal. Men depend on women by their desires; women depend on men by their desires and their needs. We would more easily survive without them then they without us. For them to have what is necessary, for them to be as they are (*dans leur état*), we have to give it to them, we have to want to give it to them, we must judge them worthy of it. They depend on our feelings. . . . [and] are at the mercy of the judgment of men. It is not enough that they be estimable, they must be in fact esteemed. It is not enough that they be pretty, they must please. . . . Their honor is not only in their conduct, but in their reputation. . . . It follows from this that the whole framework for their education must be different from ours: opinion is the tomb of virtue among men, and its throne among women.[99]

The *we* in this paragraph is multiply ambiguous. On the one hand, Rousseau knows himself sexually as a heterosexual male.[100] But now look at what he thinks himself to be in the world. Rousseau was estimable, but unesteemed. His conduct was (he knew) beyond reproach, but his reputation was miserable. It almost follows from this that womanhood is the state to which Rousseau aspired.[101] It does not quite follow because the discrepancy between what he was and how he was perceived was to be overcome by changing people's opinions of him so as to allow himself to be available as he was, directly and transparently. Perceived as a woman, as it were, he can show them he is a male. Almost no men can do this; women can never do this (in relation to men, at least), but they can maintain an appearance that is identical to their being. They still exist as an illusion, but it is a true illusion, something like the possible uses for theater and philosophy in a corrupt society that Rousseau outlines in the preface to *Narcisse*. In relation to himself, it was not a matter of giving people the "right" opinions, but of removing those opinions that were blinders. As he says in the *Narcisse* preface: "It is of no concern whether people think good or ill of me, but it is of concern that no one have the right to think ill of me."[102] It seems to me, however, clear in the preceding long citation that by the sudden interjection of the first person plural— *we*—Rousseau feels the attraction of his conception of the feminine.

An honest woman is a person in whom the mask is identical to the face. Rousseau does not think that any mask is acceptable here. The important point is that the woman be honest and he spends a good deal of time attacking women who are coquettes to men of dubious virtue. It is, I think, reasonable to say that Rousseau thinks of women here much as he thinks of theater, or the arts and sciences, in a corrupted society. Sexual attraction is for the man by definition a combining of *amour propre* and desire and is thus a kind of double unfreedom. On the other hand, sexuality is necessary, and Rousseau is quick to reject the Platonic alternative of the community of wives as engendering a "civil promiscuity" that denies a natural basis to civic virtue.[103] In the preface to *Narcisse* he writes that those whose temper has been ruined by a "careless use of medicine are forced to have recourse to doctors to stay alive." If the arts and sciences and theater destroy virtue, they nonetheless leave "a public simulacrum which is always an attractive thing." This includes politeness, an "appearance of order that prevents horrible confusion, a certain admiration for attractive things which keeps good one's from falling into forgetfulness." It is not necessary for "the love of reputation to make one forget that of virtue."[104]

It is clear that a major thrust of the last book of the *Emile* is to establish that not only is the woman's place in the home but *the home is that which can make men want to be virtuous citizens*. Rousseau is not simply saying that women should stay in their place. Their place turns out to have profound political consequences. To start with, woman-in-the-home comes to play the same role to man-as-citizen that the tutor plays to Emile.

> It is necessary for her to study profoundly the spirit of man, not by abstracting from the human spirit in general, but the spirit of the men who surround her, the spirit of the men to whom she is subject by law or by opinion. . . . They will philosophize better than she on the human heart; but she will read better than they in the hearts of men. It is to women, to find, so to speak, experimental morality, to us to reduce it into a system. . . . *The world is the book of women.*[105]

Here Rousseau ascribes to women precisely the task that he took on himself in his diagnostic writings such as the *Second Discourse*. The being of the two authors of the *Discourse on Inequality* and the *Social Contract*, when joined in one person, is a perfected sexual union, one in which sexuality no longer leads to domination and inequality. As Rousseau develops this thought one finds that it is to women that the great republics owe their virtue, indeed, that great revolutions come from women.[106] Even if all this is illusion, it makes men love virtue, beauty, nobility.

It is easy to take Rousseau to task on what he says about women. What is noteworthy and troubling about many commentators on this matter is that they seek to excuse Rousseau. In his defense, some are tempted to ask if he is not expressing here the prejudices of a bourgeois of his age, worrying about "family values" at a time that these were only coming generally into being.[107] Perhaps. But it seems to me here that such a conclusion, attractive though it be in that it gets him partially "off the hook," is misguided. It is only the reverse of blaming Rousseau for the ills of modernity. Plato haunts the *Emile* (the *Republic*, Rousseau says, is the "most beautiful book on education" that had yet been written[108]) as Rousseau's great forerunner and competitor. Women are for Rousseau the great natural source of illusion. They thus play the same role in relation to the polity that the "noble lie" did in Plato. This, however, means that it is unnecessary to have a philosopher-king to formulate illusions for the citizens. Women are, for Rousseau, sources of natural illusion. They thus make nongendered equality possible. No man (and in time no woman) need be outside the common.

Women are thus both more and less than men in Rousseau's mind. They are less because, as *women*, they are not citizens: They are closer to "nature" in that their sexual being is integrated with their self and they are not divided against themselves. But they are more than men in that their role in the polity is to be outside it, in the manner that philosophers have always been outside the polity. If nature rested in Emile thanks to the negativity of the tutor, so does the polity rest in men due to the negativity of women. It is not the case, whatever one may want to make of it, that Rousseau could simply "abandon his prejudices" and make women full citizens. Gender, according to Rousseau, leaves men more space to be citizens. Gender does not leave women alone, at least during their childbearing years.

This does not mean that those whose gender is female cannot be citizens. The Spartan woman whom Rousseau instances as a model of a citizen at the very beginning of the *Emile* has had five children, all old enough to have been killed in battle. Presumably, part of the point is that she is of an age that her sexuality leaves her alone and allows the space for citizenship.[109] I do not think there is any way around this when reading Rousseau. Sexuality can be enlisted in the service of making political life possible, but only at the cost of requiring of women that they be both more and less than citizens. Commonalty and sexuality—once no longer in the state of nature—do not sit easily together.

Rousseau's discussion of sexuality is thus closer to Aristotle's than it is to Plato's. Plato had thought to show that gender differences played no important role in any of the matters of the polity. Aristotle had argued for the importance of gender differences. He had also appeared to argue for the inferiority of women.[110] Rousseau asserts gender differences but for reasons other than those apparently Aristotle's.

In any case, this matter cannot be read away. The idea of the common has no place for sexual differences, differences that Rousseau is both unable and unwilling to declare unimportant. *However, the availability of the human is not the prerogative of males as males.* It is not that sex makes men better as males, but that their sexuality takes them less frequently away from the common. Rousseau does also think that sexuality introduces relations that are incompatible with the common political life. He is, one might say, sexist but, in contemporary jargon, not phallocratic.

All of this establishes the categories into which Sophie must fall. Rousseau now turns at some length to talking about Sophie as an embodied person. She is well born, is not pretty but interesting, sings well, has too much of an appetite (which she learns to keep under control), does not have a perfectly even temper, and so forth.[111] She appears as the perfect embodiment of European possibilities: "With the temperament of an Italian, and the sensibility of an Englishwoman, to contain her heart and his senses she has the pride of a Spaniard, who, even when seeking a lover, does not easily find one she judges worthy of her."[112]

Into the possibility of their relationship, Rousseau now introduces all the elements of a just polity. The two of them must be of relatively equal status, neither can be much richer or poorer than the other, and so forth. The forms of domination that had been rehearsed in the *Second Discourse* all return for examination, each to be eliminated from the potential relationship. The reason, of course, is that "natural qualities," qualities they have as humans, must control the relation. The key predicate of these qualities is that of social equality. It is thus the case that the human prerequisites of a good marriage have an important relation to the elements of political justice, even though, as discussed above, they are not coterminous with them.[113] All that is required is that both the male and female know how to think, not a natural art, Rousseau notes. Thus both must have had some education: This is one acquired quality that cannot be bracketed.[114]

The tutor, here explicitly compared to Athena, who appearing as Mentor accompanies Ulysses's son Telemachus to the island of Calypso (the choice of a woman disguised as a man is obviously no accident), now arranges for Emile to encounter Sophie. As in the Fénélon play to which Rousseau is making reference, like Telemachus, Emile is overwhelmed by the nymph Eucharis (whose name means "pleasing").

They court, a courtship filled with the usual tutorial delays and the little lessons learned from the passing of time. At last they become engaged. Emile discovers to his distress that the tutor thinks him a slave to his passion for Sophie, even though it is still a completely innocent passion; he is recommended a period of travel in foreign countries before marriage will become appropriate.[115] When Emile resists, the tutor invokes the pact he concluded with him at the beginning of this progress: "I would that you leave" (*je le veux*).[116] He is asked, in other words, to make the tutor's will his own. A consequence, perhaps a point of the engagement, is to give Emile the chance to abide by his contracts, something that he has not had to do until this time. Indeed, he was not capable of making a contract until well into his adolescence. Here is another step in Rousseau's implicit refutation of Hume that was seen in the last chapter. Ordinary people are indeed capable of learning how to keep their promises, even under the most difficult circumstances, but they are only capable of it if they do in fact learn how. That learning, Rousseau realized, is the natural capacity of everyone, but that does not mean that it is a capacity that everyone naturally will have. The last step into adulthood is to be able to observe one's contracts. Hume turns out to have been wrong. Emile has finally become ready for political society and will not have to accept the world that has been ready made for him by history.

His travels are a continuation of his instruction by seeing. To know others helps one to know humans, and the extension of the comparative method is now applied to political groups. This is the final step in Emile's education in preparation for political society: actually to look at different societies, again with an eye to seeing what the principles of a political society are. At the end of this process, however, he will be able to do more than even Montesquieu, who had contented himself with a comparative study of different systems of positive law. He will come back "versed in all the matters of government." Emile should be able to write or at least to grasp the "principles of political right," the *Social Contract* as it were.[117] It is thus no surprise that Rousseau initiates the closing of his book with a short summary of what Emile has learned from his travels, a summary that gives the gist of the *Social Contract*, complete with the formulation of the contract itself. Emile has learned that which is the subject matter of the book that Rousseau was writing at the same time he wrote the *Emile*.[118]

Some commentators have read the *Emile* as a description of the person who could live in the modern state, a state Rousseau conceives of as without virtue. I do not think this is Rousseau's intention at all. The *Emile* ends with Emile arriving at a formulation of the *Social Contract*, a formulation that he has achieved as the end result of his education; it is clearly an indication that Rousseau intended in his book on education to form a being who was capable of living in a just society, a capability Rousseau does not thinks each of us has naturally. At the end of *Emile and Sophie*, Emile finds himself once again participant in a more or less just society. It is not just that he is unchanged and, as Judith Shklar argues, impervious to the fears of modern society. It is that what he is *requires and will generate, come what may, a political society*. No matter what happens to him (and a lot has happened, as shown above) he is and can only be both human and citizen. Indeed, that which makes him human requires that he be a citizen. The tutor warns him that he will not live in a perfectly just society, but that his knowledge of justice will attach him to society. He is not to sacrifice the good, or even the merely acceptable, for the best.[119]

And so they marry, for now they can. In a few short pages, they are about to produce a child themselves, only to find that having become adults themselves, they do not know how to raise children. Emile implores the tutor one last time:

> Counsel us, govern us, we will be docile: as long as I shall live I will need you. I have greater needs now than ever, now that my life (*functions*) as a human (*d'homme*) begins. You have done your part, help me imitate you, and rest. It is time.[120]

The reference to the creation of the world by God is not an accident. Can God really leave his creation? It is time.

5

The Ends of Politics

Wie eng begränzt ist unsere Tagezeit
Du warst und sahst und stauntest, schon Abend ists,
  Nun schlafe, wo endlich ferne
  Ziehen vorüber der Völker Jahre

Und mancher siehet über die enge Zeit
Ihm zeigt ein Gott ins Freie, doch sehnend stehst
  Am Ufer du, ein Ärgerniß den
  Deinen, ein Schatten, und liebst sie nimmer

Und jene, die nu nennst, die Verheissenen,
Wo sind die Neuen, daß du an Freundeshand
  Erwarmst, wo nahn sie, daß du einmal
  Einsame Rede, vernehmlich seiest?

Friedrich Hölderlin, Rousseau[1]

How narrowly constrained are the days of our life.
You were and saw and marveled; evening comes so soon.
  Now sleep where, infinitely far,
  Years of the peoples pass on by.

And some see over their own time.
A god shows them to freedom, but
  Yearning you stand on the shore, a distress
  To your kind, a shadow, and love them no more

And those whom you name, promised to us,
Where are the new ones, warmed by your hand,
  Where do they approach that you,
  Lonely speaker, may distinctly be heard?

(My translation)

"One must be," wrote Rimbaud, "absolutely modern." It is not an easy imperative but I have found in Rousseau a writer of my time. He does not want to *return* to anything. Indeed, what is most noticeable about Rousseau is his acceptance of the actuality of modern conditions. The thought of the common is not therefore a thought to be recovered from a past: It is, I have argued, what Rousseau thinks as the way to deal with the present. What then is Rousseau's project? To ask this is to ask what he thought human beings were missing in the world in which they lived. For Rousseau, our initial experience—as a child, as a race—is one of lack, of not being. In the state of nature, beings were negative, they had no qualities. Infants are born capable of becoming human but without human qualities. This childish nothingness has an ambivalent position in human life. On the one hand, it tempts us to avoid acknowledgment by others and to wish to protect ourselves by imposing our own definition on them.[2] This is the world of inequality, of domination and subordination.[3] On the other hand, it is a constant reminder that we are naturally not anything in particular and that we must therefore never assume that our endowments have transcendental, that is, nonhuman, qualities. If a human being has no natural qualities, but must perforce by being *acquire* qualities, then the source of moral virtue must begin in the acknowledgment of that fact about oneself. Morality and justice could not then be based in some quality that human beings naturally have.[4] This means that the beginning of sin is the insistence that what one is, is privileged. What is unnatural is to claim that one is naturally any one thing.[5]

As I noted in chapter 2, Rousseau inveighs against those who accuse him of wanting to return "to the woods," to a kind of savage innocence. He knew, however, full well that anyone who can spell *Eden* cannot live there. The desire to remain a child in the world cannot thus truly be the desire to return to the time when we did not know that we were not any one thing. The desire to remain a child is rather the desire to protect ourselves from this knowledge by an insistence that we can know finally who we are. For Rousseau, the desire for identity is, I have argued, the desire to avoid what we have become, what we are.

I have insisted throughout this book that Rousseau grounded his thought in an experience he thought had become increasingly uncommon. For him the contemporary period was characterized by a loss of capacity on the part of one individual to find the human in an other, that is, by the loss of the capacity to acknowledge the manner in which another is exactly the same as I am. Inequality was at the origin of the loss of this capacity; however, simple inequality was not, for Rousseau, opposed to equality but to commonalty, the ordinary. When Rousseau protested that no one could see him or recognize him as a human being, he meant that they were requiring of him that he be what they could make of him. Making something of someone is, for Rousseau, domination. It is opposed to being available to an other.

Again and again Rousseau despaired of ever being seen as a human being. He hoped, I think, that the possibility of such a recognition would be raised if others were at least to notice him. I tend to think that a good deal of Rousseau's posturing derives from the belief that being noticed would at least be a start. The one text of Rousseau that has a happy ending is the *Dialogues*. The dynamics of that text are such that it is precisely the fact that the Frenchman has had to pay attention to the "Jean-Jacques" character that he eventually comes to see him as a human being. However, the dialogues are a text that Rousseau structures; they are a text of self-consolation, as if he were giving himself a scenario in which humanity might actually be recognized. They afford a possibility to life, but Rousseau never mistook the one for the other.

The Remedy and the Illness

Can it be said that Rousseau was in his life successful in his project? In a review of the *Letter to D'Alembert*, Edmund Burke wrote:

> None of the present writers have a greater share of talents and learning than Rousseau; yet it has been his misfortune and that of the world that those of his works that have made the greatest noise, and acquired to their author the highest reputation, have been of little real use or emolument to mankind. A tendency to paradox, which is always the bane of solid learning, and threatens now to destroy it, a splenetic disposition carried to misanthropy, and an austere virtue pursued to an unsociable fierceness, have prevented a great deal of the good effects that might be expected from such a genius. A satire on civilized society, a satire upon learning, may make a tolerable sport for an ingenious fancy; but if carried further it can do no more (and that in such a way is surely too much) than

to unsettle our notions of right and wrong, and lead by degrees to universal skepticism.[6]

Burke was, I cannot help but feel, impressed with Rousseau, impressed against his better judgment. His better judgment, however, warned him that society, as it was, functioned tolerably well, and that should one take seriously Rousseau's distress with persons as he encountered them (his "misanthropy"), the result would be to produce "universal skepticism," the concrete social correlative of the epistemological stance associated with thinkers like his friend David Hume.[7] That skepticism become social reality was a threat to Burke (in a way that was not actual, one should say, to Hume). He thought he saw in the French revolution a concretization of skepticism and held Rousseau responsible. The *Emile*, he says in a review of 1762, contains "not a few" ideas that were "highly blamable and dangerous both to piety and morals." In the *Letter to a Member of the National Assembly* (1791), Burke suggested that Rousseau's ideas had in fact become reality. The Jacobin leaders "all resemble [Rousseau]. His blood they transfuse into their minds and into their manners. . . . I am certain that the writings of Rousseau lead directly to this kind of shameful evil."[8]

The Jacobins do not transform his ideas; they transfuse his blood. For Burke, Rousseau's texts are alive and have become flesh, in a kind of awful sacrament. I do not want here to address the question of the relation between the thought of Rousseau and that of the leaders of the French Revolution. What is clear, however, is that for Burke the thought of Rousseau threatened to turn skepticism not just into an interesting philosophical parlor game, but into a serious social reality. Burke, in other words, accuses Rousseau of fostering precisely the sorts of things that I have tried to show he was trying to overcome.

This is not a trivial accusation. Taken at face value, Burke's accusation is that no matter what Rousseau's hopes and intentions were, the actualization of those intentions could only produce a result completely contrary to those he wished to achieve. For Burke, Rousseau's attempt at making the human available gives us Lear on the heath, "poor, naked wretches," but wretches with power, and thus exceedingly dangerous. The source of Burke's preference for artifice ("Art is nature in man") is consequent to his belief that the natural or ordinary (as opposed to the historical) is dangerous.

Why should the attempt to make the human available appear as a dangerous and irresponsible disruption of society? I think the answer must make reference to the sense that the strongest human feeling is fear. Fear, as Hobbes understood deeply, is consequent to a situation in which there is no predictable relationship between one's actions and the outcomes. One way of ensuring that an outcome will be predictable is to give its component parts adequate and ongoing definition. Hobbes thus famously spends a good deal of time making sure that all aspects of humanity are defined. In terms of human beings, this means knowing who are, reading yourself, having, I might say, the gospel of yourself.[9] (To be fair to Hobbes here, he thought that the extent of this definition was limitless in theory but highly reduced in practice.) Rousseau, however, denied that any achievement such as that of Hobbes could preserve the human as available. His thought, therefore, reintroduces questions that Burke, Hobbes, and others had presented as solved or as unquestionably true.[10] In the context of my discussion of Rousseau, this requires us to ask if any substantive definition of "the" human can be human.

Writing shortly after Rousseau, Kant will argue that for humans to be able to acknowledge their knowledge of the world in which they live, the conditions of knowledge must be human conditions.[11] It is the burden of the *Critiques* to delineate those conditions. Rousseau's enterprise, as I have read it, is parent to Kant's but also somewhat different. It is not that we need to say what the human "is." Kant was not to do this, in fact he was to keep himself from doing this by placing the full understanding of the human in the noumenal world, a world in principle inaccessible to direct human knowledge. Kant's solution, however, remains, as Nietzsche knew, too "theological." It required the positing of an inaccessible realm of solutions.[12] Rousseau wishes to impress on his readers that for us to recognize ourselves as human beings, we must only satisfy the conditions of there being other human beings in the world. This means, I have tried to show, an acceptance of both one's own and others' multiplicity, and to resist the temptation to define. For Rousseau, to define is to control is to dominate is to depend for oneself on one's domination of others or even on one's domination of oneself.[13] Hence nothing can count as myself, once and for all.

Nothing is so dissimilar to me than is myself: this is why it would be useless to try and define me other than by the singular variety.... From the start

144   JEAN-JACQUES ROUSSEAU

this should remove from the curious any hope of some day recognizing me by my personality (*mon caractère*): for they will always find me in some particular shape which will only be mine during that moment; and they will not even be able to hope to recognize me by these changes, for as they have no base period they will refer now to this moment and now to that—and sometimes I will stay for months at a time in the same state. It is this irregularity that is at the bottom of what I am (*de mon constitution*).[14]

"This irregularity": Rousseau's point, I take it, is that the requirement of regularity, predictability, fixedness is destructive of the being of a human. Say that an irregular being is a human being, and further say that most of those in this world are not like this. They are able to say who they are, or they know to what they aspire. They know what defines them. More precisely: They know themselves to be defined and that they have only to find the definition. This understanding was at the center of Aristotle's argument in the *Poetics* that Plato was wrong about the compatibility of theater with political justice. The moral function of drama was for Aristotle at the moment of αναγνορισιω. Anagnorisis is the moment in theater when the protagonist comes to recognize himself for who he is, the time his being is discovered and recovered. Aristotle points to the moment when, seeing himself for the first time, Oedipus puts out his eyes. Rousseau tacitly accepts Aristotle's understanding of the nature of drama and it becomes for him a reason to reject the centrality of the representation of the self to the self. In such a circumstance, beings are for Rousseau not (really) human.[15] From this, it would follow that a *human* being does not search for his or her identity, if only because *humans* do not have "identity."

There appears to be a paradox here, but there is not. One might ask: Who or what does Rousseau want his readers to know, if not his identity? Does not Rousseau protest again and again that no one knows him? Indeed, he does. But this protest is always against those who take some character to be the "true" Rousseau. "Character" is that which is fixed, etched, put down. It derives from the Greek word for engraving. Character is theatrical. To further grasp what Rousseau means by "irregularity" here, let me briefly compare Rousseau to another way of looking at the question of identity and politics.

The Alternative of Transparency

Partway through the second volume of *Democracy in America*, Tocqueville entertains the notion of democratic poetry: ". . . [T]he spread of equality over the earth dries up the old springs of poetry. We must try to show how other springs are revealed."[16]

Tocqueville goes on to suggest that it is only in a democratic society that "one can form a picture . . . in which a nation counts as a single citizen." Then, he continues, "all mankind can be seen together in broad daylight." Thus, in a truly sung democracy when one sees one citizen, one will see the nation. Each citizen, identical as citizen to each other, will have all the multiplicities to which anyone can aspire.

Tocqueville here reveals something central to his understanding of democracy. In the proper picture of democracy, the very identity of each citizen with each other means that in seeing one, one in fact sees all. This does not mean that there is no difference but that each of us, in Whitman's classic phrase, "contains multitudes." We are differences. A poet makes the world in words: The gift of the poet is made possible because words are (just barely) more accessible than is the world. So poetry enables those who read it. A poet of democracy makes available a world, according to Tocqueville, in which each is seen in one picture.[17] Part of the distress in Tocqueville's musings comes from the fear that no world will be available to the new democrats whom he sees as sweeping all history in front of them. Tocqueville's concern, however, is with the subject matter that this poetry must make available for it to be truly democratic poetry. The subject of the poetry of democracy, Tocqueville intimates, is neither the ideal, nor even nature; it is certainly not community and is not even properly the self. What would democratic poetry give its reader? In words that recall Rousseau's proud announcing of his own genealogy, Tocqueville asserts:

> In democratic societies where all are insignificant and very much alike, each man, as he looks at himself, sees all his fellows at the same time.[18]

I think that Tocqueville means here exactly what he says. It is not that I see a great community in the vista of democratic poetry but that I see, as I see myself, every other person as myself. This is not identity, but equality and possibility. This egalitarian vision, originally that of Hobbes,[19] holds that from the point of view of democratic politics anything that can happen to anyone can happen to me. No identity is foreclosed on the basis of race, color, creed, ethnicity, gender—on the basis of *anything*.

This is not the same position as that adopted by most liberals. John Rawls suggests that just political institutions will best be chosen from behind a "veil of ignorance," that is, by systematically bracketing all those qualities that make me different from an other. Tocqueville is rather pointing at something different in America.[20] He is not suggesting that for a just society to exist I must choose institutions without reference to my identity, but that in a democratic society I really do not have an identity that is my own, nor do I have one that is that of my "group." Rousseau would have responded to Rawls by saying that the bracketing move was not only unnecessary but that it also removed from the conditions of justice the central importance of the recognition of the acknowledgment of my commonalty and that of others.[21]

The poetry of democracy gives us the multiplicity of each human being, a multiplicity made possible and required by the identity of the citizen. The most extraordinary, some might say outrageous, moment in George Kateb's recent book, *The Inner Ocean*, comes in his final discussion of Whitman.

> All the personalities that I encounter, I already am: that is to say, I could become or could have been something like what others are. . . . I am potentially all personalities and we equally are infinite potentialities.[22]

Whatever Kateb's position is, it is not that of Rawlsian liberalism. I might say Kateb's position is certainly more exciting than such liberalisms. Kateb raises a different, less liberal, question about the democratic agent: What if the self were not "thin," in Rawls's words, but transparent, nothing? Such a self would have no historical substance—that is, it would not be defined by that which it was not. Such a self would not be Hegelian, that is, its nature would not be premised on recognition by an other. As in Rousseau, such a self could then not ever hold an other in domination, nor be subject to an other. The other is me. Such a self would be, I might say, the stuff of poetry, of art, "an abstract or epitome of the world," as Emerson wrote.[23]

In 1836 Tocqueville thought that there was as yet no American poet, but he was sure that there could be. Within 20 years there clearly was: The first edition of *Leaves of Grass* was in 1855. That Kateb finds this vision of the democratic individual available in the poetry of Walt Whitman is a confirmation of Tocqueville's anticipation. For Kateb, Whitman at his best incurs the full risk of democratic individuality: It is the risk that one runs when all need for a substantial self has been cast aside.

The passage quoted above from Kateb's essay on Whitman indicates that there is nothing any human being has become or done that I could not have become or done (Whitman does not exclude questions of gender). This is not a claim that I can be "anything I want," but that anything anyone has been has something to do with me. Any substantial fixed conclusion as to "who I am" must therefore do violence to others. Such a condition seems to me to be what is meant by "transparency." That is, the self which can be all selves has not an other, for it is transparent to them.

Humanity and Transparency

Rousseau's position is a cousin to these but more historical and less, dare I say it, aristocratic. He shares with Tocqueville (and Kateb and Whitman) the notion that in seeing oneself, the egalitarian (or democratic) individual sees all persons. (This is what it means to see oneself democratically.) But he does not think that this being is without substance, as it were, transparent. It will necessarily have substance (that is, it will exist historically); and it will gain this substance from the interaction that it will perforce have with others. Nothing is necessary but everything is given.

I fly a bit in the face here of the magisterial work of Jean Starobinski.[24] Starobinski sees transparency as the state to which Rousseau always aspired but could never achieve. Starobinski argues that the conditions that make transparency available also threaten it. In a consideration of the *Fifth Rêverie*, Starobinski notes that Rousseau at first seems to want to rid himself of his senses in order to bask only in the "feeling of existence"

(Rousseau's words), but that he soon rehabilitates externality in order to remain alive.[25] Says Rousseau:

> Absolute silence leads to sadness (*porte à la tristesse*). It presents an image of death. . . . Rest is less, it is true, but it is also more pleasant when light and pleasant ideas barely touch the surface of the soul, so to speak, without stirring its depths.[26]

Starobinski reads this as a sign of the impossible set of desires to which Rousseau has chained himself. There is certainly an important insight in that judgment. In addition, however, it seems to me that this and other passages should be looked at in conjunction with the context of the *Rêveries*. I argued above that even in the *Rêveries*, Rousseau was concerned to establish his society with himself. It is clear also that he thinks that this is a lesser state than the full society of others. *Rêverie* is an important way of making contact for those who have no (other) humans present.

> . . . [A]n unfortunate who has been removed from human society and who can here below do nothing more that is useful and good for others or for himself may find in this state [*rêverie*] compensations for all human happinesses, compensations that fortune and men will not be able to take away.[27]

If humanity cannot be compensated for, human happinesses can be, should one lack them. But it *is* a lack and the *Rêveries* seem to be written with precisely the image of the society of the *Social Contract* in mind. Rousseau is not, in this reading, so much concerned with attaining a pure and undefiled beautiful transparency as he is with the conditions under which modern persons live. The *Rêveries* are—as to a degree are the earlier texts that raise the possibility of the beautiful solitary soul as a solution—a critique of the world in which we live as well as of the beings who are of that world. It is possible that the cost of the society of the *Social Contract*, the cost of the life in which one is available in common to others, will be a loss of reverie and perhaps of other delights. The cost is hard to determine for such a loss does not presently threaten us. "The best is not to have been born, and the next best is to die quickly": Such is the wisdom of Marsyas in *Oedipus at Colonnus*. Hannah Arendt has argued that this requires that humans live politically. George Kateb has argued against her that if this were the price to pay for politics one would be better off dead.[28] Rousseau stands here unresolved, I think. Is being besides yourself the same as living with another? I can, I think, have myself for company, but I am not clear how I can be in politics with myself, unless I were quite insane.[29]

Rousseau does not see our epoch as one for humans. I take it then that to be a human being is to be able to live with others as what one is. If you remove Rousseau's question mark about ability, this was Aristotle's definition. Aristotle called it politics and meant thereby something more than we moderns do. Yet Nietzsche saw in precisely this a central question of modernity.

> To say it briefly (for a long time people will still keep silent about it):
> What will not (henceforth) be built any more, cannot be built any more,
> is—a society in the old sense of that word; to build that, everything is
> lacking, above all the material. *All of us are no longer material for a
> society*; this is a truth for which the time has come.[30]

Rousseau has much the same realization as does Nietzsche. However, living one hundred years earlier, he still thinks the material of society recoverable. What does it mean to be "material for a society"? Rousseau's concerns extend, I have said, to the grammar of human society, that is, to that which has to be the case for human beings to be such that they can live as humans with each other. The *Social Contract* presumes the existence of l'ordre civil.[31] In that book, Rousseau elaborates the institutional and structural entailments of such an order. This is not the same question as that of the qualities that citizens would have in a "well-established state."[32] So what has to be the case for humans to be capable of society? What are the requirements that a human society places on its members? To ask this is to ask the question of what has to be the case for a society to be a human society.

The Deduction of Immanence

The first requirement is that God must have left His creation. A society of Christians would, Rousseau avers, "no longer be a society of human beings."[33] Elsewhere, Rousseau indicates that there apparently are in fact no Christians on earth. "If one were allowed to draw from the actions of humans the proof of their feelings, one would have to say that the love of justice has been banished from all hearts and that there is not a single Christian on earth."[34] In fact, even if there were Christians on earth, "the words [Christian and Republic] are mutually exclusive."[35]

Rousseau's position here is not that of an atheist: Such would be to give too much attention to the question of belief. In the "Letter to M. de Franquières," Rousseau indicates that matters of religion are to be understood as beyond the "limits" of human beings.

This man who is neither a brute nor a prodigy [of philosophy] is the true human being, a median between the two extremes. . . .[36]

The centrally important thing is not to let the concern with religion delude or dilute the *sentiment interne* without which there "would soon remain no trace of truth on earth and we would be the playthings of the most monstrous opinions . . : such that we would soon be ashamed of our reason itself."[37] On these matters, Rousseau goes on to insist, there is no distinction between Jesus and Socrates. Both sought a liberating wisdom that was a human wisdom. Jesus' "noble project was to . . . make his people free and worthy of being so."[38] Again and again, Rousseau reads purely religious matters not as something to be rejected but as matters to be held outside of the dynamics of human society. Retaining the *sentiment interne* is a sign that we have yielded to neither the seduction of dogmatic assurance nor to the erosions of skepticism.

The second requirement is not to accept the immortality of the soul. In the chapter in the *Social Contract* on "Civil Religion," Rousseau refers to the "sentiments of sociability." They include not believing in the immortality of the soul,[39] which is deemed a "doctrine pernicious to the state." Why is the belief in immortality pernicious? The reason seems to be that one will no longer fear being cut off from one's co-citizens. Immortality gives one a way of being without that way being human, without being a citizen. More important, I want to say, the belief in immortality makes it both unnecessary and impossible to imagine oneself to be a (fully) human being. It tells me that what is important about me—my immortal soul—will always be immaculate. Maculation is, however, the quality of human action. What is essential to Rousseau is that the capacity for the ordinary be realizable by any person on this earth. In the notes he took on *De l'esprit*, Rousseau insists against Helvetius on the architectonic activity of human judgment.[40] Immortality allows the judgment to be passive and makes the ordinary unnecessary. It makes the ordinary unnecessary because it privileges one aspect of our self and renders it permanent. One hundred years before Rousseau, Hobbes had, in the name of civil philosophy, insisted on the mortality of the soul. Had this not been the case, some part of human life would have escaped the purview of the life with others. Hobbes was perhaps too close to religion to adopt Rousseau's veiled solution; but he knew that an immortal soul would make citizenship and this world secondary. Thus he had joined the ranks of those theologians who held that the soul and the body were one in death and in resurrection.[41]

The concern with the politically nefarious consequences of the doctrine of the immortality of the soul is at the root of Rousseau's hostility to theater and representation. Solon had fled in despair from one of the early theatrical representations in Athens. When Thespis argued to him that it was after all not real and only a game, he is purported to have responded that it would not be long until one saw the effects of such games on the citizens.[42] This is at the base of Rousseau's perception: The most important thing about theater seems to lie precisely in the fact that the characters on stage do, in some way, escape the limits of being human, specifically, the limits of mortality. Although actors-as-characters are not gods, they are clearly beings above the ordinary human run. As Michael Goldman notes: "While on stage, the actors enjoy a kind of omnipotence, a privilege and protection not unlike that accorded sacred beings."[43] Humans, as opposed to actors-as-characters, live their lives, and to be lived those lives must, all of them, come into being and to an end. Actors-as-characters are, in Goldman's words again, "phenomenologically immortal." They are fixed, given, defined in the sense that all they can and ever will say is already said. They always rehearse eternity and do not die, and this is precisely their attraction and seduction for us.[44] To want to be fixed once and for all is to want to be a god. Against this, Heidegger suggests that to be capable of death is a prerequisite for actually dwelling on the earth.[45]

If the first criterion for being "material for society" is that God be absent from one's world and the second that one not hold the soul to be immortal, the third is to marvel that the earth is. It is for this reason that

Hölderlin thought Rousseau a "son of the earth," not, that is, a child of heaven.[46] As was seen, the very word *human* derives from the word for earth and is used to signal a distinction from the divine.[47] In the second of the letters Rousseau addresses to Malesherbes, he describes himself as feeling the voluptuousness of being weighed down by the heaviness of this universe.[48] Whence this ecstasy? It is no wonder that much of the first part of Emile's education is spent teaching him to sense.

> Oh! that the fate that I have enjoyed would be known to all. Each would want a similar destiny; peace would reign on earth; humans would no longer think to harm each other and there would be no more evil persons when no one would have an interest in being so. But what did I enjoy at last when I was alone? My self, the whole universe, all that is, and that can be, all that the sensible world has that is beautiful, and all that the intelligible has that is imaginable.[49]

Rousseau's transfigurative ecstasy in the Vincennes woods not only gave him the *Discourse on Arts and Sciences*, it gave him a touchstone by which to recognize an experience that was human by virtue of being of this earth. The astonishment that the world is, what Hannah Arendt called "the love of the world," is central to the grammar of the human. In such a state, says Rousseau, "I did not think, I did not reason, I did not philosophize. . . . "[50] These multiple negations of our capacity to make the world are negations of the individual will, that is, of the temptation to fix the world as mine. It is this process that makes the human available, that gives the human a home.

A Human Home

What can be home for a human being? Rousseau's work pursues two ends. The first is to make available to his readers a sense of what a human home would be. The second is to awaken in them the recognition that they are in fact, and all appearances to the contrary, homeless.

How is it when society is a human home? Here my suggestion that the *Social Contract* is to be seen as the working out of the grammar of human society needs to be unpacked further. One, not unusual, way of thinking about Rousseau's endeavor in the *Social Contract* is to suggest that he is telling us what we should as rational beings consent to—what elements of the social system can command our moral assent. The rest—all that is not agreed to—is either one of the marks of social imperfection we must endure or else not part of the "conversation of justice" (the phrase is from Rawls). Yet this reading, plausible though it be, is, I think, quite wrong. If we are speaking the language of justice, then we do not consent in part to that language, as if we would deny the grammaticality of the past tense.[51] If this is true, then the *Social Contract* gives us that of which we are members, were we to acknowledge it, merely by the fact of our existence. It gives us the human. It does not give us only that to which we explicitly consent, as a more "liberal" reading would have it; it gives us that to which we do in fact, must, consent.[52] It gives us a home.

But this is not a home that we have, in which we live. Rousseau's distress with Paris is that it makes role and pretense central and attractive. It turns our lives into theater, rather than, as with the experience in St. Gervais, bring theater into our lives. What has happened is that in modern society persons devour themselves. Paris is for those who "can no longer forgo eating humans."[53] Where do we not devour each other? The society of inequality is a kind of mutual self-consumption in that each seeks to make the other part of him- or herself. Domination is the requirement that others be me. Marcel Hénaff has pointed out that the model of society that Rousseau often employs draws on its exaggeration. If cannibalism is the sign of the wasteland of Paris, eating *with* others, he argues, is the paradigm of civility.[54] This is certainly true, although there is more. The end of the fourth book of the *Emile*, which contains an extensive discussion of shared feasts, also describes a generally bucolic society, available to all, as Rousseau says. This is indeed a kind of picture of a human society; but it is not intended by Rousseau as a final word. (Here I differ from Hénaff, who sees these as the only two contrasting models in Rousseau). It is no accident that Rousseau places this description at the end not of the entire *Emile*, but of the fourth book. At this point, however, Emile still lacks two experiences: that of sexuality and that of politics. These will provide the subject matter of the next book. Eating with others (as opposed to eating others) is preparatory to living with them; but that does not make it Rousseau's final model.[55]

The communal feast, although a counter to the cannibalistic world of
Paris, is thus not sufficient. One is forced to raise the question of the final
elements of Emile's life. Are gender and politics compatible with a world
of human beings? Can a person retain experience of gender and politics
and to that degree still be human—still acknowledge that which he or she
(the necessity of two pronouns gives us pause) has in common?

When is a person not a human being? This is one formulation of the
central question that informs all of Rousseau's work. This is what I might
call a peripheral question, peripheral in the sense that it is generated by
the core of Rousseau's concern, the concern with the common. There are
two ways of looking at peripheral questions. One approach—perhaps its
best known exponent today is John Rawls—is to suggest that the important matter is to get the central questions answered correctly. Once that is
done, this position holds, then the rest is simply mopping up. A second
approach values the periphery because it reveals the tensions of the center.
In this view, the periphery is precisely that which keeps one from thinking
that the center has the quality of holding.

I propose then to look at the *inhuman*, a category required by Rousseau's
thought of the human. His explorations are thus in part at least investigations
into the inhuman. Here these questions are spectator to Rousseau's concerns, required by it but not more part of it than the audience is part of
the play. I have tried to let the questions I have raised about Rousseau lead
me naturally around his texts. This book is the paths into which his
thought leads my questions. But in doing so, I have left questions like
those that follow until here for a number of reasons. On the one hand, they
sometimes would have been digressions from the narrative, an interrup-
tion of the spectacle. On the other, they would have required recasting
the entire chapter in a manner and with a concern that I think would
have been inappropriate to Rousseau's text, as if one wanted to make
the audience reaction part of the text. On a divine third hand, many of
them could not have been explored without considerations that came
in later chapters. So to investigate them then and there would have been
to lift them out of their natural framework in Rousseau's presentation. To
consider them here is not simply to tidy up: Here is where this book has
led me.

I see these issues outstanding: (a) What is the not-human as it relates
to Rousseau's understanding of politics and women? (b) What is the

relation of the not-human to the legislator figure who appears in the second book of the *Social Contract*? (c) Is there an end to the demands of the human, to politics? To answer all of these, I must first say something about the inhuman and not-human and their relation to the human.

Who Has No Home?

When is a person not a human being? In Rousseau, some of the answers are clear: A slave is not a human being, which means that if a human being becomes a slave he or she no longer is a human being. A king is not a human being, and neither are the rich or the powerful. What is meant here by a human being is then not a "natural" quality in the sense that any featherless biped (the term is famously Plato's) has it merely by virtue of being alive. Rousseau's understanding of the human had to do with the capacity to allow others to be available to you in the same manner and as one might be to oneself. (This was not itself without problems.) This means further that there is nothing about the human that provides a kind of irreducible residue to protect against the encroachment of the inhuman.

Take the following, admittedly extreme, case. In the late 1930s the psychologist Bruno Bettelheim was imprisoned for about a year in Dachau and Buchenwald.[56] He details the various techniques of domination that were used to disrupt the ordinary world of the inmates and replace it with a world determined by the administration of the camps. What he found was that prisoners were unable over a long period of time to resist molding themselves to camp structures unless they consciously and with fore-thought drew some mental line over which they would not allow themselves to be moved. Their humanity, says Bettelheim, was in their own hands and its loss could be prevented only by the insistence that one would retain some human acts for one's own. André Malraux, in his *Antimémoires*, writes of those in the camps:

> Humanness, that is what they wanted to rip out of them. The human condition is the condition of creaturehood, the condition that im-poses destiny on human the way that a mortal illness imposes it on

human beings. The destruction of this condition is the destruction of
life; to kill. But the extermination camps, by trying to transform the
human into a beast, have made us feel that one is not human simply by
living.[57]

The camps are only the most unavoidable question of the human in our time.
The world of the camps is one of organized dislocation, where persons
were led to have nothing in common, not even death. Violence was
economically applied to disrupt the ordinary world, the world of human
beings. Rousseau details life in the Parises of his world as a constant
seduction away from humanness. Without in any way diminishing the
horror of the world of the camps, that Paris is a seduction and not violence
makes little difference to the fact that being human can be lost or be taken
away. Furthermore, such dynamics are built into the world in which we
(in the West, whites more than not, males more than not) live. This is the
point that Marx made when he wrote: "By working, the [laborer who sells
his labor-power] *becomes* actually what before he was only potentially,
labor-power in action, a laborer"; and in fact, with the addition of tech-
nology, the laborer "*becomes* the appendage of a machine."[58] Marx means
the *becomes* seriously—this is literally what happens. It is like what
Rousseau says about slavery: They are not human beings.[59]

In neither Marx nor Rousseau is there an opposition to the division of
labor per se. The concern is for what the clarity and fixity that the division
of labor affords human identity. Marx did not perhaps understand as fully
as he might have the security of relations of inequality. In the passage
cited from *The German Ideology* at the beginning of the previous chapter,
the important thing to realize is that after the revolution, a human being
will be able to engage in all these activities, without ever becoming identified
in terms of his or her performance. Being a hunter, or a fisherman, or even a
critic is the problem. Marx and Engels want to oppose such a state to that
of a human who hunts, fishes, or criticizes. So also Rousseau argues that
anyone who is defined in terms of roles cannot at the same time be a
human being. Such a concern was, I argued, at the root of Rousseau's
hostility to representation, both in the theater and in politics. The character on stage, the character that stands for us: Such are fixed, once and for
all. Yeats knew, even if he half approved:

> Though Hamlet rambles and Lear rages
> And all the drop-scenes drop at once
> Upon a hundred thousand stages,
> It cannot grow by an inch or an ounce.[60]

To be a character, to become a role: These are the seductions and requirements—the discipline—of modernity for Rousseau. It is important to see that his hostility here is not to theater but to the theatricalizing of everyday life. If to be an official is not to be a human being, it is because what an official is is defined: It cannot grow by an inch or an ounce. It is not just to play a part, but to become that part. In response to our anxiety over identity, modernity makes available a wide range of parts—"you can be anything you want to be." This is the stuff of theater. Theater, being a role, is very seductive: It allows us to deny that I have anything common to you.

In the worlds in which we live, the most usual form of theatricalization is rationalized roles, what Max Weber called bureaucracy. This link may seem strange: The dull routine of office seems distant from the mimesis of the stage. But bureaucracy has its attractions. Weber, as often, got it right:

> Entrance into an office, including one in the private economy, is considered an acceptance of a specific obligation of faithful management *in return for a secure existence.* It is decisive for the specific nature of modern loyalty to an office that, in the pure type, *it does not establish a relation to a person.* . . . Modern loyalty is devoted to impersonal and functional purposes.[61]

> Bureaucracy develops the more perfectly, the more it is 'dehumanized,' the more completely it succeeds in eliminating from official business love, hatred, and all purely personal, irrational and emotional elements which escape calculation.[62]

"The more completely it . . . eliminat[es] . . . all . . . personal . . . elements." What Weber means by "personal" is what Rousseau means by "human": As it is not defined but acknowledged, it is precisely that which cannot be calculated, ordered, predicted, disciplined. The genealogy of

modernity for Weber was one of progressive *Entzauberung*, of demagifi-
cation. Key to both thinkers here is the recognition that the theatricality
of the modern world—the roles that it provides all of us and in which we
find ourselves secure—is desirable. It is not surprising that Rousseau
appear as a kind of Alceste to Burke, except that Rousseau is serious and
cannot, as was Molière's character, be exposed as as much of a pretender
as the rest of us.

What is normally meant by the romantic response to this situation
would consist in counterpoising a real or natural self to the demands of
the rationalizing world. Judith Shklar's hostility to a "politics of identity"
comes from her realization that such a response will always betray
itself.[63] The "real self" is too weak to stand against society, something
Rousseau knew very well. She is quite right that Rousseau resists this; but
for me, he does not, as she argues, resist in the name of a number of
different institutional solutions. Against the politics of identity, Rousseau
does not advocate finding the real me, but the root of his teaching is not
one or another form of authoritative institution. The burden of his argument in the *Second Discourse* is that, in nature, humans are nothing. He
proposes to draw on this understanding, not to determine what humans
really are, but to make it possible for them to acknowledge that they are
not anything. Institutions should be consequent to this acknowledgment.

Against this, the modern world offers the temptation of being someone.
What is attractive about being a king, or even a slave, is that you know
who you are. So far is he from offering his readers a picture of what they
really, truly, are, Rousseau is warning them *not* to take up such opportu-
nities. Rousseau is, I might say, concerned with the project of making a
common sense, not with determining a specific individual identity.[64]

The first thing then to say about not being human is that the inhuman
is fixed, given, not only present. The human, contrariwise, resists or has
no definition. The deep significance of whatever is romantic in Rousseau
is not his pursuit of the "real me." It is that each person, in order to be
human, always chooses the others he or she also is. When Rousseau
embraces his multiplicity, as in the passage cited above, he is requiring
for his humanity the recognition of an other as himself. What Cavell calls
"the acknowledgment of a relationship" with an other is always, Rousseau
indicates, possible with an other, with oneself.[65]

Is Sex Human?

It is because of these considerations that Rousseau finds himself in a quandary with the question of sexuality. If the capacity for human society and citizenship rests on there not being any defining substantive characteristic, what are we to make of the fact that sex seems unavoidable? This is not precisely the problem of gender: The example of the Spartan mother is a clear indication that Rousseau thinks that citizenship is possible for both men and women. Nor can Rousseau simply say that we have two kinds of human beings, male and female, for this would fly in the face of the whole argument for the common. He does pretty clearly assume that if any one is to be human, those with male sexuality are the least interruptive of the grammar of the human. Both male and female are, so to speak, out of the realm of the common when sex is on their minds; but, Rousseau seems to think, sex is more constantly on the minds of young women.

So the question is if the human is compatible with sex. Insofar as Rousseau answered this question—and from the previous chapter, it must be that he did to a very great extent—his answer is that it is not. But I think that one can, even in terms of Rousseau's understanding, return to Rousseau's distress with the politics of identity and push the question in a different direction. The question could be phrased as follows: Is sex necessarily defining of identity? That is, does sex give one an identity, *volens nolens*, no matter what? Sex here must mean sexual orientation and imply a repeated limited and specific identification of self and other. (I mean: If one is heterosexual one looks to an other of the other sex; if homosexual, an other of the same.) This is pretty clearly what Rousseau assumed would have to be the case. Can one construct a Rousseauian argument without this assumption? I do not want here to answer this question although some recent work seems to be moving in that direction.[66] What is clear is that sexuality would have to be divorced from questions of identity, and that a politics of identity would have to be rejected.

Rousseau sought to remove sexuality from the realm of the common and was willing to assume that insofar as sex was a determining part of a person's identity that such an individual was uncommon. He thought that sex was sometimes a separate, valuable part of life, even though it was not fully human. In this case, Rousseau shows a strong sense that the common would not be sufficient to all aspects of human life. I noted earlier the possibility that the world of the household would have such qualities. But it must be said, this is interpretative of what is at best suggestion in Rousseau's texts. It is the case that in the first version of the *Social Contract*, the supposed rights deriving from families, relations between mother and father, as well as conquest or usurpation, are all designated as "false notions of the social bond." "There is," writes Rousseau, "nothing of all this in political society."[67]

What Is the Legislator?

Are there, however, beings who have traffic with the realm of the common yet are not and cannot be part of it? I do find such considerations in Rousseau in his understanding of the legislator figure. The legislator is presented in both versions of the *Social Contract* as a nonhuman being, with no real relations to anything or anyone in his (or her) time and place. What the legislator does, however, is to remove from all individuals any qualities that he or she might have on his or her own. Referring to the work of the legislator, he says:

> Thus . . . each citizen is nothing, can do nothing, except by others . . . This work which is constitutive of the republic is not part of its constitution: it is a particular and superior function which has nothing in common with the human world.[68]

Rousseau goes out of his way in these passages to dehumanize the legislator. The reason, I think, is that no thing and no one can be superior to the world we have in common and still be part of that world. The authority of the common and the ordinary is such that it must be the only recourse. This is the reason that the Legislator has no other, that is, has nothing in common with human beings. There can be no access for humans to anything that transcends our world.

Why not? I think the reason has to do with Rousseau's anxieties about philosophy. If we ground our world on knowledge rather than on senti-ment—human feeling—we will necessarily reintroduce inequality into that world. Therefore if the common were to require that knowledge be grounded, or needed extraordinary means to come into being, that ground and those means would necessarily be epistemologically unavailable to the common folk.

What is Rousseau's relation to the legislator? One might think that Rousseau is elaborating an understanding for humans of humans. Once again, I cannot enter into the complexities of Rousseau's relation to Kant. Suffice it to say that Kant shares much of Rousseau's understanding of the common, but that Kant thinks that one needs philosophy to establish that understanding, and a philosophy so complex that you must be a philosopher to understand it. Kant is the beginning of a profession of the human. Along this line, Rousseau might think of the legislator as a kind of philosopher-king and himself as the bearer of knowledge.

Is this what Rousseau is himself doing—being a legislator? This is a tempting answer,[69] but I think it quite wrong. Rousseau is neither God, nor the tutor. In my analysis of Rousseau's relation to authorship and of the tutor's relation to Emile, I tried to suggest that in both cases the effect of the writing was to empower the reader of those texts—that is, that they were written not to reproduce the situation of Emile with the tutor, but to authorize the understanding of the reader. They require of the reader that he or she allow Rousseau to be available. But they do not privilege Rousseau, in the way that the tutor is privileged with Emile. In fact, they show us what is wrong with such privilege.

So the most important thing about the legislator is that we will never see one. We must recognize the possibility that there has been, is, might be such a being, but also that no one of us could ever claim to anyone else to be such a being. Nor could anyone make a legitimate claim to us. The possibility of such figures exists, but not for us.

Why does Rousseau even mention it then? Some commentators think that Rousseau here reattaches himself to orders of rank, to nobility, to the classics. I rather think this is precisely to what Rousseau is calling our attention: to the fact that we will be tempted to find answers in beings that claim superiority. Rousseau has two motives. One is somewhat Burkean: We may think of our political institutions as if they had been instituted by a genius, an overman. This is, he suggests, somewhat like what religions could do for us, but not in the end the same thing.[70] The second motive, I think, is Weberian. Weber too knew the attractions that those making a

claim to genius would have in a disintegrating world. When the ordinary
becomes uncommon, then claims to the extraordinary will fall on ready
ears. A society is "ordered" for Rousseau when it is ordinary. But this will
not last; it is not lasting. He writes:

> My life's experience has been the apparent breakdown of this [moral]
> order, and so it will begin after my death.[71]

In such a realm, the temptations away from the ordinary to the realm of the
defined are great and close to irresistible. By legitimating the political realm
on the basis of the common, Rousseau is hereby, I think, forewarning us
against the temptations of the inhuman. Weber was to do the same.[72]

Ends to the Human

Are there then limits to the human realm, the realm we have in common?
One might say, "Of course—there are the realms that constitute our
individuality." But this miscasts the problem. The realm of our individuality will become the realm of the inhuman and fix and define us if we do
not live all the time in the world of the common. If that world is a kind of
grammar to each individual sentence we speak, then it is with us always.
It reveals the human to us and keeps us with other humans. It is the end
of the world.

The implication here in Rousseau is that others, be these the others in
our person, or the others in the world in which we live, need to be liberated
from what we (as we are as historical beings) make of them. The human
needs to be cast loose from the inhuman. At the beginning of this book, I
noted my experience in classrooms where students would deny, often
vigorously, that they ever could really know another person. Certainly
they neither did nor would make this claim about their knowing the
requirements of the roles or characters that they found played in front of
them. With that, there was no question. It was simply not a problem to
know what the clerk in the window is thinking when he or she takes your
money for registration. But there is comfort to be drawn, I think, from the
fact that they denied that they could ever really know another human

being. It meant, at least, that my students sensed that there was something different between knowing another human and knowing a clerk (or a king, or a slave). Their denial reflects at least the dim sense that there is something about human beings that raises this question. If that is not forgotten, perhaps Rousseau's hopes that he might be an other for the world were not without some foundation.

Chapter 1 Notes

1. Citations from Rousseau are, when available, from Jean-Jacques Rousseau, *Oeuvres Complètes.* Edited by Bernard Gagnebin and Marcel Raymond. Five volumes. (Paris: Gallimard, 1959ff.). These are cited as volume number (roman numerals) and page number (arabic numerals). In order to permit recovery of the text from any source, particular works by Rousseau are cited by title and internal subdivision. The following titles are abbreviated:

AS: *Discourse on the Arts and Sciences*

CC: *Correspondance Complète,* R. A. Leigh, ed. (Geneva. Institut Voltaire, 1965).

DOI: *Discourse on the Origin of Inequality*

ESOL: *Essai sur l'origine des langues. [Essay on the Origin of Languages.]* As it is hard to get otherwise in the United States, this text is cited from Victor Gourevitch's translation (New York: Harper & Row, 1986) and referenced as VG.

LA: *Letter to d'Alembert*

SC: *On the Social Contract*

Other titles are given by name. Those works of Rousseau not appearing in *OC* are listed in the edition from which I took the text. Thus SC i 6 *OC* iii 362 is *Social Contract,* book 1, chapter 6 in *Oeuvres Complètes,* volume iii, page 362. A number of excellent translations have appeared in the last 20 years, many of which I have consulted. The translations, however, are mine, unless specifically noted. All readers of Rousseau owe a great debt to the extensive notes and *Apparatus,* that accompany the Gallimard volumes.

2. I do mean "all." However, an interpretation is not an easy thing to give. There are only as many interpretations as there are: To the claim that there are other possible

ones, the only response is "do it!" See Alexander Nehamas, *Nietzsche: Life as Literature* (Cambridge, MA: Harvard University Press, 1985).

3. Arthur Melzer's recent book *The Natural Goodness of Man* (Chicago: University of Chicago Press, 1990) gives an excellent overview of these with, however, the intention of resolving them. See also Georges Davy, *Thomas Hobbes et Jean-Jacques Rousseau* (Oxford, UK: Clarendon Press, 1953), 3-7.

4. I leave *modern* undefined except to note that it means at least Anglo-American-European white, more or less male, in the 19th and 20th centuries. However, Rousseau was read and put to use elsewhere: See Timothy Kaufman-Osborne, "Rousseau in Kimono," *Political Theory, 18*(3) (August 1990).

5. Robert Dérathé, *Jean-Jacques Rousseau et la science politique de son temps* (Paris: Vrin, 1970). Dérathé is aware of the anachronism and tries to provide an argument justifying his choice.

6. Though one should never go too quickly on these matters: Hobbes (in chapter 16 of the *Leviathan*) is at some pains to insist that in public matters the author and the persona are identical, thus, in the end, raising the question he wants to deny. See my "How to Write Scripture: Words, Authority, and Politics in Thomas Hobbes," *Critical Inquiry, 20*(1) (Autumn 1993), 128-178.

7. The most complete account of his life is now the biography of Maurice Cranston of which two volumes have appeared as of this writing. See *Jean-Jacques: The Early Life and Work of Jean-Jacques Rousseau, 1712-1754* (London: Allen Lane, 1983) and *The Noble Savage: Jean-Jacques Rousseau, 1754-1762* (London: Allen Lane, 1991). See also Ronald Grimsley, *Jean-Jacques Rousseau: A Study in Self-Awareness*, 2nd ed. (Cardiff, UK: University of Wales Press, 1969).

8. Generally speaking, inhabitants were *citoyen* and/or *bourgeois*, or foreign-born *habitant*, or *natif*. A *citoyen* is a child of a *bourgeois* and can become a magistrate. A *bourgeois* is a child of a *bourgeois* or of a *citoyen* but born in a foreign country and who has received the right of the *bourgeoisie* from the magistrature. A *bourgeois* can be a member of the *conseil générale* or of the *grand conseil*. An *habitant* is a foreigner who has received permission to live in the city; a *natif* would be the child of an *habitant*. Rousseau cites D'Alembert's article on Geneva in the *Encyclopédie* approvingly in SC i 6 *OC* iii 362. See also Michel Launay, *Jean-Jacques Rousseau: Ecrivain politique, 1712-1762* (Cannes: C.E.L., 1971). I owe this reference to Pamela Mason, "The Genevan Republican Background to Rousseau's *Social Contract*" (unpublished manuscript) from which I have learned a good deal. For a good summary see Jean Daniel Candaux, "Introduction, *Lettres écrites de la montagne*," *OC* iii clvi ff.

9. Ebauche des Confessions 6 *OC* i 1159.

10. He finds "the remedy in the evil," as he notes in the *Confessions* (1 *OC* i 19). See Jean Starobinski, *Le remède dans le mal* (Paris: Gallimard, 1989), 165ff.

11. *Confessions* 2 *OC* i 58.

12. *Confessions* 2 *OC* i 84-85.

13. The date of the sexual consummation of the relationship was, however, probably not until 1733. See Cranston, *Jean-Jacques*, 107.

14. *Confessions* 3 *OC* i 106.

15. *Confessions* 4 *OC* i 159.

16. *Correspondance Complête*, R. A. Leigh, ed. (Geneva: Institute Voltaire, 1965), vol. 1, 59; see 59-73 (henceforth *CC*).

17. See the account in Cranston, *Jean-Jacques*, 156-229.

18. The whole episode is in *Confessions* 8 *OC* i 374-380.

19. *Lettre à de Beaumont* (Archbishop of Paris) *OC* iv 928.

20. Denis Diderot, ed., *Encyclopédie*, vol. 5 (Stuttgart: Froman, 1966), 646.

21. Letter to Paul Moultou, *CC* vii 318.

22. Letter to Leniepps 7/15/1764 (*CC* xi 186); *Lettres écrites de la montagne* ix *OC* iii 897.

23. *Lettre à Philopolis, OC* iii 231.

24. For an ongoing comparison between these two books see Sarah Kofman's recent book on *Ecce Homo, Explosions I* (Paris: Galilée, 1992). See Chapter 5 notes.

25. See, for instance, Melzer, *The Natural Goodness of Man*; J. L. Talmon, *The Rise of Totalitarian Democracy* (Boston: Beacon, 1952); I. Berlin, "Two Concepts of Liberty," *Four Essays* (Oxford, UK: Oxford University Press, 1969).

26. E.g., Talmon, op. cit.; Karl Popper, *The Open Society and Its Enemies* (New York: Harper & Row, 1963), vol. 1, 121, 293; vol. 2, 45 ("collectivist mysticism of Rousseau's making").

27. See Robert Darnton, "Readers' Response to Rousseau," *The Great Cat Massacre and Other Episodes in French Cultural History* (London: Penguin, 1991), esp. 235ff. In addition, the claim of having had personal friendship with Rousseau was seen as a possible help to those in political trouble during the French revolution. The claim in 1790 by the Count d'Antraigues, then under indictment, to have received from Rousseau an outline of a sequel to the *Social Contract* on federations is almost certainly false. See R. A. Leigh's account in *CC* vol. 37, 370.

28. Cited in Darnton, 240; The writer was male: Rousseau notes that he abstained from exploiting the women who offered themselves to him after reading his writing.

29. "Rousseau put me right," says Kant in the *Observations on the Feeling of the Sublime and the Beautiful*, cited by Hannah Arendt in her *Lectures on Kant's Political Philosophy*, R. Beiner, ed. (Chicago: University of Chicago Press, 1982), 29.

30. There are questions here then for postmodernism as a universal textual strategy. See the exchange between myself and Victoria Silver following my "How to Write Scripture: Words, Authority, and Politics in Thomas Hobbes," *Critical Inquiry, 20*(1) (Autumn 1993), 128-178.

31. "Fragment sur dieu et la révélation," *OC* I xx.

32. *Dialogues* 2 *OC* i 808.

33. See Monique Cottret, "Les jansénistes jugent de Jean-Jacques," in Catherine Maire, ed., *Jansénisme et revolution* (Paris: Bibliothèque Mazarine, 1990), 81-102, esp. 89.

34. "Fragments autobiographiques—Mon portrait," *OC* i 1124.

35. *Dialogues—Sujet et forme de cet ecrit OC* i 663.

36. *Dialogues* 1 *OC* i 673.

37. Although he would be horrified at finding himself in Rousseau, George Kateb has gotten Whitman right on this. See his "Walt Whitman and the Culture of Democracy," in Tracy B. Strong, ed., *The Self and the Political Order* (Oxford, UK: Blackwells, 1992).

38. *Dialogues* 2 *OC* 1 778.

39. I shamelessly take over the term from Stanley Cavell, "Knowing and Acknowledging," *Must We Mean What We Say?* (New York: Scribner, 1969), chapter 9. In Ludwig Wittgenstein's *On Certainty* (New York: J. & J. Harper, 1969), par. 378, a book published only after Cavell wrote his text, we find—no surprise—"Knowledge is in the end based on acknowledgement."

40. *Dialogues—Histoire du précédent récit OC* i 982.

41. See ibid., 282, and for the *billet circulaire,* ibid., 990ff. Boothby, incidentally, behaved honorably and kept his agreement with Rousseau about the conditions of publication.

42. *Testament* (1763) *OC* i 1225-1226.

43. *Confessions* i *OC* i 543. See Jean Starobinski, "The Accuser and the Accused," *Daedalus, 107*(3) (Summer, 1978), 43-44.

44. I am asking here for indulgence until chapter 4 on my equivocation between *human* and *man.* Questions of sexuality in Rousseau risk draining his multiplicities. In any case, the relation is not parallel to that in English between man and human, where Teutonic usages identify *man* and *male human.* In Old English, gender distinction were other: *wer* and *wif. Homme* has an etymological relation to *humain;* more important, they are both derived from the word for *earth* and the root is a term used to make an opposition to the divine. See Emile Benveniste, *Le vocabulaire des institutions indo-européenes* (Paris: Editions de Minuit, 1969), vol. 2, 180.

45. *Confessions* 1 *OC* i 5.

46. "Fragments autobiographiques," *OC* i 1185, 1184.

47. *Rêveries du promeneur solitaire* (henceforth *Rêveries*) 1 *OC* i 995.

48. "Letter about a new refutation" *OC* iii 102 (The letter is addressed to the refutation offered by the Dijon academician Lecat who had voted against Rousseau.).

49. Thus Aristotle's definition of friend is "another myself." (*Ethica Nicomachia* 1166[a]31; see *Eudemian Ethics* 1245[a]30).

50. *Confessions* 3 *OC* i 109. This passage has been subject to a famous and brilliant analysis (Why is this the one we remember?) by Jacques Derrida, *De la grammatologie* (Paris: Editions de Minuit, 1967), 203-234, esp. 220-221. Derrida links masturbation and writing; while not rejecting his analysis I think Rousseau is more aware of what he is doing than does Derrida and that the *différe(a)nces* of his text are there consciously. In turn this makes the politics of authorship more complex in my reading.

51. This reading is common and often forms part of important books. See Arthur Melzer, *The Natural Goodness of Man,* 90; G. Lanson, "L'unité de la pensée de Rousseau," *Annales de la société Jean-Jacques Rousseau,* 8 (1912), 1-13; N. Wahl, "La bipolarité de Jean-Jacques Rousseau," *Annales de la société Jean-Jacques Rousseau, 33* (1962), 49-55; Judith N. Shklar, *Men and Citizens: A Study of Rousseau's Social Theory* (Cambridge, UK: Cambridge University Press, 1969, 1985). Cf. the remarks in Jean Starobinski, *The Living Eye* (Cambridge, MA: Harvard University Press, 1989).

52. *Emile (manuscript Favre) OC* iv 57.

53. Ibid., 58. Judith Shklar has made the man/citizen opposition into the structure of her book; it is for me its strength and its flaw.

54. *Ebauches des Confessions* 1 *OC* i 1154.

55. *Ebauches des Confessions* 5 *OC* i 1159.

56. I am reminded that Nietzsche subtitles his autobiography *Ecce Homo,* "How to Become *What* You Are."

57. Cf. *The New Heloise* v II *OC* 523.

58. *Emile (manuscript Favre) OC* iv 57.

59. *Ebauches des Confessions* 3 *OC* i 1158.

60. Idem (my italics).

61. *Narcisse* preface *OC* ii 962-963.

62. Voltaire was, as usual, right, if for the wrong reasons, in focusing on this episode as among the most troubling in Rousseau.

63. On speaking with a human voice see Stanley Cavell, "The Politics of Interpretation," in *Themes Out of School* (Chicago: University of Chicago Press, 1984), 48-49, 53.

64. *Lettre à Lecat, OC* iii 102. These are similiar considerations in Victor Gourevitch, "Rousseau on Lying: A Provisional Reading of the Fourth Reverie," *Berkshire Review*, 15 (1980), pp. 93-107. Thanks to Michael Roth for pointing me to this essay.

65. Ludwig Wittgenstein, *Philosophical Investigations* (New York: Macmillan, 1958), par. 118. I would not have remembered to put this passage here had I not reread the essay by Cavell mentioned in note 63.

66. See the excellent discussion in Cranston, *Jean-Jacques*, 230-244.

67. *Confessions* 8 *OC* i 351; Diderot's account of the episode is slightly different but not contradictory (*Oeuvres Complètes*, II [Paris: Gallimard, 1964], 485).

68. *La découverte du nouveau monde*, act iii, scene 4 *OC* ii 839.

69. *Lettre à Lecat, OC* iii 102. The Plutarch essay is "How to Profit from One's Enemies" and is also cited by Rousseau in *Rêveries* 4 *OC* i 1024.

70. *AS* i *OC* iii 6-7.

71. M. de Montaigne, "Du pédantisme," *Essays*, book 1, chapter 25 in *Oeuvres complètes* (Paris: Editions du Seuil, 1967), 72: "The study of the sciences weakens and feminizes the will and the spirit (*les courages*) more than it hardens and seasons them" (my translation).

72. *AS* 1 *OC* iii 8.

73. *AS* 1 *OC* iii 15.

74. Analogies between himself and Socrates in fact appear 14 separate times in the *First Discourse* and the various responses that Rousseau makes to his critics.

75. *Lettre à l'abbé Raynal, OC* iii 33.

76. This scene has been given an exhaustive and (?!) definitive reading by Jacques Derrida, "Plato's Pharmacy," *Disseminations* (Chicago: University of Chicago Press, 1981), 61-172.

77. *AS* 2 *OC* iii 28 and n.

78. *AS* 1 *OC* iii 17.

79. Ibid., 25.

80. Observations *OC* iii 36.

81. See Leibniz's letter to Thomas Burnett from 1696 in G. W. Leibniz, *Saemtliche Schriften*, vol. 1 (Berlin: Akademie Verlag, 1987). I am indebted here to the learning and kindness of my friend Pat Riley, who, however, will be horrified at the use to which I have put his scholarship.

82. *AS* 2 *OC* iii 27. The philosophers mocked are probably Bishop Berkeley, D'Holbach, Mandeville, and Hobbes.

83. *Confessions* 6 *OC* i 237.

84. *Observations OC* iii 1259, 40 n. B (my italics).

85. But already in the *"Dernière réponse"* (*OC* iii 94) Rousseau sketches it out in the discussion of bringing up a child.

86. *"Dernière réponse," OC* iii 73.

87. *"Dernière réponse,"* 170 *OC* iii 95.

88. *AS* 2 *OC* iii 25.

89. *"Dernière réponse," OC* iii 80.

90. The status of the *Essay on the Origin of Language* is in dispute. The *Second Discourse* passes over language briefly and makes reference to a text to come. Is this the text? It is clear that Rousseau worked on this essay repeatedly and that its origins are

contemporaneous with his work on music and the *Dictionary of Music*. Robert Wokler, *Rousseau on Society, Politics, Music and Language*, doctoral thesis, Nuffield College (Oxford, UK, 1987), is by far the most extended treatment of these issues. See also Jacques Derrida, *De la grammatologie*, 235-378. In the next several paragraphs I owe a debt of provocation to Thomas Kavanagh, *Writing the Truth: Authority and Desire* (Berkeley and Los Angeles: University of California Press, 1982), especially chapter 3. I do not agree with Kavanagh but it led me to think in ways I would not have. See his discussion of these matters. After I completed this book, Michael Roth introduced me to Victor Gourevitch, "The Political Argument of Rousseau's Essay on The Origin of Languages," *Pursuits of Reason: Essays in Honor of Stanley Cavell*, eds. Ted Cohen, Paul Guyer, Hilary Putnam (Texas Tech University Press, 1993), pp. 21-35. I wish I had seen it before.

91. *ESOL* 4 OC v 383; in chapter 3 I discuss similar ideas in conjunction with the figure of the legislator.

92. *ESOL* 7 OC v 392.

93. *ESOL* 16 OC v 421.

94. *ESOL* 19 OC v 427.

95. I thing that one can argue that Rousseau is wrong here about painting and that the difference between representational and nonrepresentational painting (a distinction of which he did not know) is not as great as one would conclude. But to come to this conclusion he would have had to look at representational painting in conjunction with nonrepresentational. See here Michael Fried, *Realism, Writing, Disfiguration* (Chicago: University of Chicago Press, 1987) and especially his *Absorption and Theatricality: Painting and Beholder in the Age of Diderot* (Berkeley and Los Angeles: University of California Press, 1980), 167-171.

96. *Sic,* although possibly a slip for *emotions*?

97. Idem; I hear here the anticipation of Schopenhauer, Wagner, and Nietzsche.

98. I cannot resist here drawing attention to how similar this analysis is to that of Nietzsche in *The Birth of Tragedy*. Rousseau even goes on to discuss how music degenerated among the Greeks with Socrates and Plato.

99. *ESOL* 19 OC v 436-427.

100. I was helped in this formulation by the top paragraph on p. 9 of Stanley Cavell, "The Thought of Movies," *Themes Out of School*.

101. *DOI* 1 *OC* iii 156-157.

102. This is precisely (part of) Nietzsche's position on the same issue. See my *Friedrich Nietzsche and the Politics of Transfiguration* (Berkeley and Los Angeles: University of California Press, 1975, 1988), chapter 6.

103. *"Dernière réponse," OC* iii 96; *"Préface d'une seconde lettre," OC* iii 104.

104. *Emile* iv *OC* iv 610. I have put Rousseau's text into indented paragraphs to bring out its dialogue form.

105. S. Kierkegaard, *On Authority and Revelation* (New York: Harper & Row, 1966), 92-142, and "Of the Difference between a Genius and an Apostle" in *The Present Age* (New York: Harper & Row, 1962), 87-108.

106. Kierkegaard, *On Authority and Revelation*, 110.

Chapter 2 Notes

1. See Victor Gourevitch, "Rousseau on Arts and Sciences," *Journal of Philosophy*, *69* (1972), 7531.

2. *DOI* preface *OC* iii 122. Rousseau draws the image of the statue from Plato (*Republic,* 611) but emphasizes the defacement much more than Plato to the point that there is a question if the original survives at all.

3. *AS* 2 *OC* iii 30.

4. The Academy's formulation of the question is usually given, even by Rousseau, as asking for the "origin." For the accurate title, see *OC* iii 1300. See Bronislaw Baczko, *Rousseau: Solitude et communauté* (Paris: Mouton, 1974), 61.

5. As early as January 30, 1750, he had signed himself in this manner to Voltaire.

6. Compare to Aristotle, *Politics*, vols. 1, 2 (1252a): Rousseau's usage is like the Greek *arché*. Cf. contra, Deena Goodman, *Criticism in Action* (Ithaca, NY: Cornell University Press, 1991), 108, to which, however, I owe a good dealing of prompting. See the discussion in Pierre Burgelin, *La philosophie de l'existence chez Jean-Jacques Rousseau* (Paris: Presses universitaires de France, 1951), 509.

7. *DOI* 1 *OC* iii 131.

8. *DOI* 1 *OC* iii 132.

9. *DOI* dedication *OC* iii 118.

10. *Dialogues* 2 *OC* i 887-888.

11. *Fragments de la lettre à de Beaumont, OC* iv 1025.

12. Though I do not share it completely I am informed and prompted by Jean Starobinski's magisterial "Introduction" to the *Second Discourse* in *OC* iii.

13. It is worth noting that Persius lived at the time of Nero and was known for his moralizing condemnations of the mores of his time. Persius also provides the epigraph for the *Confessions*.

14. I am sure it is a not an accident, but there are 19 laws of nature in Hobbes's *Leviathan* and 19 chapters to Locke's *Second Treatise of Government.*

15. *DOI OC* iii 133. Jean Starobinski's analysis of the progression of the first part of the *DOI* remains the most incisive. See his introduction to *DOI* in *OC* iii.

16. *Fragments politiques I, OC* iii 474.

17. *Lettre à de Beaumont OC* iv 966-967; similar passages can be found in the *Emile, OC* iv 454 (except for Robinson Crusoe: See the discussion in Allan Bloom's "Introduction" to his edition and translation of the *Emile* (New York: Basic Books, 1979), 7ff. See *Emile OC* iv 568.

18. *Emile 3 OC* iv 454.

19. This is not to say that Rousseau was alone in the 17th century in his hostility to books. Diderot's article on "Livre" for the *Encyclopédie* is also an attack. Relations between Rousseau and Diderot are beyond the scope of this essay. Generally speaking, they tend either to contrast the two, or to point out resemblances generally to the detriment of Rousseau's originality. The articles of George Havens, "Diderot and the Composition of Rousseau's First Discourse," *Romantic Review* (1939) and "Diderot, Rousseau, and the Discours sur l'inégalité," *Diderot Studies, 3* (1961) find the most similarities. The complexity of their relationship has been exceptionally well described by Maurice Cranston, *The Noble Savage: Jean-Jacques Rousseau 1754-1762* (London: Allen Lane, 1991).

20. R. W. Emerson, "Experience," *Essays and Lectures* (New York: Library of America, 1979), 476.

21. *SC* ii 6 *OC* iii. I first saw the importance of vision in Rousseau from reading James Miller, *Rousseau, Dreamer of Democracy* (New Haven, CT: Yale University Press, 1984) and Jean Starobinski, *Jean-Jacques Rousseau: La transparence et l'obstacle* (Paris: Gallimard, 1971) (Translation: *Jean-Jacques Rousseau: Transparency and Obstruction,*) trans. Arthur Goldhammer (Chicago: University of Chicago Press, 1988).

22. *Mon Portrait OC* i 1120. In the *Fragments pour un dictionnaire,* Rousseau claims that botany has greatly suffered as a science from having been thought part of medicine (*OC* iv 1201). Rousseau's *Lettres sur la botanique* place a great deal of emphasis on being able to really see the plants in their complexity. E.g., *OC* iv 1152-1153.

23. *DOI, OC* iii 125.

24. See Miller, *Rousseau, Dreamer of Democracy,* 6-7 and *passim.*

25. *ESOL* 1 OC v 376.

26. *ESOL* 5 OC v 388.

27. *Dialogues* i *OC* i 755.

28. *The New Heloise* preface *OC* ii 5.

29. *Confessions* 12 *OC* i 591.

30. *DOI* 1 *OC* iii 134-135.

31. Questions about films, as reflections on moving reflections, automatically raise questions of ontology. See Stanley Cavell, *The World Viewed: Reflections on the Ontology of Films* (New York: Viking, 1972).

32. *DOI,* 1 *OC* iii 132-133.

33. *DOI* 1 *OC* iii 132.

34. "Fragment on the State of War," as reconstructed by Grace Roosevelt, *Reading Rousseau in the Nuclear Age* (Philadelphia: Temple University Press, 1990), 388. The version of this piece given in *OC* iii 600ff. is completely out of order.

35. Some of the material in the next three paragraphs draws on my *The Idea of Political Theory: Reflections on the Self in Political Time and Space* (Notre Dame, IN: University of Notre Dame Press, 1990), 28ff.

36. See C. B. Macpherson, *The Political Theory of Possessive Individualism* (Oxford, UK: Clarendon Press, 1962); Leo Strauss, *Natural Right and History* (Chicago: University of Chicago Press, 1965); Peter Laslett, "Introduction," *Two Treatises on Government* (New York: Mentor, 1965); John Dunn, *The Political and Social Thought of John Locke* (Cambridge, UK: Cambridge University Press, 1982); Richard Ashcraft, *Revolutionary Politics and Locke's Two Treatises* (Princeton, NJ: Princeton University Press, 1983).

37. *Lettre à de Beaumont, OC* iv 936.

38. *DOI* preface *OC* iii 125-126.

39. *DOI* 1 *OC* iii 155.

40. *DOI* 1 *OC* iii 155.

41. *ESOL* 9 OC v 395.

42. *ESOL, idem.*

43. *DOI* preface *OC* iii 126, see *DOI* note xv *OC* iii 219.

44. *Emile* 2 *OC* ii 322; cf *OC* ii 491.

45. *Dialogues* 1 *OC* i 668-669.

46. John Locke, *Second Treatise*, par. 34 (Laslett, 333).

47. *Fragments politiques* 2 7 *OC* iii 476.

48. *Lettre à de Beaumont, OC* iv 936.

49. *DOI* 1 *OC* iii 151.

50. G. Havens, "Voltaire's marginalia on the pages of Rousseau," *Ohio State University Studies,* vol. 6 (Columbus, 1933), 14; as usual, Voltaire was on to something if off the mark in his criticism of Rousseau.

51. *DOI* 1 *OC* iii 160-161.

52. Pierre Burgelin, *La philosophie de l'existence chez Jean-Jacques Rousseau* (Paris: Presses universitaires de France, 1951), 251, notes that man was "*une monade qui reflete un univers sans le distinguer de soi.*"

53. *DOI* 2 *OC* iii 166.

54. *The New Heloise* V, 3 *OC* ii 571.

55. *Premier Contrat, OC* iii 283.

56. *ESOL* 2 OC v 380.

57. *ESOL* 9 PC v 395-6.

58. *Fragment sur l'histoire des moeurs* 4 *OC* iii 555.

59. *Lettre à Philopolis, OC* iii 2323.

60. See, e.g., *DOI* 1 *OC* iii 162.

61. *SC* ii 7 *OC* iii 381.

62. Cf. contra, A. O. Lovejoy, "The Supposed Primitivism of Rousseau's *Discourse on Inequality,*" in *Essays on the History of Ideas* (New York: Putnam, 1960), 14-17. This is a brilliant essay marred by its assimilation of Rousseau to Hegel.

63. *Emile* 1 *OC* iv 249.

64. See the extended comparison in Burgelin, *La philosophie de l'existence chez Jean-Jacques Rousseau,* chapter 19.

65. *Emile* 4 *OC* iv 500; see the discussion of Robinson Crusoe in J. H. Broome, *Rousseau* (London: Arnold, 1963).

66. The best discussion of this is in Burgelin, *La philosophie de l'existence chez Jean-Jacques Rousseau,* 509.

67. *DOI* preface *OC* iii 126.

68. *DOI* note 2 *OC* iii 195-196.

69. *Emile* preface *OC* iv 242.

70. *Pygmalion, OC* ii 1230-1231.

71. *Emile* 5 *OC* iv 857.

72. Few writers have seen how key this play is to Rousseauian themes. Among those who have are Michael Brint, *Tragedy and Denial: The Politics of Difference in Western Political Thought* (Boulder, CO: Westview Press, 1991) and Jean Starobinski, *The Living Eye* (Cambridge, MA: Harvard University Press, 1989), 67-71.

73. The philosophical importance of this has been explored in Stanley Cavell, *Pursuits of Happiness: The Hollywood Comedy of Remarriage* (Cambridge, MA: Harvard University Press, 1981).

74. Starobinski makes a similar point, *The Living Eye,* 68.

75. *Narcisse* 6 *OC* ii 995.

76. *Narcisse* 9 *OC* ii 1002.

77. *Dialogues* preface *OC* i 665 (my italics).

78. See the discussion in Robert Osmont's introduction to the *Dialogues OC* ii p. l.

79. *Dialogues* 2 *OC* i 773.

80. *Dialogues* 2 *OC* i 826.

81. *Dialogues* 2 *OC* i 903.

82. *Dialogues* 3 *OC* i 926.

83. *Dialogues* 3 *OC* i 935-937; 940.

84. *Portrait, OC* i 1121.

85. *Emile* 1 *OC* iv 249 (my italics).

86. *DOI* 2 *OC* iii 168; *DOI* 1 *OC* iii 135.

87. *SC* first version *OC* iii 283.

88. *Lettre à Philopolis, OC* iii 232.

89. The source of these reflections lies in what has been called various "romanticism" or "moral perfectionism." Cf. Phillippe Lacoue-Labarthes and Jean-Luc Nancy, *L'absolu littéraire* (Paris: Editions du Seuil, 1978); Stanley Cavell, *This New Yet Unapproachable America* (Chicago: University of Chicago Press, 1989); and *In Quest of the Ordinary* (Chicago: University of Chicago Press, 1988).

90. Cf. Lovejoy, "The Supposed Primitivism of Rousseau," 28.

91. The expression is Judith Shklar's in her "The Liberalism of Fear," in Nancy Rosenblum, ed., *Liberalism and the Moral Life* (Cambridge, MA: Harvard University Press, 1989) and *Montesquieu* (Oxford, UK: Oxford University Press, 1987), 68-69.

92. *Emile* 4 *OC* iv 550-551.

93. *Emile* 1 *OC* iv 259-260; cf. *Confessions* 8 *OC* i 388-389 x.

94. *DOI* note 9 *OC* iii 204.

95. Judith N. Shklar, *Men and Citizens: A Study of Rousseau's Social Theory* (Cambridge, UK: Cambridge University Press, 1969, 1985).

96. Hence in the end her head, if not her heart, is with Montesquieu.

97. *DOI* note 9 *OC* iii 205.

98. *DOI* 1 *OC* iii 158.

99. *Emile* 4 *OC* iv 491.

100. Rousseau did not invent the terms nor the distinction. For references and a brief discussion see Dérathé's note on p. 1376 of *OC* iii.

101. *DOI* note xv *OC* iii 219.

102. *Emile* 4 *OC* iv 523.

103. This occurs precisely in *Emile* iv *OC* iv 522.

104. *Emile* 4 *OC* iv 505.

105. *DOI* 2 *OC* iii 166.

106. Ibid.

107. *DOI* 2 *OC* iii 169-170.

108. *DOI* 2 *OC* iii 174.

109. Ibid., 177.

110. Ibid., 187.

111. Ibid., 189 (my italics).

112. Ibid., 191.

113. The most interesting and completely developed of these commentaries are those of Marcel Hénaff, "The Cannibalistic City: Rousseau, Large Numbers, and the Social Bond," *Substance*, 67 (Spring 1992), 3-23, and "Rousseau et l'economie politique: Système rustique et système de finances," *Etudes françaises, 25*(2/3) (1989), 103-129.

114. These are only available with difficulty as the fifth volume of the *Oeuvres Complètes* has not yet appeared. The complete text (with notes) of *Du Principe de la mélodie ou Response aux erreurs de la musique* has been given in the appendix to Robert Wokler, *Rousseau on Society, Politics, Music and Language*, doctoral thesis, Nuffield College, Oxford, UK, 1987 (henceforth Wokler). This is Rousseau's response to Rameau's attack on his *Lettre sur la musique française* (in *Oevres de M. Rousseau de Genève*, Vol. 2, Neuchâtel, 1764, pp. 212-304). Wokler's thesis contains an important discussion of the writings on music.

115. *Dialogue* 2 *OC* i 872-873.

116. *L'origine de le mélodie OC* v 333. See *Du principe de la mélodie*, Wokler, 450.

117. *Dialogue* 1 *OC* i 683. This is the basis of Rousseau's praise of Italian opera. It is referred to in *The New Heloise* (I, letter 48 *OC* ii 133) and discussed in Wokler.

118. *L'origine de la mélodie OC* v 333-334; See *Du principe de la mélodie*, Wokler, 450-451.

119. Ibid., 456-457.

120. ESOL 20 OC v 429.

121. LA OC v 123-124. I have occasionally modified the translation that can be found in Allan Bloom's edition of this essay. See his *Politics and the Arts* (Ithaca, NY: Cornell University Press, 1968). The citation here is Bloom 232-233.

122. ESOL 19 OC v 424.

123. LA OV v 33-34 (Bloom 26ff).

124. Letter to D'Alembert, Bloom, 26ff. Whether or not Rousseau was right about Molière, it is worth noting that what he found in the St. Gervais festival is remarkably like what Nietzsche says can be or was realized in classical Aeschylean tragedy. There the chorus permits the audience to "overlook" (in both senses of the word) the "entire realm of culture." See my *Friedrich Nietzsche and the Politics of Transfiguration*, chapter 6, and *The Idea of Political Theory: Reflections on the Self in Political Time and Space* (Notre Dame, IN: University of Notre Dame Press, 1990), chapter 2.

125. See George Kateb, "Walt Whitman and the Culture of Democracy," in Tracy B.

Strong, ed., *The Self and the Political Order* (Oxford, UK: Blackwells, 1992), 208–229; also reprinted as the last chapter in his *The Inner Ocean* (Ithaca, NY: Cornell University Press, 1992).
    126. See *Emile* 5 *OC* iv 831. See Hénaff, "The Cannibalistic City," *Substance, 67* (Spring 1992).
    127. *Emile et Sophie* 2 *OC* iv 912.
    128. *Emile et Sophie* 2 *OC* iv 913.
    129. Ibid., 918.
    130. *Rêveries* 1 *OC* i 996.
    131. Ibid., 999.

Chapter 3 Notes

1. *SC* i 1 *OC* iii 351.
2. *Emile* 2 *OC* iv, 308; see also *Lettres écrites de la montagne* 8 *OC* iii, 841.
3. *DOI OC* iii, 191.
4. *SC* iv 2 *OC* 439.
5. *SC* i 4 *OC* iii 357-358.
6. Ibid., 356.
7. *SC* iv 2 *OC* iii 440.
8. The origins of the use of the idea of a social contract are in some dispute. It certainly appears in Grotius on the continent (see Richard Tuck, *Philosophy and Government, 1572-1651* (Cambridge, UK: Cambridge University Press, 1993), 175ff.). It also appears, in what I see as a more fruitful use, in the Puritans and other Calvinists. The key recognition that the terms under which a community is governed are determined arbitrarily, by human beings, rather than drawn from some suprahuman source, can be found already in a text like John Cotton, "Limitation of Government," in Perry Miller, ed., *The American Puritans* (New York: Anchor Books, 1956), 85-88.
9. Manegold of Lautenbach, *Ad Gebehardum Liber,* translated by Ewart Lewis in her *Medieval Political Ideas* (New York: Cooper Square, 1974), 165.
10. E.g., John Preston: "There being a compact and covenant between God and him, that if Adam stood, all his seed should stand with him; but if he fell, then that all that were born of him should by virtue of that covenant, compact, or agreement have his sin imputed to them. . . . " And Thomas Hooker: "Adam in innocence represented all mankind, he

176

stood (as a Parliament man doth for the whole country) for all that should be born of him." Cited in Perry Miller, *The New England Mind: The Seventeenth Century* (Cambridge, MA: Harvard University Press, 1961), 401.

11. Although I cannot develop here, one consequence of this would be that the arguments that John Rawls, for instance, advances against "the principle of perfection" in *A Theory of Justice* (Cambridge, MA: Harvard University Press, 1971), 325-332, need to be rethought.

12. John Locke, *Second Treatise on Government,* par. 116.

13. David Hume, "Of the Original Contract," *Political Essays* (Indianapolis: Bobbs-Merrill, 1953), 45.

14. David Hume, "Of the Original Contract," *Political Essays,* 56.

15. I. Kant, *Critique of Pure Reason* (New York: St. Martin's, 1953), 128.

16. Hume, *Political Essays,* 24.

17. The most brilliant dissection of this kind of history is by J. G. A. Pocock, *The Ancient Constitution and the Feudal Law* (New York: Norton, 1967).

18. *Confessions* 12 *OC* i 625.

19. David Hume, *A Treatise on Human Nature,* II, ii, 3 (London: Penguin, 1983), 463.

20. Kant, *Critique of Pure Reason,* 55 (B 20); see also 44 and 127-128.

21. See Kant, *Critique of Pure Reason,* 127 (B 127).

22. For instance, the arguments in *SC* iv 8 (*OC* III 460) seem clearly aimed at Hume's comments on pagan religion in *The Natural History of Religion,* chapter 5. The *Essays* had been translated into French in 1752; Dérathé reads the reference in the *Fragments politiques* (*OC* iii 518) to *"deux hommes cherchant à se rendre célèbres"* as referring to Hume. The definition of miracles in *Lettres écrites de la montagne* (*OC* iii 734) is the same as that of Hume in the *Inquiry;* he almost makes verbatim use of Hume's argument in the *Lettre à Charles de Beaumont* (*OC* iii 104). In the *Lettres* (*OC* iii 740), he raises the possibility of an example of miracle that is the same as that used by Hume. Marguerite Richebourg, however, in "La bibliothèque de Jean-Jacques Rousseau," *Annales de la société Jean-Jacques Rousseau, 21* (Geneva: Editions Jullien, 1932), 181-241, at 222 argues that Rousseau neither owned nor read Hume's *Inquiry.*

23. *SC* i *OC* iii 351.

24. *OC* iii 1410.

25. *DOI OC* iii, 192-193.

26. *SC* first version i 2 *OC* iii 283.

27. *Fragments* 10 *OC* iv 1019.

28. Ibid., 284.

29. *SC* ii 1 *OC* iii 368.

30. See Emile Benveniste, *Le vocabulaire des institutions indo-européenes* (Paris: Editions de Minuit, 1969), vol. 1, 96f., 186f. "[C]*ommunis* does not mean 'who divides the loads,' but properly 'who has the *munus* [duties] in common.' When this system of compensation is at play inside a circle, it determines a 'community,' an ensemble of men tied together by this link of reciprocity" (96-97).

31. A realization shared by, for instance, Andrew Levine, in *The End of the State* (London: Verso, 1987), 14, although I share little else with the argument of this book.

32. *SC* i 6 *OC* iii 361 (Rousseau's italics).

33. This usage of *portion* has been established by Stanley Cavell in *The Senses of Walden* (New York: Viking, 1972) and is what Jean-Luc Nancy means by *le partage* in *"La comparution*/The Compearance," *Political Theory, 20* (August 1992).

34. As it is for not unrelated reasons with Hobbes. As such, although I do not think that his thought resembles that of Hobbes (not as much, at least, as writers like Cranston and Viroli do): See Maurice Cranston, *The Noble Savage* (London: Allen Lane, 1991), 302 ff.; Maurizio Viroli, *Rousseau and the Well-Ordered Society* (Cambridge, UK: Cambridge University Press, 1986); Peter Winch, "Man and Society in Hobbes and Rousseau," in Maurice Cranston and Richard Peters, eds., *Hobbes and Rousseau* (New York: Doubleday, 1972), 233-253. I do find parallels in the misreadings they each give rise to.

35. William Connolly, *The Terms of Political Discourse* (Lexington, MA: Heath, 1974), 38-39. See my discussion of this passage in my *The Idea of Political Theory*, chapter 1.

36. If I understand them correctly this realization is at the heart of Ernesto Laclau and Chantal Mouffe, *Hegemony and Socialist Strategy* (London: Verso, 1985).

37. *Rêveries* 3 *OC* i 1016 (my italics).

38. *SC* i 3 *OC* iii 354.

39. *SC* i 6 *OC* iii 361. Note how the meaning is altered if we translate (with Masters) as "an indivisible part of the whole" (Rousseau's italics).

40. *SC* ii 4 *OC* iii 373.

41. *Political Economy, OC* iii 242f; *SC* first version i 5 *OC* iii 297.

42. See the discussion of acting *hekon* in A. W. H. Adkins, *Merit and Responsibility* (Oxford, UK: Clarendon Press, 1960), 10ff., 319ff.; and especially in J. P. Vernant et Pierre Vidal-Naquet, "Ebauches de la volonté," *Mythe et tragédie en grèce ancienne* (Paris: Maspéro, 1972), esp. 53ff.

43. Cite Augustine, *City of God,* chapter 19. A short but useful history of the idea of will can be found in Patrick Riley, *Will and Political Legitimacy* (Cambridge, MA: Harvard University Press, 1982), chapter 1. See also his "The General Will before Rousseau," *Political Theory, 6* (November 1978), 485-516.

44. Hobbes, *Leviathan* (Oxford, UK: Clarendon Press, 1953), 38.

45. For instance, Steven Ellenburg, *Rousseau's Political Philosophy: An Interpretation from Within* (Ithaca, NY: Cornell University Press, 1976), 103n.; and Lester Crocker, *Rousseau's Social Contract: An Interpretative Essay* (Cleveland, OH: Western Reserve, 1968) read it as collectivist (the first favorably, the second not). Judith N. Shklar, *Men and Citizens: A Study of Rousseau's Social Theory* (Cambridge, UK: Cambridge University Press, 1969, 1985) and Patrick Riley, *Will and Political Legitimacy* (Cambridge, MA: Harvard University Press, 1982) read it as individualist, the first psychologically, the second morally.

46. *SC* iv 2 *OC* iii 440.

47. Ibid., 440-441.

48. It comes to accomplishment with Nietzsche. See my *Friedrich Nietzsche and the Politics of Transfiguration,* (Berkeley and Los Angeles: University of California Press, 1975, 1988), chapter 8, and Hannah Arendt, *Willing* (New York: Harcourt Brace Jovanovich, 1978), 178-194.

49. The distinction can be found in Emile Durkheim, *Montesquieu and Rousseau* (Ann Arbor: University of Michigan Press, 1960) and in (e.g.) I. Berlin, "Two Concepts of Freedom," *Four Essays on Liberty* (Oxford, UK: Oxford University Press, 1984).

50. *SC* ii 4 *OC* iii 373.

51. Bertrand de Jouvenel, *De la souveraineté* (Paris: Presses universitaires de France, 1955), 124.

52. *SC* iv 1 *OC* iii, 437.

53. *SC* ii 3 *OC* iii 37.

54. Alexis Philonenko, *Théorie et praxis dans la pensée morale et politique de Kant et de Fichte en 1793* (Paris: Vrin, 1968), 197-198, has argued convincingly that Rousseau is here using the language of integral calculus.

55. *Political Economy OC* iii 245.

56. *SC* ii 4 *OC* iii 374.

57. C. E. Vaughan, ed., *The Political Writings of Jean-Jacques Rousseau,* vol. 1 (Cambridge, UK: Cambridge University Press, 1915), 242-243.

58. Amelie Oksenberg Rorty, "Self-deception, Akrasia and Irrationality," in Jon Elster, ed., *The Multiple Self* (Cambridge, MA: Harvard University Press, 1987), 115-122.

59. *Emile* (manuscript Favre) *OC* iv 57. See the remarks on this issue in Jean Starobinski, *The Living Eye* (Cambridge, MA: Harvard University Press, 1989), 61.

60. David Hume, *Treatise on Human Nature* I, 6 ("Of Personal Identity") (New York, 1985); reprinted in Tracy B. Strong, ed., *The Self and the Political Order* (Oxford, UK: Blackwells, 1992).

61. As holds Shklar, *Men and Citizens.*

62. Patrick Riley, *Kant's Political Philosophy* (Totowa, NJ: Rowman & Littlefield, 1983).

63. *SC* ii 3 *OC* iii 371. In *A Theory of Justice,* Rawls tends to treat Rousseau as an afterthought and a precursor of Kant and Kohlberg. John Chapman has seen the relation of Rousseau for Rawls' thought. See his "Rawls's Theory of Justice," *American Political Science Review, 69*(2) (June 1975), 588-593.

64. Robert Axelrod, *The Evolution of Cooperation* (New York: Basic Books, 1984).

65. *Lettres écrites de la montagne* 6 *OC* iii 808.

66. *Pygmalion, OC* ii 1228.

67. See Jacques Derrida, "Ce dangereux supplément," *De la grammatologie* (Paris: Editions de Minuit, 1967).

68. *ESOL* 2 OC v 380 (VG 245). The argument that it was needs had been made by Condillac. See the discussion in Robert Wokler, 176ff.

69. *ESOL* 3 OC v 381 (VG 246-7). Stanley Cavell saw the importance of this passage in *The Claim of Reason* (Oxford, UK: Clarendon Press, 1979), 466ff.

70. *ESOL* 1 OC v 375 (VG 240).

71. In the Third *Rêverie,* Rousseau indicates that most people live happy in illusions and wishes, not very seriously, that he had himself been able to. See *Rêveries* iii *OC* ii 1011.

72. *SC* iii 11 *OC* iii 425.

73. *Emile* 1 *OC* iv 249; Cf. C. E. Vaughan, ed., *The Political Writings of Jean-Jacques Rousseau,* vol. 2, 366: "We are forced to admit that the popular image of Rousseau . . . as the determined foe of all historical institutions . . ." is pure illusion.

74. *SC* ii 4 *OC* III 373.

75. *Emile* 5 *OC* iv 842.

76. *SC* first version i 7 *OC* iii 310.

77. *SC* ii 6 *OC* iii 379.

78. See the very important work by Jean-Luc Nancy, *La communauté desoeuvrée* (Paris: Christian Bourgeois, 1984) and *"La comparution/Compearance," Political Theory, 20* (August 1992).

79. Stanley Cavell, *Must We Mean What We Say?* (New York: Scribner, 1969), 39.

80. Or, more precisely, they overcome that distinction.

81. *SC* ii 1 *OC* iii 369.

82. See here Michel Foucault's parallel discussion of what would be a right that one had no right to claim in his posthumously published text in *Libération* (June 30-July 1, 1984), 22.

83. *SC* i 7 *OC* iii 362-363.

84. Hence Rousseau has no need for what Rawls calls "the principle of fidelity" (i.e., of the continuity over time of a rational choice to the chooser) (*A Theory of Justice*, 346) that would underlie and ensure the morality of the institution of, e.g., promising.

85. Ibid., 363.

86. *SC* i 9 *OC* III 367.

87. *Fragments politiques, OC* iii 485.

88. *SC* iii xi *OC* iii 424.

89. For an extensive discussion of all these issues, see my *The Idea of Political Theory*, chapter 2, from which I draw on in this section.

90. Nietzsche makes the same point about "overlooking" in *The Birth of Tragedy*, chapter 8; see my discussion in *Friedrich Nietzsche and the Politics of Transfiguration*, chapter 6.

91. *Narcisse* preface *OC* i 965-966.

92. *Narcisse* preface *OC* i 972n.

93. *SC* ii 12 *OC* iii 394.

94. *SC* ii 7 *OC* iii 383.

95. Idem.

96. Cf. R. W. Emerson's remarks on "provocation" in "The Divinity School Address," *Essays and Lectures* (New York: Library of America, 1983), 79. There is an obvious relation here to the Kantian *Kritik*.

97. *SC* ii 7 *OC* iii 381.

98. *Political Economy OC* iii 244.

99. *SC* ii 4 *OC* iii 373.

100. *SC* iii 1 *OC* 396.

101. *CC, vii, 373.*

102. *SC* iii 16 *OC* iii 432.

103. E.g., Benjamin Barber, *Strong Democracy* (Berkeley and Los Angeles: University of California Press, 1984).

104. *SC* iii 1 *OC* iii 398.

105. *SC* iii 1 *OC* iii.

106. This is discussed in detail in M. Françon, "Le language mathématique de J-J Rousseau," *Cahiers pour l'analyse, 6* (1966), 84ff.

107. *SC* iii 1 *OC* iii: "Thus to be good the government must be relatively more powerful."

108. *SC* iii 7 *OC* iii 414.

109. *SC* iii 1 *OC* iii.

110. *SC* iv 1 *OC* iii 437.

111. *Fragments politiques* iv 7 *OC* iii 493.

112. *SC* iii 15 *OC* 111 429.

113. John Rawls, "Two Concepts of Rules," *Philosophical Review, 64* (January 1955), 3-32.

114. *SC* iv 2 *OC* iii.

115. *SC* iii 13 *OC* iii 427.

116. *SC* iii 15 *OC* iii 430. See Government of Poland 7 *OC* iii 975: "What has until now conserved the legislative authority? It is the continual presence of the legislator."

117. *SC* iii 12 *OC* iii 425.

118. Though my analysis differs from his in important ways, it is a delight to me that I come back here to themes I first encountered in Pierre Burgelin, *La philosophie de l'existence chez Jean-Jacques Rousseau* (Paris: Presses universitaires de France, 1951).

119. *SC* iii 1 *OC* iii.

120. *SC* iv 2 *OC* iii.

121. In *De legibus* iii 15.

122. *SC* iv 4 *OC* iii.

123. *SC* iv 7 *OC* iii.

124. *SC* iv 8 *OC* iii.

Chapter 4 Notes

1. *Emile* 4 *OC* iv 499.
2. *AS* 1 *OC* iii 15.
3. *Emile* 5 *OC* iv 836-853.
4. *Emile* 1 *OC* iv 252.
5. *Emile* 5 *OC* iv 692.
6. *Emile* 1 *OC* iv 249-250.
7. Ibid., 251.
8. See, e.g., Corsica *OC* iii 943; Poland *OC* iii 955. See the interesting book by Francis Imbert, *L'Emile, ou l'interdit de la jouissance* (Paris: A. Colin, 1989), 13ff.
9. I continue to learn despite and because of my differences from the opposite point of view in Judith N. Shklar, *Men and Citizens: A Study of Rousseau's Social Theory* (Cambridge, UK: Cambridge University Press, 1969, 1985).
10. One should resist the temptation to make too much of the absence of the birth-mother. The giving over of children to wet-nurses or nannies was a common practice among the aristocratic and upper-middle classes in his time. See, even with all its faults, Phillippe Ariès, *Centuries of Childhood: A Social History of the Family* (New York: Knopf, 1962).
11. *Emile* preface OC iv 242.
12. *Emile* iii *OC* iv 434.
13. Jean Starobinski, *Jean-Jacques Rousseau: Transparency and Obstruction,* trans. Arthur Goldhammer (Chicago: University of Chicago Press, 1988).

182

14. The *locus classicus* of this is J. L. Talmon, *The Rise of Totalitarian Democracy* (Boston: Beacon, 1952).

15. In the *Lettre à de Beaumont*, Rousseau was to indicate that the world he was dealing with was one that existed whether or not individuals had been rescued from original sin through baptism, and by extension that existed without concern for original sin (or religion).

16. *Emile* preface *OC* iv 242.

17. *Emile* preface *OC* iv 241-242.

18. *Emile* 1 *OC* iv 348.

19. *Lettres écrites de la montagne* 5 *OC* iii 783.

20. *Emile* preface *OC* iv 241.

21. *Emile* (manuscript Favre) iv 7 *OC* iv 237.

22. Idem.

23. Cf. Phillipe Ariès, *Centuries of Childhood*.

24. *Emile* 1 *OC* iv 247.

25. Cf. L. S. Vygotsky, *Mind in Society: The Development of Higher Psychological Processes* (Cambridge, MA: Harvard University Press, 1978); A. R. Luria, *The Making of Mind* (Cambridge, MA: Harvard University Press, 1979); the work of Michael Cole, e.g., *The Cultural Context of Learning* (New York: Basic Books, 1971) is an American development from this basis.

26. *Emile* 1 *OC* iv 259-260.

27. Relations between Freud and Rousseau are complex. On this understanding of neurosis see, for instance, Paul Ricoeur, *Freud and Philosophy* (New Haven, CT: Yale University Press, 1970). There is an unelaborated parallel on 211.

28. *Emile* 1 *OC* iv 282.

29. *Emile* 1 *OC* iv 254.

30. Ibid., 261.

31. Ibid., 260-261.

32. *Emile* 1 *OC* iv 304.

33. Ibid., 282; Rousseau often inveighs against habits too quickly acquired: see *Dialogues* 2 *OC* i 846-847. See J. Derrida, "Ce dangereux supplément" in *De la grammatologie*, 203-234.

34. *Emile* 1 *OC* iv 298.

35. I cannot pursue the relations to Kant here, but this is clearly Rousseau's version of autonomy. It is, however, firmly this worldly and not transcendental, at least in the sense generally understood to be Kantian.

36. *Emile* 1 *OC* iv 407-408.

37. *Emile* 1 *OC* iv 323.

38. *Emile* 1 *OC* iv 301.

39. *Emile* 1 *OC* iv 362.

40. Idem, 364.

41. Ibid., 356.

42. *Emile* 2 *OC* iv 426.

43. Ibid., 466.

44. Ibid., 469ff.

45. *Emile* 4 *OC* iv 489.

46. *Emile* 4 *OC* iv 494.

47. Ibid., 505.

48. Idem.
49. Ibid., 505.
50. Stanley Cavell, *Must We Mean What We Say?* (New York: Scribner, 1969), 266.
51. *Emile* 1 *OC* iv 500.
52. Ibid., 497.
53. The difference with John Rawls here is instructive. Rawls claims that justice requires as a prerequisite that one not envy the lot of those whose lot is improved more than one's own is. Rousseau suggests that a just person can only be developed by avoiding situations from which envy would "naturally" result.
54. The reference to King Lear calls to mind "Lear's prayer," just before he goes mad.

> O I have ta'en
> Too little care of this! Take physic pomp;
> Expose thyself to feel what wretches feel,
> that thou mayst shake the superflux to them
> And show the heavens more just
> Act III, iv, lines 32-36.

See Stanley Cavell, *Must We Mean What We Say?*, last chapter

55. *Human* here is *homme*. As noted in chapter 1, I have used *human* and *man* depending on the sense and requirements of the context. The text of the three maxims and supporting citations are *Emile* 1 *OC* iv 506-510.
56. *Emile* 4 *OC* iv 550.
57. *Emile* 4 *OC* iv 522-523.
58. There is a very complex question here of what proximity means in the modern world. For Emile, it means at least the Bey and fellow slaves in Algiers. But what shall we make of a world of television, E-mail, airplanes? Perhaps the most interesting beginning of thought here is Donna Haraway, "A Manifesto for Cyborgs," reprinted in my *The Self and the Political Order* (Oxford, UK: Blackwells, 1992).
59. Ibid., 525. Emile had been shown masks as part of his first education in others. In *The New Heloise*, Saint Preux will make the same point about faces (*The New Heloise* ii 21 *OC* ii 273).
60. *Emile* 4 *OC* iv 606.
61. Karl Marx, "Contribution to the Critique of Hegel's *Philosophy of Right,*" *Collected Works*, vol. 3 (New York: International Publishers, 1975), 175.
62. *Emile* 4 *OC* iv 558.
63. Ibid., 558. I give "priest" for *vicaire*. This is Cranston's usage and is more accurate than the standard *vicar*, which has both too hierarchical and too Anglican overtones. One might also use *curate*.
64. See my discussion of this distinction (which I borrow from Stanley Cavell, *The World Viewed*, 157) in *The Idea of Political Theory*, 119-127.
65. One was an abbot Jean-Claude Gaime (*Confessions* 1 *OC* i 90-94) and the other the abbot Jean-Baptiste Gatier (ibid., 118-119). The story of Rousseau's running away and the hospice is ibid., 42ff.
66. Shklar, *Men and Citizens*, 114 and note.
67. R. W. Emerson, "The Divinity School Address," *The Portable Emerson*, 52.
68. *Emile* 4 *OC* iv 571.

69. See *Dialogues* 3 *OC* i 972; *The New Heloise* 7 *OC* ii 683; *The New Heloise* 6 *OC* ii 641; *Emile* 1 *OC* iv 248.

70. See the parallel understanding of Wittgenstein in Stanley Cavell, *Must We Mean What We Say?*, 71.

71. *Emile* 4 *OC* iv 648.

72. *Emile* 4 *OC* iv 601-602. The notes to the Pléiade edition trace out a genealogy of this idea in Rousseau's texts, omitting, however, the key relation with pity in the *Second Discourse* (*OC* iv 1561-1563).

73. *Idem.*

74. *Idem.*

75. *The New Heloise* iii, 18 *OC* ii 358.

76. *Emile* 4 *OC* iv 599.

77. *Lettres morales* 3 *OC* iv 1096.

78. *Emile* 4 *OC* iv 606.

79. *Emile* 4 *OC* iv 606.

80. Ibid., 635.

81. *Idem.*

82. Ibid., 628.

83. Ibid., 610 (my italics).

84. Ibid., 614ff.

85. *OC* iv 1577. See my discussion at the end of chapter 1 of Kierkegaard's distinction between an "apostle" and a "genius."

86. *Emile* 4 *OC* iv 617.

87. *Emile* 4 *OC* iv 651-652.

88. There is the opening here of a complex comparison to Michel Foucault.

89. Ibid., 653.

90. Ibid., 657.

91. Ibid., 670.

92. Ibid., 671.

93. Ibid., 689. The phrase comes in a discussion of why Emile will eschew blood sports such as hunting.

94. The question of Rousseau's judgment on women has in recent years occupied many pens. He is an "inexhaustibly rich, if vexing thinker," as Jean B. Elshtain put it in *Public Man, Private Woman: Women in Social and Political Thought* (Princeton, NJ: Princeton University Press, 1981) 148, although the weight has fallen differentially on "rich" and "vexing." The crux of the question seems to come on the discrepancy between his apparent emphasis on freedom and autonomy in the citizen and his apparent relegation of woman to the home. See, inter alia, Susan Okin, *Women in Western Political Thought*, (Princeton, NJ: Princeton University Press, 1979), 99-196; Elizabeth Rapapport, "On the Future of Love: Rousseau and the Radical Feminists," in Carol Gould and Marx Wartofsky, eds., *Women and Philosophy* (New York: Putnam, 1976); Margaret Canovan, "Rousseau Two Concepts of Citizenship," in Ellen Kennedy and Susan Mendus, eds., *Women in Western Political Philosophy* (Chicago: University of Chicago Press, 1987); Joel Schwartz, *The Sexual Politics of Jean-Jacques Rousseau* (Chicago: University of Chicago Press, 1984); Lynda Lange, "Rousseau and Feminism," *Social Theory and Practice, 12* (1981); Allan Bloom, "Introduction" to his edition and translation of the *Emile* (New York: Basic Books, 1979).

95. Ibid., 691.

96. *Emile* 5 *OC* iv 693.

97. Ibid., 695.

98. Ibid., 697.

99. Ibid., 702-703.

100. Does he sometimes defend himself too much? We know from the *Confessions* that he was approached homosexually while an adolescent.

101. See the discussion of Rousseau's sexuality in Ronald Grimsley, *Rousseau. A Study in Self-Awareness* (Cardiff, UK: University of Wales Press, 1961), 97ff; see Schwartz, op. cit.; see J. Derrida, "Ce dangereux supplément," *De la grammatologie.*

102. *Narcisse* preface OC ii 959.

103. *Emile* 5 *OC* iv 700.

104. *Narcisse* preface *OC* ii 973-974.

105. *Emile* 5 *OC* iv 737 (my italics).

106. Ibid., 742.

107. See, e.g., Elshtain, *Public Man, Private Woman.*

108. *Republic* quote in *SC.*

109. *Emile* 1 *OC* iv 249.

110. See the discussion of women in Aristotle in S. Salkever, *Finding the Mean* (Chicago: University of Chicago Press, 1990), 185-199.

111. *Emile* 5 *OC* iv 746-754.

112. Ibid., 758.

113. Susan Moller Okin has some arguments against this point in her sympathetic discussion of Rawls in *Justice, Gender and the Family* (New York: Basic Books, 1989).

114. *Emile* 5 *OC* iv 764-766.

115. Ibid., 814-820.

116. Ibid., 824.

117. *Emile* 5 *OC* iv 836. "Principles of political right" is of course the subtitle to the *Social Contract.* The description of a just political society occupies, 836-849.

118. Ibid., 840.

119. Ibid., 858.

120. Ibid., 868.

Chapter 5 Notes

1. Thanks to Frank Sposito for bringing this poem to my attention.

2. What is the language of temptation in a postreligious age (which is not to say an age without religion)? Most notably it may be found in Freud and Wittgenstein.

3. This is the focus of Hegel's famous analysis of "Lord and Bondsman." Alexandre Kojève's reading of Hegel in *Introduction to the Reading of Hegel* (New York: Basic Books, 1969) is a Rousseauist reading in that he places this passage at the core of all of the *Phenomenology*.

4. This realization is at the source of Kant's insistence that human *nature* is not the source of morality and that the qualities of morality must apply to all rational beings, as rational beings. See I. Kant, *Fundamental Principles of the Metaphysics of Morals* (Indianapolis, IN: Bobbs-Merrill, 1949), 64.

5. The most extensive investigation of this understanding of the moral has been made in relation to some aspects of Greek ethics in Martha Nussbaum, *The Fragility of Goodness* (Cambridge, UK: Cambridge University Press, 1986). What she finds in Aristotle, I see in Rousseau.

6. Edmund Burke, Review of the *Letter to D'Alembert* in the *Annual Register* (1762), in Peter Stanlis, ed., *Edmund Burke: Selected Writings and Speeches* (New York: Anchor, 1963), 89.

7. Hume had first admired Burke with the publication of *A Philosophical Inquiry into the Origin of our Ideas of the Sublime and the Beautiful* (1757). Burke had given a

188   JEAN-JACQUES ROUSSEAU

glowing review to Hume's *History of England* ("No man perhaps has come nearer to that so requisite and so rare a quality in an historian of unprejudiced partiality").

8. Edmund Burke in Stanlis, op. cit., 93, 512, 516.

9. See my "How to Write Scripture: Words, Authority, and Politics in Thomas Hobbes," *Critical Inquiry, 20*(1) (Autumn 1993) and my exchange with Victoria Silver that follows.

10. On a distinction between the "unquestioned" and the "unquestionable," see my *Friedrich Nietzsche and the Politics of Transfiguration* (Berkeley and Los Angeles: University of California Press, 1975, 1988), chapter 1.

11. My formulation here owes something to Stanley Cavell, *In Quest of the Ordinary* (Chicago: University of Chicago Press, 1988), 66, where he in turn is drawing on Martin Heidegger, "The Thing," *Poetry, Language, Thought* (New York: Harper & Row, 1971), 163-186.

12. Thus in the *Metaphysical Elements of Justice* (Indianapolis: Bobbs-Merrill, 1967), 128, Kant can write that "[T]o assume that the moral law within us might deceive us would give rise to the disgusting wish to dispense with reason altogether and to conceive of ourselves and our principles as thrown in together with all the other species of animals under the same mechanism of nature."

13. Thus Nietzsche asserts that "the categorical imperative reeks of cruelty." Friedrich Nietzsche, *On the Genealogy of Morals,* essay ii, chapter 6 (New York: Vintage, 1969), 65.

14. *Le persifleur* (The Mocker), *OC* i 1108-1109. This text dates from 1749, when Rousseau, Diderot, and Condillac were still friends. For a commentary see Jean Starobinski, *Jean-Jacques Rousseau: La transparence et l'obstacle* (Paris: Gallimard, 1971). (Translation: *Jean-Jacques Rousseau: Transparency and Obstruction*), trans. Arthur Goldhammer (Chicago: University of Chicago Press, 1988). I cite from the translated edition, 50-53.

15. For an elaboration of the strengths and problems in this position see chapter 2 of my *The Idea of Political Theory: Reflections on the Self in Political Time and Space* (Notre Dame, IN: University of Notre Dame Press, 1990).

16. Alexis de Tocqueville, *Democracy in America* (New York: Anchor, 1969), 484. My thanks to my student Sonia Alonso Saenz de Oger for recalling this passage and discussing the relation of Whitman and Tocqueville with me. Some of the material in the next several paragraphs draws on my essay "Politics and Transparency," in Austin Sarat and Dana Villa, eds., *Liberal Modernism and Democratic Individuality* (Princeton. Princeton University Press, 1996).

17. The frontispiece to Hobbes's *Leviathan*, in which the body of the whole is made up of the individually distinguishable members, is thus a clue to the democratic aspirations of that book.

18. Tocqueville, ibid.

19. Thus in the frontispiece to the *Leviathan,* each individual is severally distinct in the body of giant Sovereign. See my "How to Write Scripture: Words, Authority, and Politics in Thomas Hobbes," *Critical Inquiry, 20*(1) (Autumn 1993). See also George Kateb, "The Irrationality of Politics," *Political Theory, 17*(3) (August 1989).

20. There is a complex thought here that I cannot pursue. Rawls claims to rely a great deal on American constitutional history for his understanding of justice in political, not metaphysical, terms. (See J. Rawls, "Justice as Fairness: Political not Metaphysical," in Tracy B. Strong, ed., *The Self and the Political Order* [Oxford, UK: Blackwells, 1992].) Suppose he were wrong about the nature of American constitutional history? See Patrick Neal, "Vulgar Liberalism," *Political Theory, 21*(4) (November 1993).

21. This is decidedly not the point of Rawls's so-called communitarian critics. It is not that we are thick selves and that Rawls denies our being by circumventing our historicity. Rather for Rousseau it is that Rawls takes the human out of the experience of justice. Throughout this book, I have denied that Rousseau is a communitarian.

22. George Kateb, *The Inner Ocean* (Ithaca, NY: Cornell University Press, 1992), 247.

23. Ralph Waldo Emerson, "Nature," *Essays and Lectures* (New York: Library of America, 1981), 18.

24. Cf. Jean Starobinski, *Jean-Jacques Rousseau: Transparency and Obstruction.*

25. Starobinski, 259-260.

26. *Rêveries 5 OC* i 1047-1948.

27. Ibid., 1047.

28. George Kateb, Hannah Arendt. *Politics, Consciousness, Evil* (Totowa, NJ: Rowman & Littlefield, 1984), 1f.

29. Nietzsche's insanity is instructive here. See my "Nietzsche's Political Aesthetics," in M. Gillespie and Tracy B. Strong, eds., *Nietzsche's New Seas* (Chicago: University of Chicago Press, 1988).

30. Friedrich Nietzsche, *The Gay Science* (New York: Vintage, 1968), par. 356.

31. *SC* i *OC* iii 351.

32. The expression (*un état bien constitué*) occurs in the preface to *Narcisse* (*OC* ii 965). The qualities of this society are the focus of Maurizio Viroli, *Jean-Jacques Rousseau and the "Well-Ordered Society"* (Cambridge, UK: Cambridge University Press, 1988). That he translates "bien constitué" as "well-ordered" gives a sign of his Hobbesian biases.

33. *SC* iv 8 *OC* iii 465.

34. *Narcisse* preface *OC* ii 962.

35. *SC* iv 8 *OC* iii 467.

36. *Lettre à M. de Franquières OC* iv 1137-1138.

37. Ibid., 1139.

38. Ibid., 1146.

39. *SC* iv 8 *OC* iii 468n. Again, a position he shares with Machiavelli.

40. Notes on 'De l'esprit' *OC* iv 1129.

41. See my "How to Write Scripture: Words, Authority, and Politics in Thomas Hobbes," *Critical Inquiry, 20*(1) (Autumn 1993).

42. J.-P. Vernant recounts this in *Mythe et tragédie en grèce ancienne* (Paris: Maspéro, 1973), 13-17.

43. Michael Goldman, *An Actor's Freedom* (New York: Viking, 1965), 13.

44. The above paragraph draws on my *The Idea of Political Theory: Reflections on the Self in Political Time and Space*, 44-45.

45. Martin Heidegger, "Building Dwelling Thinking," *Poetry, Language and Thought,* 149-150.

46. It is interesting to note that when Romain Rolland spoke of an oceanic feeling that Freud responded to him that he knew himself to be only a "terrestrial beast." See my "Psychoanalysis as a Vocation: Freud, Politics and the Heroic," *Political Theory, 13*(1) (February 1984).

47. See Emile Benveniste, *Le vocabulaire des institutions indo-européenes* (Paris: Editions de Minuit, 1969), vol. 2, 180.

48. *Lettres à Malesherbes* 3 *OC* i 1141 (Starobinski also cites this letter [263n]).

49. *Lettres à Malesherbes* 3 *OC* i 1138-1139.

190   JEAN-JACQUES ROUSSEAU

50. Ibid., 1141. See here Hannah Arendt's critique of the will in *Willing: The Life of the Mind*, vol. 2 (New York: Harcourt Brace Jovanovich, 1978), esp. 172.

51. This is a point that hearkens back to Plato in the *Protagoras*, where Socrates insists against Protagoras that one cannot have just one part of virtue.

52. I am prompted here by Stanley Cavell, *Conditions Handsome and Unhandsome: The Constitution of Emersonian Perfectionism* (Chicago: University of Chicago Press, 1990), 107-108.

53. *Emile* v *OC* iv 831. See the very interesting discussion of this passage in Marcel Hénaff, "The Cannibalistic City: Rousseau, Large Numbers, and the Abuse of the Social Bond," *Substance, 67* (Spring 1992), 3ff.

54. Hénaff, op. cit., 22-23.

55. Eating together is thus a form of Eucharist, but not a Church.

56. See Bruno Bettelheim, "Individual and Mass Behavior in Extreme Situations," *Journal of Abnormal and Social Psychology, 38*(4) (October 1943), 417-452, reprinted in Tracy B. Strong, ed., *The Self and the Political Order* (Oxford, UK: Blackwells, 1992).

57. A. Malraux, *Antimémoires* (Paris: Gallimard, 1967), 587 (my translation).

58. Karl Marx, *Capital*, vol. 1 (New York: International Publishers, 1967), 177 (my italics).

59. Aristotle, too, denied that slaves were human beings. Do we resist the claim in the same way in each?

60. W. B. Yeats, "Lapis Lazuli," in M. L. Rosenthal, ed., *Collected Poems* (New York: Collier, 1969), 292.

61. Max Weber, "Bureaucracy," in Gerth and Mills, eds., *From Max Weber* (New York: Oxford University Press, 1968), 199 (my italics).

62. Max Weber, *Economy and Society* (Berkeley and Los Angeles: University of California Press, 1973), 975.

63. Judith N. Shklar, *Men and Citizens: A Study of Rousseau's Social Theory* (Cambridge, UK: Cambridge University Press, 1969, 1985).

64. I am informed here by the discussion in Frank Sposito's doctoral dissertation, University of California-San Diego, Department of Political Science, La Jolla, 1993.

65. Stanley Cavell, *Conditions Handsome and Unhandsome*, 31.

66. See Judith Butler, *Gender Trouble: Feminism and the Subversion of Identity* (New York: Routledge, 1990), and William Connolly, *Identity\Difference* (Ithaca, NY: Cornell University Press, 1991) as well as Wendy Brown, *Manhood and Politics: A Feminist Reading in Political Theory* (Totowa, NJ: Rowman & Littlefield, 1988).

67. *SC* first version 5 *OC* iii 299; see 297-305.

68. *SC* ii 7 *OC* iii 382.

69. It is implicit, for instance, in Starobinski. See also John Chapman, "Rawls' Theory of Justice," *American Political Science Review, 69*(2) (June 1975), 588-593.

70. *SC* ii 7 *OC* iii 384.

71. Letter to Moultou, February 14, 1769, *CC xxxvii, 57* (also cited in *Viroli, 15*).

72. See my essay "Max Weber and the Bourgeoisie," in T. Maley et al., eds., *The Barbarism of Reason* (Toronto: University of Toronto Press, 1994).

Bibliographical Afterword

I have kept footnotes on secondary sources to a minimum. The reasons are several. First and determinative, although perhaps least important, is the limitation of the format of this series. The books in the *Modernity and Political Thought Series* are intended to be short and provocative, rather than exhaustive. Second, my desire was to let the text speak for itself as much I was able to and not to interpose myself between the reader and Rousseau with disquisitions on variations, contrarities, or agreements. Lastly, when considering the Rousseau secondary literature, it was not clear where to start nor where to end.

Nevertheless, having refused to tread, I shall rush in a bit here. It is not my intention to be complete—even if I were capable of it. I have avoided mentioning here texts that are in the notes, except when they are necessary to make my point. The volumes of the *Annales de la Sociète Jean-Jacques Rousseau* contain exhaustive bibliographies and are an excellent source of essays about Rousseau, on topics both general and arcance. Another

191

excellent source of articles on Rousseau has been the journal *Studies on Voltaire and the Eighteenth Century*.

Rousseau, however, appears increasingly everywhere—philosophy, literature, literary criticism, feminist studies, political theory, history, and anthropology.

The following seem to me the *categories* of criticism that are most prevalent. Perhaps the most important general approach in the last 2 decades is that which starts from a concern for how a text works—"affective stylistics," as Stanley Fish called it. My text is clearly influenced both positively and negatively by these writings. (See Fish, 1980, *Is There a Text in This Class?* Cambridge, MA: Harvard University Press and especially "Literature in the Reader: Affective Stylistics," *New Literary History.* vol. II (Autumn, 1970, pp. 123-162). I have also been moved by the work of Wolfgang Iser, starting with *The Art of Reading,* Baltimore, MD: Johns Hopkins Press, 1978).

The key text on Rousseau in this general vein is probably Jean Starobinski's *Jean-Jacques Rousseau: La transparence et l'obstacle* (1957, 1971), all the more impressive for having been written before Derrida, Fish, Deman, and the others. It was not only magisterial in its time, but has held up exceptionally well. More recently, the works of Jacques Derrida (cited in the text) have been of utmost importance. Paul Deman's work (especially in *Blindness and Insight,* New Haven, CT: Yale University Press, 1979) paralleled many aspects of Derrida's.

As I note in the first chapter, the affect of Rousseau's texts on his readers has been remarked on from early on. One might consult here Robert Ellrich, *Rousseau and His Reader: The Rhetorical Situation in the Major Works* (Chapel Hill, NC: University of North Carolina Press, 1969). More recently Raymond Trousson, *Jean-Jacques Rousseau: Le deuil éclatant du bonheur* (Paris, 1989) has given some more extended idea of these reactions. Rousseau's multiple relations to women, gender, and sexuality have also proven exceptionally fruitful terrain for the text-oriented approach. Peggy Kamuf, *Signature Pieces* (Ithaca, NY: Cornell University Press, 1988) and *Fictions of Feminine Desire: Disclosures of Heloise* (Lincoln, University of Nebraska Press, 1982) and Sarah Kofman, *Le respect des femmes* (Galilée, Paris, 1982) are only three important texts. After finishing this book, I read Judith Still, *Justice and Difference in the Works of Rousseau* (Cambridge, UK: Cambridge University Press, 1993) and wished that I had been able to read it earlier. She raises several of the questions that I raise about sexuality and difference.

A second approach to Rousseau consists in locating him in the context of his times. I have done this when I thought it necessary, but I am aware of insufficiencies. Dérathé's *Jean-Jacques Rousseau et la science politique de son temps* (1950) as well as his *Le rationalisme de Jean-Jacques Rousseau* (1948) are central in this enterprise. Following Lévi-Strauss's admission that he never started a piece of work without rereading the *Discourse on the Origins of Inequality,* a literature placing Rousseau in the context of *la science* of his (and our) time has developed. See Ronald L. Meek, 1976, *Social Science and the Ignoble Savage* (Cambridge, UK: Cambridge University Press); Michèle Duchet, *Anthropologie et Historie au siècle des lumières* (Paris, 1971). Also excellent in placing Rousseau in the context of the discussions of this time is the work of Robert Wokler, in particular his *Rousseau on Society, Politics, Music and Language,* D. Phil. thesis, Nuffield College, published in facsimile in 1987.

In Chapters 3 and 4, I have partly worked in the vein to which I was introduced by Judith Shklar. Indeed, political theorists, rather than philosophers, have been the most sympathetic to Rousseau's writing as a substantive theoretical contribution. Roger Masters' *The Political Philosophy of Rousseau* (Princeton, NJ: Princeton University Press, 1958) and Judith Shklar, *Men and Citizens: A Study of Rousseau's Social Theory* (Cambridge, UK: Cambridge University Press, 1969) dominated discussion for over 10 years. John Charvet gave a more analytical reading in *The Social Problem in the Philosophy of Rousseau* (Cambridge, UK: Cambridge University Press, 1974). More recently, we have seen political theoretical reading of particular texts, of which an excellent example is Christopher Kelly, 1987, *Rousseau's Exemplary Life: The Confessions as Political Philosophy* (Ithaca, NY: Cornell University Press).

A final group reads Rousseau in the context of the history of ideas. Ernst Cassirer, *The Question of Jean-Jacques Rousseau* (trans. and edited by Peter Gay, New York, 1954) makes a determined effort to find everything of worth in Rousseau as anticipatory of Kant. Patrick Riley's work on *The General Will Before and After Rousseau* (Princeton, NJ: Princeton University Press, 1986) is a first-rate account of the secularization of the divine, starting with Pascal and culminating in Rousseau. George A. Kelly gave an account of the period that started with Rousseau in *Idealism,*

Politics, History: Sources of Hegelian Thought (Cambridge, UK: Cambridge University Press, 1969). It is here that my text satisfies me the least, as I have been content with pointing, at Kant, Hegel, Marx, and others, rather than elaborating. I can only hope that the arrows I have cast were in the right direction.

That Rousseau can be read with profit in each of these modes seems to me central to his importance for our times. He permits a voice to each of us: This, if nothing else, is the mark of a great thinker, a great person.

Name Index

Index of Major Discussions
of Texts From Rousseau

(The most important discussions of major texts are in bold.)

About the Author

Tracy B. Strong is Professor of Political Science at the University of California, San Diego. He was educated at the Collège de Genève, Oberlin College, and Harvard University. His books include *Friedrich Nietzsche and the Politics of Transfiguration, The Idea of Political Theory: Reflections on the Self in Political Time and Space, The Self and the Political Order,* and *Right in Her Soul: The Life of Anna Louise Strong* (with Helene Keyssar), and his essays have appeared in numerous journals. His interests include the relation between philosophy and literature, the uses and abuses of ordinary language for political theory, and philosophy of social science. He is presently working on a book on aesthetics and political thought in the early part of the twentieth century. From 1989 until 2000 he was editor of *Political Theory*.